Beyond Evidence-Based Psychotherapy

COUNSELING AND PSYCHOTHERAPY: INVESTIGATING PRACTICE FROM SCIENTIFIC, HISTORICAL, AND CULTURAL PERSPECTIVES

A Routledge book series
Editor, Bruce E. Wampold, University of Wisconsin

This innovative new series is devoted to grasping the vast complexities of the practice of counseling and psychotherapy. As a set of healing practices delivered in a context shaped by health delivery systems and the attitudes and values of consumers, practitioners, and researchers, counseling and psychotherapy must be examined critically. By understanding the historical and cultural context of counseling and psychotherapy and by examining the extant research, these critical inquiries seek a deeper, richer understanding of what is a remarkably effective endeavor.

Published

Counseling and Therapy With Clients Who Abuse Alcohol or Other Drugs
Cynthia E. Glidden-Tracy

The Great Psychotherapy Debate
Bruce Wampold

The Psychology of Working: Implications for Career Development, Counseling, and Public Policy
David Blustein

Neuropsychotherapy: How the Neurosciences Inform Effective Psychotherapy
Klaus Grawe

Principles of Multicultural Counseling
Uwe P. Gielen, Juris G. Draguns, Jefferson M. Fish

Cognitive-Behavioral Therapy for Deaf and Hearing Persons With Language and Learning Challenges
Neil Glickman

Forthcoming

The Pharmacology and Treatment of Substance Abuse: Evidence and Outcomes Based Perspective
Lee Cohen, Frank Collins, Alice Young, Dennis McChargue

Making Treatment Count: Using Outcomes to Inform and Manage Therapy
Michael Lambert, Jeb Brown, Scott Miller, Bruce Wampold

The Handbook of Therapeutic Assessment
Stephen E. Finn

IDM Supervision: An Integrated Developmental Model for Supervising Counselors and Therapists, Third Edition
Cal Stoltenberg and Brian McNeill

The Great Psychotherapy Debate, Revised Edition
Bruce Wampold

Casebook for Multicultural Counseling
Miguel E. Gallardo and Brian W. McNeill

Culture and the Therapeutic Process: A Guide for Mental Health Professionals
Mark M. Leach and Jamie Aten

Beyond Evidence-Based Psychotherapy

Fostering the Eight Sources of Change
in Child and Adolescent Treatment

George W. Rosenfeld

Routledge
Taylor & Francis Group
New York   London

Routledge
Taylor & Francis Group
711 Third Avenue
New York, NY 10017

Routledge
Taylor & Francis Group
2 Park Square
Milton Park, Abingdon
Oxon OX14 4RN

© 2009 by Taylor & Francis Group, LLC
Routledge is an imprint of Taylor & Francis Group, an Informa business

International Standard Book Number-13: 978-0-415-99336-4 (Softcover) 978-0-415-99335-7 (Hardcover)

Library of Congress Cataloging-in-Publication Data

Rosenfeld, George W., 1945-
    Beyond evidence-based psychotherapy : fostering the eight sources of change in child and adolescent treatment / George W. Rosenfeld.
        p. ; cm.
    Includes bibliographical references and index.
    ISBN 978-0-415-99335-7 (hardbound : alk. paper) -- ISBN 978-0-415-99336-4 (pbk. : alk. paper)
    1. Child psychotherapy. 2. Adolescent psychotherapy. 3. Evidence-based psychiatry. I. Title.
    [DNLM: 1. Psychotherapy--methods. 2. Adolescent. 3. Child. 4. Evidence-Based Medicine. 5. Mental Disorders--therapy. WS 350.2 R813b 2008]

RJ504.R67 2008
618.92'8914--dc22   2008015242

Visit the Taylor & Francis Web site at
http://www.taylorandfrancis.com

and the Routledge Web site at
http://www.routledge.com

This book is dedicated to Jean Rosenfeld, LCSW, BCD, whose thinking has blended so much with mine over the years that I am not sure which ideas are hers and which are mine. Her contributions of content and editing are on every page. Thank you for your support and patience.

Contents

Part 2 Case Studies

Series Editor's Foreword

This innovative new series is devoted to grasping the vast complexities of the practice of counseling and psychotherapy. As a set of healing practices delivered in a context shaped by health delivery systems and the attitudes and values of consumers, practitioners, and researchers, counseling and psychotherapy must be examined critically. By understanding the historical and cultural context of counseling and psychotherapy, and by examining the extant research, these critical inquiries seek a deeper, richer understanding of what is a remarkably effective endeavor.

Delivering psychotherapy to children and adolescents is a complex undertaking because of the institutional, political, and social context in which these services are provided. One of the pervasive influences in the current context is the notion of evidence-based practice in mental health services. Narrowly interpreted, evidence-based practice has become a rationale for mandating particular treatments for youth. George Rosenfeld, in *Beyond Evidence-Based Psychotherapy: Fostering the Eight Sources of Change in Child and Adolescent Treatment,* cogently proposes principles for conducting psychotherapy for children and adolescents that value evidence but recognize the broad context in which services are delivered. His years of experience as a therapist bring to this volume the clinical wisdom that supplements the research evidence; this synthesis yields a remarkably important contribution that should interest clinicians and scientists alike.

Bruce E. Wampold, PhD, ABPP, Series Editor

University of Wisconsin–Madison

Introduction

Psychotherapy is an art influenced by science. The art involves developing and maintaining rapport with clients; using clinical judgment in applying therapeutic approaches supported by research, while incorporating the therapist's clinical knowledge and experience into treatment; respecting and using clients' beliefs and intentions; and deciding how to proceed when the research literature provides no, ambiguous, or conflicting guidelines. This text will review the psychotherapy research and fill in the gaps with personal experience to identify the factors that contribute to change in psychotherapy and build on these factors to identify an evidence-supported, theoretically eclectic approach to psychotherapy.

Political and economic forces are defining psychotherapy in our society. Psychotherapy is expected to follow the medical model that dictates that the therapist is responsible for diagnosing the patient and then selecting and implementing "the treatment of choice" for the diagnosis. The patient's primary role is to comply with the therapist's directions. The treatment is expected to be evidence based, which means that several studies using the highest standard of research (randomly assigned, double-blind, controlled clinical trials) have proved the intervention to be effective for the client with that particular diagnosis. "There are presently 145 officially approved, manualized, evidence-based treatments for 51 of the 397 possible *DSM* diagnostic groups" (Miller, Hubble, & Duncan, 2007, p. 31). Because almost all the present evidence-based treatments are cognitive-behavioral and behavioral, these are seen as the most effective treatments. When clients do not benefit, their dropping out and lack of progress are viewed as resistance, lack of motivation, or entrenched psychopathology. This model has led textbooks and continuing education classes to be obsessed with teaching diagnostically related treatment techniques.

Traditionally, textbooks in child and adolescent psychotherapy have been organized in two main ways. They have been based on the medical model and have presented the evidence-based "treatments of choice" for youths according to their diagnosis. They have claimed that the power of therapy lies in the treatment offered by the therapist, whose job it is to direct the course of treatment by identifying the problems and selecting the proper, often manualized, treatment. Other textbooks have presented a particular theoretical orientation that is then applied to youths with particular diagnoses. These approaches assume that the best preparation for seeing clients involves being armed with proven techniques and/or the best theoretical orientation. However, they misinterpret and ignore the research, so the complexity of psychotherapy, if not the practice itself, is being threatened.

This book focuses on the other 85% to 90% of psychotherapy that is marginalized by textbooks and the medical model. It reviews the therapy research and offers an evidence-based alternative to the medical model. It identifies a variety of factors that have an even more powerful effect on treatment outcome than the presently favored theoretical orientations and techniques and describes techniques and strategies therapists can use to allow these factors to improve outcome. This book is intended to be a companion and complement to the typical text that emphasizes cognitive-behavioral and evidence-based treatments.

The research supports an alternative approach to psychotherapy that is more client driven and collaborative and focuses on the factors that most affect outcome. This leads to a different formulation of the therapy process and the roles of the therapist and client. The research indicates that (a) many theoretical approaches are equally effective, not just cognitive-behavioral and behavioral; (b) the treatment techniques supplied by the therapist contribute a small part to the change generated by psychotherapy; and (c) other factors are a greater contributor to change than therapist-selected treatment techniques. The research on psychotherapy supplies answers to the therapist's questions that are very different from those suggested by the medical model: What causes change? What is the therapist's role in helping the client? What should the therapist do and say during therapy?

The number of effective therapies has led to eclecticism and integrationism (Downing, 2004). Eclecticism has challenged therapists to seek

reduces traditional psychodynamic

strategies to inform choosing the most appropriate treatment. This text will describe a strategy for selecting the treatments based on particular client characteristics and desires, the problems being remediated, the abilities of the particular therapist, the strengths and resources in the client's environment and the state of the client–therapist relationship, and adjusting their treatment to the client's progress.

Integration has spawned an exciting exploration to identify the elements that are common in effective treatments. Many of the common factors that account for change in effective treatments have been identified. This text will present a treatment approach that evolves from these sources of change. In comparison to the medical model, it is a more client-driven approach in which the client's view of the problem and goals and the client's and therapist's resources and characteristics contribute to the choice of intervention. It is an approach that attends to the relationship between the client and therapist and de-emphasizes treatment techniques as change agents.

Despite the research that indicates that no particular theory or orientation is more effective than others, graduate training has traditionally fostered a commitment to a particular theoretical orientation, under the assumption that beginning therapists could not handle the overwhelming tension of treating clients without being grounded in a predominant theoretical orientation. The lack of a widely accepted unifying theory of psychotherapies and the lack of a theory for determining which treatment to select from the smorgasbord of possible approaches have been seen as two problems that have to be resolved before beginning therapists can abandon being guided by a predominant theoretical orientation. In this vein, Stricker and Gold suggested that student therapists should begin by learning "one approach thoroughly rather than many approaches simultaneously" (Norcross & Goldfried, 2005, p. 453). Then, after beginning therapists become more experienced, they can, as more seasoned therapists tend to do, incorporate different approaches into their repertories and eventually create their own integrated, eclectic style.

Only recently have some graduate programs come to believe that beginning therapists need not adopt premature identities to cope with uncertainty; that they can benefit from knowing early in their careers that no single approach fits all clients, problems, and situations; that students should have respect for a wide variety of orientations because there are multiple approaches that could benefit a client; and that tolerating uncertainty is an unavoidable part of being a therapist (Lampropoulos & Dixon, 2007). Given these guidelines, this book will help therapists navigate through a complex, exciting, and meaningful career. Without a single theory to cling to, therapists are not adrift. The research does offer guidance to inform the choice of technique and the therapist's contribution to treatment. This book presents guidelines for selecting treatment strategies from a wide variety of orientations and directing the therapist's input based on maximizing the factors that promote client change. This text will present a theoretical frame that will allow therapists to incorporate into their work techniques from a variety of orientations.

Now, particularly in the public sector and with managed-care clientele, goal-driven, client-directed, and rapid treatment is expected. In this confusing environment child and adolescent therapists are expected to diagnose, identify factors that will help the client change, develop realistic goals and expectations, formulate treatment plans that incorporate evidence-based techniques, appropriately select and time interventions, adjust treatment to client feedback, manage the therapy hour, and then be evaluated by their clients. Therapists are expected to help clients tolerate the frustrations of treatment, manage their ambivalence to change, feel motivated to change, help direct treatment by contributing to the choice of goals and identifying how they will support accomplishing them, ameliorate problems, and successfully terminate. Without clear guidelines from the research, our daily practice requires us to develop our unique balance between self-disclosing and being neutral; between allowing sessions to be client driven and therapist directed; between supporting and confronting the client; between focusing on problems or strengths; between choosing to focus on the client's past, present, or future; and between dealing with behavior, cognitions, or affect. Therapists are expected to cope with the emotional effects of dealing with traumatized clients; balance personal, organizational, legal, and ethical demands; and use transference and countertransference reactions to improve outcome. We struggle with a stressful occupation characterized by conflicting theories and demands. No wonder beginning therapists, armed with only a favored theoretical orientation, meet clients with trepidation.

Part 1 of this book offers practical advice to guide therapists through these common struggles by identifying the factors that cause change in psychotherapy, presenting treatment techniques supported by the literature and clinical experience, and describing an evidence-based rationale for selecting and timing therapist interventions. Part 2 presents a typical day of treatment cases and describes their progress over a 3-month period in which many of the treatment approaches are demonstrated. The reader can get a realistic sense of a therapist's day and the pace of change in a typical session and over a 3-month period.

The youths' problems are interwoven with the parents' problems, so in most treatments the caretakers need to actively participate and therapists need the skills to keep them productively involved. Child and adolescent therapists need to form relationships with family members of all ages, and, therefore, they need the skills of an adult therapist as well as the ability to treat youths. Although this is a book about treating children and adolescents, much of the research that is reviewed and the suggestions provided also apply to the treatment of adults.

George Rosenfeld, PhD

PART 1

Research and Theory

CHAPTER 1

What Are Reasonable Expectations
for Psychotherapy?

What I Wish I Knew When I Started Being a Therapist 35 Years Ago

As a clinical psychologist I have completed almost 40,000 hours of psychotherapy in the past 35 years. These sessions have been in relative isolation, with input from a few colleagues and mentors and sporadic explorations of the treatment literature. My excellent graduate education at the University of Minnesota helped me start but became outdated as knowledge expanded and trends changed. I was educated before the field was aware of the pervasive impact of sexual abuse, domestic violence, fatherless households, and the methamphetamine epidemic that has swept the western United States. Cultural diversity was not addressed. This was in a time before brain imaging, managed care, the deinstitutionalization of the mentally ill, and the domination of evidence-based and cognitive-behavioral approaches. The feminization, desecularization, manualization, medicalization, and deprofessionalization of psychotherapy were still yet to come. It seems probable that these trends will continue to mold the development of psychotherapy, leading a panel of experts to forecast the "expansion of evidence-based therapy, practice guidelines, behavioral medicine, and pharmacotherapy" (Norcross, Hedges, & Prochaska, 2002, p. 316). No matter what direction the field takes, 35 years from now, new perspectives and discoveries will make today's education and practice standards seem as antiquated as my training now seems to me, and the thoughts about treatment presented here will seem just as primitive as the treatment methods to which I was exposed. Being a psychotherapist clearly requires adapting to constant change and constantly changing.

When I began as a therapist, my focus was on quieting my anxieties. I worried about being competent and accepted by colleagues and clients. I greeted clients with the hope of curing them or making them "normal." Now I am not even sure what normal is. As the saying goes, "Normal is what you think people are until you get to know them." I tried to take away their problems, but being problem free is not a realistic goal. Life can involve moving from one damn thing to another. Clients are going to have more problems and continue to struggle with many of their same issues.

Clients were not born yesterday with a blank slate and infinite capacities to change. This is not a depressing or hopeless view. It describes the realistic boundaries in which we operate and makes improvement in clients' lives so much more significant. A great deal is accomplished when therapy helps clients to reduce their symptoms, become more realistic, advance to the next developmental stage, become less trapped in repetitive patterns, tolerate more affect so they do not subsequently resort to as many destructive behaviors and defenses, carry fewer unexamined secrets (often forged under stress in childhood), feel less worried, and be more able to participate and find pleasure in work, play, and relationships.

My interventions were initially aimed at making the most useful interpretations and understanding connections to the past. With experience I found that interpretations were rarely necessary or sufficient to create change, that often what I had to say was not as powerful as what the client had to say, and that dealing with the past was not always appreciated, possible, or helpful. As I developed as a therapist, I focused on acquiring a wide range of other techniques. Now I value many approaches but see their usefulness as depending on the client's situation and the therapeutic relationship. I focus less on pathology and resistances and more on the therapeutic relationship and getting to know the client's background, hopes, strengths, feelings, relationships, present struggles, and achievements. Because the influence of family members is so powerful, I rely more on family and conjoint (parent with youth) treatment than individual therapy for treating youths, especially when the client is young, unmotivated, or difficult to engage or believe. I now look for skills to build, and I focus more on the present and future than on the past.

Now I observe not only the client and I but our interaction and progress along a more mapped-out path. I watch us struggle with engaging in the therapeutic relationship, developing a treatment plan that meets our expectations, trying to accomplish our goals without being thrown off course by our personal needs and biases, and finally ending when the clients and I are enjoying each other the most. I find myself trying to understand, attend to, and respond to so many aspects of the treatment process, the client, myself, and our interaction that being a therapist seems an unmasterable task. It is similar to the tension-reduction exercise I try to teach to some clients. I ask them to place their hands almost together with the goal of making all five opposing fingertips almost, but not quite, touch each other. As they focus on one or two pairs of opposing fingers, others stray apart and need to be attended to and brought closer. It is an absorbing, mentally and emotionally taxing task that cannot be fully mastered.

If Change Were So Easy to Accomplish, the Client Would Have Done It Already

Change Is Not as Easy to Accomplish as We Have Been Led to Expect

Our interventions are not as powerful as outcome studies would lead us to believe. Often the data supporting our techniques are derived from research on populations that are different from our typical clients because these studies usually exclude people who have more severe or multiple psychological problems, comorbid physical problems, suicidal ideation or intention, or a personality disorder; abuse substances; or are an ethnic minority (March et al., 2004; Westen & Morrison, 2001).[1] Therefore the research may not be relevant to the typical outpatient who would fail to be included in most outcome studies. Because outcome studies carefully preselect subjects that are most likely to benefit from treatment and exclude the most treatment-resistant subjects, the efficacy of a treatment technique or manual in the laboratory does not ensure that the findings are transferable to the more complex clinical environment. Also, many outcome studies give an exaggerated view of the effectiveness of treatment because they do not count dropouts as treatment failures, and the more subjects who drop out of studies, the more effective the treatment is reported to be (Bradley, Greene, Russ, Dutra, & Westen, 2005). Furthermore, they typically measure only short-term change, so we do not know the shelf life of the changes created by these techniques.

In the child and adolescent psychotherapy research, many of the studies on the efficacy of treatment are completed on nonreferred school populations rather than on groups seeking treatment. Many studies compare treatment with a specific technique to a no-treatment (waiting list) control group (Weisz, Doss, & Hawley, 2005),[2] so that the technique being evaluated is confounded with the therapeutic relationship, which is a significant contributor to the effectiveness of the technique. Therefore, outcome studies on specific techniques seem unrealistically optimistic.

It is naive to feel we should be able to fix (or even understand) all the people who walk into our office, irrespective of their age, intelligence, sexuality, and gender; their cultural, medical, neurological, genetic, ethnic, spiritual, and educational backgrounds; their social class; the intensity and duration of their problems; and their resources to overcome the obstacles to regularly participate in therapy. Generally, we might anticipate that the longer the client has had the problem, the more severe the problem is the more complicated it is by comorbid conditions; likewise, the less support for change there is outside of the therapy session, the more complex and difficult treatment will be.

For years I told clients not to expect magic, and it took me years to understand what I was really saying. I know how difficult it is for me to change myself and my habits, fears, and expectations, even when I have the resources and social support and am highly motivated to change. Imagine how difficult it is to help others change who may lack motivation, knowledge, and emotional resources and may be embedded in an environment that does not support or even frustrates change. We can make some progress in 1 hour a week, but we may be working with people who fear the unknown and cling to their problems, which have become part of their identity and their familiar friend. Many clients are actually ambivalent about change. They may believe that the devil they know is preferable to the devil they do not know. For many clients change can take time and cause discomfort. Some clients will need to expose themselves repeatedly to their fears. They may have to experience uncomfortable feelings involved in risking intimacy, correcting well-ingrained misconceptions and thought patterns, exposing felt deficits, learning new skills, revisiting painful experiences, or accepting responsibility for poor choices they made. Changing a behavior could require eliminating exposure to many triggers, a task akin to discarding an identity and forging another.

Some clients build their world around their problems and do not want to abandon them, despite the pain they cause. They may take pride in behaving the way their parents acted and get special treatment for their fears and threatening behaviors. They may have learned to adapt to their pain, as many depressed clients do, because they do not recognize how depressed they are since the depression has increased so gradually over time. Clients may not be motivated to change because they do not believe they have a problem, even though everyone else in the universe knows they do. They may believe their problems and defenses allow them to avoid or escape from greater pain, as an overeater may be escaping from boredom, an isolate may be avoiding anticipated rejection, or a thief may be stealing to compensate for loneliness. Just because clients seek therapy and attend sessions does not mean they are ready to change. Clients can be reluctant to abandon their present patterns of behaviors and beliefs without some hope that new patterns will be better. I do not pressure clients to give up their defenses and coping mechanisms until they have alternatives on which they can rely. It is dangerous to leave a sinking lifeboat until another comes along.

We cannot expect clients to easily abandon the behaviors and defenses that repeatedly have been useful solutions to their previous problems, even though these solutions have now become problems themselves. For instance, an abused child might have successfully survived her chaotic environment by being self-reliant and controlling in relationships. Later this pattern could be detrimental by interfering with being intimate or vulnerable in her present relationships. Furthermore, clients cannot erase the genetic and biological contributions to their problems, and they cannot eliminate the effects of the repeated failure, abuse, rejection, chaos, deprivation of nurturance, missed opportunities for training, and dysfunctional models and values to which they have been exposed. Some problems are chronic. For example, depression is often a recurrent disorder (Consensus Development Panel, 1985; Keller, Lavori, Lewis, & Klerman, 1983).[3]

At times therapists have to handle their feelings about helping someone accept and manage a worsening condition. Physicians are trained to do this. They can even say to a patient, "I think that is all I can do for you." Therapists are not trained to give up. However, we have to monitor our hope and persistence with a rational evaluation of our progress. I try to recognize when treatment is not working and adjust the goals and treatment plan as I gain a more realistic understanding of the client and his or her situation. Similarly, I may raise the bar when additional strengths and potentials surface. Therapy is the art of the possible; we have to figure out what is doable. When I cannot generate an achievable goal, I consider seeking consultation or adding additional resources, such as medication, including significant others in the treatment plan, adding another treatment modality, or referring to a higher level of care or a different therapist. Sometimes I might orient the client toward acceptance rather than toward change.

The good news is that the same interconnectedness that makes progress difficult can allow a small change to ripple through many domains and multiply. Often I feel as if I am planting and nurturing seeds when I facilitate small changes in cognitive, emotional, and behavioral patterns. Sometimes therapists have a great deal of influence against powerful forces. Sometimes we do have some magic. Some problems respond well to hope generated by treatment, reassurance, psychoeducation, behavior management, environmental changes, cognitive-behavioral techniques, and/or a corrective emotional relationship. Sometimes explaining the nature of a disorder, reframing the client's problem, or correcting cognitive distortions can generate a cascade of changes. Sometimes irreversible changes flow from teaching parents to use time-out instead of threats, to use "I messages" instead of passivity or aggression, or to emotionally connect to their child. Similarly changes can multiply by helping a depressed person be a little more angry and assertive or an angry person be a little more depressed, mindful, or aware of others' feelings.

For most clients their problems manifest in an inability to form and maintain relationships, including the therapeutic relationship. So relationship difficulties often connect problems, goals, and treatment. Developing and maintaining the therapeutic relationship is a major part of treatment, because what the client learns from this relationship can affect all other relationships, and often the potency of interventions depends on the therapeutic relationship.

Rapid Change Is Not a Goal—Make Haste Slowly

Clients live in a world of fast food, microwave ovens, and instant text messaging and World Wide Web searches. Some expect quick solutions and immediate gratification. The glimpses of therapy they have been exposed to may have come from the popular media gurus who greet and treat before the next commercial. Therefore clients may not appreciate that the therapist wants to begin with an assessment and ask so many questions. Part of slowing clients down involves helping them postpone their desire to obtain advice, reassurance, and rapid relief. Some clients may need to accept more realistic expectations about change. Change can occur rapidly or require preparation, progress in bursts, and have setbacks. Identifying and removing the patterns that have gotten in the way of the clients' past attempts to change can be required.

Of course we want to remediate symptoms as soon as possible. There are costs to attending therapy sessions. The following are just a few: missing school and extracurricular activities, having problems with the caretaker's employer due to taking time off for meetings, becoming overdependent on the therapist to the exclusion of developing other relationships, dealing with the financial expense, experiencing sibling jealousy, having to cope with stigmatization and embarrassment, being the identified patient, feeling at fault for the family's problems, and feeling stress created by trying new things and dealing with previously avoided patterns of thoughts, feelings, and behaviors.

But some clients need to be slowed down, especially at the start of treatment. Perhaps believing that therapy involves telling painful secrets and facing the uncomfortable past, they, in their zeal to be good clients and get well, can open up too early and expose too much. Then they may become overwhelmed with anxiety and might not return. This can be a surprise to the therapist, who may have felt the session was quite successful, because the client appeared to trust, disclose, and express intense feelings. Actually, the client was allowed to move too quickly without the therapist's assessing the client's capacity to handle the impact of his or her disclosures.

Before exposing clients to these stresses, I try to make sure they have established the skills and resources necessary to handle these uncomfortable feelings, so they do not go home and dissociate or act out and then avoid therapy. Clients who are not able or ready to contribute to regulating the speed and intensity of therapy, do not have the skills to self-soothe and modulate their affect, do not have emotional support outside of the therapeutic relationship, or do not have the ability to use relationships to regulate their affect need to first focus on acquiring these and other ways of coping with stress before adding more stress to their lives. If we succumb to the temptation to try to be the client's only support for handling stress, we could be committing ourselves to always being available, possibly with no limits on time, cost, expectations, and liability. Such ventures can lead to client disappointment and therapist burnout.

As We Slow the Client, We Slow Ourselves

There are benefits to slowing down treatment, but progressing slowly can be uncomfortable for both the therapist and the client. The client expects the therapist to offer something, and the therapist wants to give something. There are many pressures on the therapist to rush to closure, provide solutions, and offer suggestions as soon as possible. Therapists are exposed to a treatment literature that extols brief, even one-session, treatments (Bloom, 2001; Hoyt & Talmon, 1990) in which the clinician teaches a technique (perhaps having the client constantly ask himself or herself, "How does this make me feel?"), prescribes the symptom (worry before you go to bed instead of while you are in bed trying to get to sleep), reframes the narrative, and provides a paradoxical suggestion or a behavioral prescription; then the client is almost cured. We are pressured to intervene rapidly before the client's money, insurance, or patience run out or the client becomes even worse. We might feel anxious and incompetent when we do not give them something.

Early comments and interpretations by the therapist can be destabilizing and disrupt the initial goal of engaging the client. Some clients are not ready to be seen or be seen as the therapist sees them. Comments that we think are obvious may be earth shattering, even such comments as, "You're being abused," "He may be retarded," "You may need medication," or "Do you have a drug problem?" Sometimes therapists mistakenly believe that the sooner they offer interpretations or suggestions, the more helpful and competent they are.

Moving too rapidly can be ineffective. Premature suggestions can be perverted by the client's established belief system. For instance, I once educated an authoritarian, punitive father about natural consequences in an attempt to help him develop priorities about the behaviors he would try to control in his son. I wanted him to understand that natural consequences would teach the lesson if he did not intervene. He returned the next session to proudly tell me how he allowed his son to decide for himself what time he would be home and how the son got the natural consequence—a good spanking.

Often changes create countervailing forces. For instance, helping someone become more assertive without the proper preparation can lead to painful consequences because the person to whom the client expresses his or her assertiveness might be threatened and respond with hostility. Different systems tolerate different amounts of change. If the family is not prepared to appreciate the new behavior, it can be squashed like a bug. Especially at the start of treatment, therapist-generated solutions can be uninformed, create dependency, and prevent the client from developing the skills to solve problems independently. Advice can cut off communication and exploration.

However, with experience, patterns emerge and become familiar. Because I have traveled the same roads with other clients, I may well have useful suggestions, insights, and warnings to offer. When I do offer suggestions, I try to be constantly vigilant that they fit the client's situation and are not the recycled solutions I relied on with other clients or in my life. When the client seems familiar, I proceed with caution, because I do not want to treat the wrong client. The best treatment happens when I ask clients the right questions that lead them to discover the solutions themselves. Then they are more motivated to implement these changes, but I may not be in total agreement with the course they are taking.

Therapists observe robust patterns and assume that the new client will fit that mold. After we hear perpetrators deny abusing others and then eventually acknowledge their abusive behavior, it is natural to believe the accuser and assume the accused is guilty. After we see abused children recant and then reaffirm their disclosure, it is understandable to not believe their denials. After we see drug addicts repeatedly return to their habit, it is reasonable to discredit their promises. Predicting from the base rates is one of the helpful things therapists do. However, we must be on the lookout for the exception. For example, after seeing many grandmothers repeatedly provide money and housing to their drug-addicted children only to see them return to the streets after emotionally harming the grandchildren that the grandmother is raising, I was quick to try to protect the children. I tried to persuade one grandmother to refuse to allow her son to return home again. The grandmother reported that her alcoholic son appeared at the door with his pregnant meth-addicted girlfriend and asked if they could live in her home. I instantly pointed out the pattern of his using her home to clean up and then return to the streets, how it hurt her finances and the children, how she was not really helping them but enabling them to go in the direction their addiction was leading them, and that there were other resources she could help them obtain. She agreed and felt guilty but let them stay without even making their stay contingent on any bench-mark behaviors. She said she just had to help them. At subsequent sessions I continued to pressure her to look more realistically at her choice and codependent behavior. We had a strong relationship, so she tolerated me. Six months later her son had a job, was parenting the children, and was bonding to his new daughter. They were substance free, and the girlfriend had become the grandmother's best friend.

Therapists Can Be an Obstacle to Change if We Cannot Be Flexible and Tolerate Uncertainty

The basic premises of psychotherapy are still being debated. There are conflicting theories about the nature of human beings that generate differ-ent treatment models that focus on different methods of creating change. Behaviorists use behavior modification and believe that feelings do not play a part in causing behavior. Dialectical behavior therapy focuses on changing feelings and contends that feelings cause thoughts and pathology. Psychoanalysis focuses on bringing the unconscious into awareness and contends that the unconscious causes feelings, whereas rational-emotive and cognitive-behavioral models focus on changing cognitions and stipulate that conscious cognitions cause feelings. Some theorists focus on the ante-cedents of behaviors, some focus on the behaviors, and some focus on the consequences. Psychiatrists emphasize that the client's biology causes feel-ings and behavior, and they focus on creating chemical changes.

Some therapies focus on the past, others focus on the present or future. Some focus on problems, some focus on solutions (Gingerich & Eisengart, 2000). Some ignore problems, and emphasize installing character strengths and virtues. Some encourage expressing feelings to reduce them (abreaction and catharsis), whereas others emphasize suppression and control. Some think the cure is in the therapeutic relationship, whereas others emphasize evidence-based techniques. Some focus on insight to achieve behavioral change, whereas others do not think insight is a necessary or sufficient pre-condition to change. Some challenge and confront, whereas others nurture and support. Some emphasize change, some emphasize acceptance. For the same problem, therapists recommend different modes of therapy (medica-tion, individual, child guidance counseling, family, group, etc.). Therapists have different models for how long therapy should last and who should choose the problem to remediate. It is rare to find one generally accepted theory or approach to a client's problem. Senior therapists will disagree on how to prioritize the many interventions that are currently available.

We have to deal with the mother of uncertainty; the effectiveness of psychotherapy in clinical practice continues to be debated. It is unclear if, how much, for what problems and clients, and under what conditions treatment enhances outcome.

We have to be open to changing and adapting our approach from session to session. At times we need to be guided by our client's present needs. Often I have to postpone or abandon my plans for a session to deal with what the client is or should be focused on. At the same time I do not want to get into the trap of constantly putting out fires and not dealing with core issues and treatment goals. When I feel comfortable doing my routine, I wonder if I might be ignoring important aspects of my client and not adjusting to his or her needs. Beware the overconfident therapist; he or she may be delusional.

Sometimes I do not know if I am helping or making things worse. Progress in therapy and our contribution to it are difficult to measure. We are not engaged in a business where success can be easily measured by a monetary bottom line. We cannot count on clients to tell us why they terminated or if we have been helpful; they can just quit without a word. Sometimes they tell us, and we cannot believe them. Often clients present themselves initially as worse than they are to justify to themselves and the therapist their need to obtain services. Then they exaggerate improvement to justify leaving treatment. We have to live with very poor ways to measure outcomes. I recently received a letter from an adult whom I saw as a 14-year-old, Hispanic, fatherless gang member from a chaotic family. I treated her for 6 months and ended feeling that I had accomplished little. She argued with almost everything I said, defended her behaviors, and sometimes yelled at me and left the session. I knew I liked and cared about her, but I was not sure she had a connection with me, even though she kept coming back to complain about the treatment she received from family and peers until the family moved without notice. The letter described how well she was doing and thanked me for being so helpful in turning her around, and she apologized for having been so rude and oppositional. I was shocked and reminded that I cannot be too confident in my judgments about what is happening in therapy. Sometimes I think I am being helpful, whereas the client thinks I am not. Often clients report that they really appreciated what I said in a previous session, and I do not recall saying it or at the time did not feel my comment was particularly significant. Sometimes I might be the last to know what is really going on.

CHAPTER 2

The Eight Sources of Change in Psychotherapy

Therapists need to be critical consumers of the treatment research. When we carefully review the research on evidence-based treatments, we find that methodological problems, biases, and political and economic forces have distorted the findings. This examination leads to questioning the field's present reliance on the medical model in which evidence-based techniques are applied to particular diagnoses. The problem with relying on evidence-based interventions is not with the concept of evidence-based treatment. Clinical practice should be based on treatments that are backed by research, because research is the best protection against inadequate treatments. As Alan Kazdin (2008, p. 157), the president of the American Psychology Association, stated, "The best practice will continue to be based on the best science." The problem is that much of the research is biased, flawed, indiscriminately applied, and ignored. There is considerable research to aid the clinician in developing a strategy for selecting and timing interventions that improve outcome. The research indicates that eight elements account for change in psychotherapy. Each can be sufficient to determine outcome. Therefore the therapist's mission is to contribute to fostering change by maximizing the impact of these forces.

These eight forces are described as distinct entities, but in reality they can be indistinguishable from each other. For instance, the distinction is vague between therapeutic techniques and the therapist's characteristics that contribute to change. As Leitner (2007) explained, "Becoming a psychotherapist is not about assembling a bag of tricks and learning the formula for matching tricks (i.e., techniques) with problems. What you do as a therapist emerges from who you are in the therapy room. ... Theory and technique wind up so integrated into who the therapist is as a person that they lose their meanings" (p. 35). He contended that when techniques are not fully integrated, they are perceived by the client as an ingenuous reaction and feel like the therapist is doing something to the client. However, when they are fully incorporated into the therapist, the techniques become effective because they are seen as a spontaneous exposure of the therapist's genuine reaction to the client.

What Are the Factors That Contribute to Change in Psychotherapy?

1. Evidenced-Based Techniques

Evidenced-based techniques might be incorporated into treatment when the timing is appropriate. The research guides us to favor some interventions and to avoid others.

There are evidence-based interventions that have become the standard of care for some diagnostic categories. Research has shown at least the short-term effectiveness of cognitive-behavioral therapy (CBT) and exposure and response prevention for compulsions; applied behavior analysis and the TEACCH program for autism (Mesibov & Shea, 2006); CBT, exercise, and medication for depression; dialectical behavior therapy for borderlines; penile squeeze and stop–start techniques for premature ejaculation (Kilmann & Auerbach, 1979); Wet-Stop and similar devices for enuresis (Glazener, Evans, & Peto, 2005); behavior modification for encopresis; cognitive therapy for panic disorder and bulimia; medication, classroom- and home-based behavior modification, education about the disorder, and educational advocacy for attention-deficit/hyperactivity disorder (ADHD); parent behavioral training involving contingency management, anger management, and problem-solving and assertiveness training for youths with behavior disorders; and exposure, relaxation, medication, systematic desensitization, and (for adolescents and older) CBT for fears and anxiety. Because of our present political and economic climate, it may be unethical, and increasingly nonreimbursable, to exclude such interventions from our client's treatment plan (Lonigan, Elbert, & Bennett-Johnson, 1998).[1] There are many resources to guide the therapist in applying evidence-based treatments using the medical model. At least five books have recently been published for therapists on evidence-based treatments for children and adolescents (reviewed by Ginsburg, 2006), and there are treatment guidelines that are readily available for most diagnostic categories (e.g., the American Association of Child and Adolescent Psychiatry guidelines).[2]

The research also supports excluding treatments (Lilienfeld, 2005), such as insight-oriented psychotherapy for conduct disorder, ADHD, and schizophrenia. "Studies of psychosocial interventions among children and adolescents for autism, anorexia and bulimia, PTSD, bipolar disorder, obsessive-compulsive disorder, panic disorder, and substance abuse have not yet met the criteria for being considered well-established or probably efficacious" (Hoagwood, Burns, Kiser, Ringeisen, & Schoenwald, 2001, p. 1180). The use of cognitive-behavioral techniques has not been shown to be helpful in mastering impulses in youths with ADHD. They do not seem to benefit from the frequently offered "stop-reflect-and-then-act" interventions or from diets that reduce or eliminate sugar and additives or increase vitamins and supplements.

The experts polled in the Delphi study on the future of psychotherapy (Norcross, Koocher, & Garofalo, 2006) "considered as *certainly discredited* 14 psychological treatments: angel therapy, use of pyramid structures, orgone therapy, crystal healing, past lives therapy, future lives therapy, treatments for post-traumatic stress disorder (PTSD) caused by alien abduction, rebirthing therapies, color therapy, primal scream, chiropractic manipulation for mental disorders, thought field therapy, standard prefrontal lobotomy, and aroma therapy. Another 11 treatments were consensually designated as *probably discredited*" (p. 517), including Erhard Seminar Training, age-regression methods for treating adults sexually abused as children, craniosacral treatments for anxiety and depression, preventive interventions for "born criminals," sexual reorientation therapy for homosexuals, holding therapy for reactive attachment disorders, treatments for mental disorders resulting from Satanic ritual abuse, healing touch therapy for mental disorders, therapy based on the schizophrenogenic theory of schizophrenia, reparenting therapies, and treatments based on Bettleheim's theory of autism, which blamed autism on the failure of parents to supply adequate emotional support and nurturance.

Some treatments have been found to harm some clients. They include critical-incident stress debriefing, recovered-memory techniques, treating dissociative identity disorder with techniques that create more alters, grief counseling for individuals with normal bereavement reactions, expressive-experimental therapies such as encounter groups, Drug Abuse Resistance Education (D.A.R.E.) programs,[3] and relaxation treatments for panic-prone patients (Lilienfeld, 2007, p. 58). Scared Straight (Petrosino, Turpin-Petrosino, & Buehler, 2002) and boot-camp (MacKenzie, Wilson, & Kider, 2001; Wilson, MacKenzie, & Mitchell, 2005; Zhang, 1999) interventions for conduct disordered clients and holding and rebirthing therapies for attachment disordered clients have not been shown to be helpful and can cause harm.

In treating attachment disordered youths, "Treatment techniques or attachment parenting techniques involving physical coercion, psychologically or physically enforced holding, physical restraint, physical domination, provoked catharsis, ventilation of rage, age regression, humiliation, withholding or forcing food or water intake, prolonged social isolation, or assuming exaggerated levels of control and domination over a child are contraindicated because of risk of harm and absence of proven benefit and should not be used" (Chaffin et al., 2006, p. 86).

Some peer group and educational treatments have been shown to be harmful. Peer group treatment for adolescent conduct disorders can increase delinquent behaviors (Dishion, McCord, & Poulin, 1999; Rhule, 2005), perhaps by supplying inappropriate modeling, peer pressure, and reinforcement of delinquent appearance, behaviors, cognitions, and affect. Some researchers have reexamined the literature and found little evidence for concluding that group treatment can cause harm to delinquent youths (Weiss et al., 2005). Probably some youths benefit, and some are harmed; we lack the research to identify characteristics of clients, groups, and treatments that predict positive or negative outcomes. There is always a danger that when clients with the same disorder get together, they will reinforce each other's defenses and share pathological techniques to incorporate into their repertoires. For example, clients with eating disorders love to reinforce each other's values about body image and share ways to lose weight and conceal their dieting and exercise. I have had clients who received support to maintain their anorexia or bulimia from the Internet. When I searched Google (September 9, 2005) for "pro ana," (anorexia), I found 6,750,000 citations, many offering "thinspiration tricks and techniques." There is similar Internet support for "pro mia," or bulimia, and for cutting (Whitlock, Powers, & Eckenrode, 2006) and peer support for skin burning and erasing. Providing educational interventions to inadequately screened populations can create problems. As a client with a substance abuse disorder responded after being exposed to a D.A.R.E.-like school-based drug education program, "It was helpful. I learned that you can make a bong out of a Coke can."

There is evidence that some clients get worse during treatment, because psychotherapy can cause harm and because treatment cannot prevent the client's deterioration. One study found that one fifth of youths treated in outpatient settings showed signs of deterioration (Tam & Healy, 2007), and the estimate of prominent psychotherapy researchers was that 10% of clients get worse from psychotherapy (Boisvert & Faust, 2003).[4] The mechanisms have not been identified by which treatments fail to benefit or harm clients. However, some treatments may harm because they create false memories or personality alters, sensitize clients to dangers and personal deficits, arouse anxiety that the client is unable to successfully process and desensitize to, or provide deviant role models or well-intended information that the client uses in a detrimental manner.

Evidence-based treatments can fail or harm because the sources of change have not been adequately addressed. Problems with any of the eight sources of change can be sufficient to subvert therapy. The therapist can contribute to a poor outcome by failing to recognize and remediate problems in the forces of change. My most serious treatment mistakes (that I am aware of) have been as follows: (a) presenting techniques to inadequately motivated clients, (b) offering treatments based on recognizing and then developing more adaptive cognitions and feelings when clients lack the ability to observe their cognitions and emotional states or cannot process their feelings and cognitions in language, (c) offering relationship-based treatments to clients who cannot form relationships, (d) providing a treatment rationale that conflicts with the client's theory of change, (e) inadequately engaging caretakers or youths, (f) working on goals that are different from those of the youth or parents, (g) not adequately dealing with barriers to treatment, (h) creating disappointments by inadequately providing a treatment frame, (i) alienating a client by presenting values that clash with his or her values or otherwise being unattuned to countertransference feelings, (j) inadequately dealing with transference tests and relationship ruptures, (k) making clients uncomfortable by pushing them in response to resistances, and (l) allowing the client to experience too much anxiety or frustration.

The vast majority of treatment approaches have not been subjected to sound outcome research. Only a few treatments have been studied empirically. For instance, in a review of outcome studies on youths in the past 40 years, 71% involved learning-based (cognitive-behavioral and behavioral) interventions (Weisz, Doss, & Hawley, 2005). "Family therapy, and parent work in parallel with individual treatment for the child, have rarely been evaluated, despite the fact that these are probably the most frequent psychosocial approaches in routine clinical work" (Roth & Fonagy, 2006, p. 423). These researchers concluded, "In many respects the field is at too early a stage to make many evidence-based recommendations about which treatments show the most benefit for which disorders [for youths]" (p. 424). Because treatments are not supported by research, it does not necessarily mean that they are not effective. At this time we do not know their effectiveness. Therefore we cannot make valid claims as to which techniques are the most effective.

Evidence-based treatments cannot be automatically applied in daily practice because of a variety of reasons. The research supporting their superiority over other techniques has flaws that lead to questioning the power of the techniques and whether it is the technique that really causes the improvement. Messer and Wampold (2002) argued that evidence-based techniques are embedded in a therapeutic relationship, which is what actually accounts for much of the treatment effect. Furthermore, they contended that faulty research underlies the advantage attributed to many evidence-based techniques, even when the studies tried to control for the benefits of the therapeutic relationship. They found that in the typical study, the specific "successful" treatment was compared to a nonactive treatment control group that attempted to provide the common relationship factors without the specific treatment technique. When these control treatments were divided into bona fide treatments and non–bona fide treatments ("vaguely described as 'verbal therapies,' 'non-specific therapies,' or 'non-psychiatric treatment' "), these controls were "foils to establish the efficacy of a particular treatment ... and were not meant to be therapeutic in the sense of an active treatment backed by theory, research, or clinical experience" (p. 18).

Applying this analysis to treating depression, Wampold, Minami, Baskin, and Tierney (2002) meta-analyzed therapies for depression and found CBT to be superior to noncognitive and nonbehavioral therapies until they separated these therapies into two groups: those that were bona fide treatments (i.e., treatments supported by psychological theory and provided with a specified protocol) and those that were not intended to be therapeutic. Then the superiority of CBT to these other therapies was an artifact of including non–bona fide therapies in the comparisons. "CBT was not significantly more beneficial than non-cognitive, non-behavioral treatments that were intended to be therapeutic." Furthermore, the authors pointed out that to measure effectiveness, these studies often used rating scales (e.g., the Hamilton Depression Inventory or the Beck Depression Inventory) that were overweighed on cognitive aspects of depression so they favored the cognitive treatment being tested (p. 163). Other meta-analysis (Spielmans, Pasek, & McFall, 2007; Weisz, McCarty, & Valeri, 2006) of the effectiveness of cognitive-behavioral treatments for anxious and depressed children replicated Wampold et al.'s findings and concluded, "CBT was no more efficacious than bona fide non-CBT treatments."

To review, evidence-based techniques may appear superior to controls because control groups have been inadequate. When evidence-based treatments are compared to well-designed controls, they have not been found to be superior (Baskin, Tierney, Minami, & Wampold, 2003).[5] For example, in a meta-analysis of 64 child psychotherapy outcome studies, behavioral therapies were far superior to client-centered and psychodynamic treatments until the authors excluded studies whose outcome measures were highly similar to the specific activities that were focused on in treatment. Then the superiority of behavioral treatments disappeared (Casey & Berman, 1985). Likewise, when evidence-based psychotherapies for youths were compared to "treatments as usual" in a meta-analysis of 32 studies where all subjects were randomly assigned to treatment groups, the authors concluded, "Evidence-based treatments outperformed usual care" (Weisz, Jensen-Doss, & Hawley, 2006, p. 671).

However, almost all the studies reviewed were on conduct disordered males whose evidence-based treatment was compared to ineffective treatments. The "treatments as usual" that the evidence-based treatments were superior to included probation services and correctional facility or residential care where psychotherapy may or may not have been provided.

Another problem with the research supporting the superiority of evidence-based treatments for specific diagnostic categories is that the research has not adequately controlled for client and experimenter expectations. It may not be the particular technique that leads to client progress, but the client and therapist's belief in the treatment (Beutler & Clarkin, 1990). Similarly, the researcher's belief in the effectiveness of the treatment being evaluated can alter the outcome of studies. In fact, it has been estimated that almost 70% of the variance in the effect sizes found in studies that compared one treatment to another may have been caused by the researchers' alliance to the treatment (Luborsky et al., 1999).

Another reason evidence-based treatments cannot be automatically relied on in clinical practice is that even though treatments have been shown to be effective in controlled experiments with screened subjects, it does not mean that these interventions are transportable to clinical practice. Clients are a different species than research subjects. Comorbidity runs rampant in clinical practice while researchers seek subjects who have only one diagnosis. Probably 50% of patients can be expected to have at least one comorbid diagnosis (Wittchen et al., 1998). Twenty-one percent of people with one *DSM-IV* (*Diagnostic and Statistical Manual of Mental Disorders–Fourth Edition;* American Psychiatric Association, 1994) diagnosis might meet the criteria for three or more disorders (Andrews et al., 2002).

Furthermore, as discussed above, evidence-based treatments may not be transportable to everyday clinical practice because the subjects in these studies are preselected to benefit from the intervention. The effectiveness of these techniques is partly a function of excluding two thirds of the most difficult to treat clients (Westen & Morrison, 2001).[6] These researchers found, "The more patients excluded in a given study, the higher the percent of patients that showed improvement." In addition, "Subjects who come to treatment for clinical trials via advertisement (versus clinical referral) may show more favorable treatment responses" (Brent et al., 1998, p. 906). As James Prochaska noted, research outcome studies recruit "the most compliant clients by requiring multiple assessments and permission before treatment starts, requiring that people be willing to accept placebos or no treatment, and making access to treatment difficult, such as always being clinic-based rather than having an option for home-based treatment" (Norcross & Goldfried, 2005, p. 422). As others have observed, to foster significant results the first law of research may be "Don't use real patients" (Goldfried & Wolf, 1996).

Evidence-based techniques cannot automatically be adapted to clients who have the diagnosis that the techniques are supposed to treat, because clients with the same diagnosis are a very heterogeneous group. To be acceptable to clients, techniques need to be compatible with the client's theory of change, so they make sense to him or her. The techniques also need to be perceived by clients as potentially beneficial and capable of being carried out, and clients must be ready to tolerate the stress that these techniques might generate. For instance, research indicates that exposure-based treatments using the learning principle of desensitization effectively treat PTSD and panic disorders in the laboratory. But in my practice it is rare to find a client who can begin to expose himself or herself to anxiety without significant preparation. Much of the art of therapy involves judging the client's readiness and ability to tolerate evidence-based interventions as well as deciding if such interventions can be used at all.

Clients with the same diagnosis differ dramatically in their level of motivation, which helps determine the choice and timing of interventions (Prochaska & DiClemente, 1992). Probably my most frequent mistake is to offer an intervention before the client is ready. Often clients progress from denying and minimizing their problems to acknowledging them and then seeking solutions with varying degrees of commitment to the treatment process. We have to make our choice of intervention fit their present awareness and motivation to change.

A major concern about evidence-based treatments is that the *Consumer Reports* survey ("Mental Health," 1995), the National Institute of Mental Health (NIMH) Treatment for Depression Collaborative Research Program (Elkin et al., 1989), and meta-analyses of comparisons of active treatments (Luborsky et al., 2002)[7] indicated that there is not a significant difference in the effectiveness of different treatments based on different theoretical orientations. "Study after study, meta-analysis after meta-analysis, and Luborsky et al.'s meta-meta-analysis have produced the same small or non-extent difference among therapies … the evidence points to all active therapies being equally beneficial" (Messer & Wampold, 2002, p. 19).

This finding that most forms of psychotherapy do about equally well is known as the dodo bird verdict based on the dodo bird's quote in *Alice in Wonderland* that "everybody has won so all shall have prizes." These research findings have led to the belief that the most powerful forces in treatment are not the specific interventions but the common factors in effective treatments, especially the therapeutic relationship (Lambert & Barley, 2001). These authors concluded that empirically validated techniques account for less than 15% of the variance in the treatment outcome. They contended that 30% of outcome variance is accounted for by the therapeutic relationship, client characteristics and other extratherapeutic change forces contribute

40% of the outcome variance, and 15% is accounted for by placebo effects (the client's expectations).

The similarity in effectiveness of treatments is further confirmed by evidence that treatments, which are assumed to be effective because of their unique elements, are just as effective when the unique features are removed. Therefore, the "theoretically purported important components are not responsible for [the] therapeutic benefits" (Ahn & Wampold, 2001). So the unique therapeutic ingredients of favored treatments might not account for the client's improvement. For example, the back-and-forth eye movement in eye movement desensitization and reprocessing therapy (EMDR) may not be a necessary or sufficient cause of the improvement attributed to using this treatment (Spector & Read, 1999).

Tallman and Bohart suggested that the dodo bird verdict is evidence that successful clients are self-healers. They concluded, "The dodo bird verdict occurs because the client's abilities to use whatever is offered surpass any differences that might exist in techniques or approaches. ... Clients utilize and tailor what each approach provides to address their problems. Even if different techniques have different specific effects, clients take these effects, individualize them to their specific purposes, and use them. Thus, for example, a client can use cognitive or interpersonal techniques ... or emotional exploration procedures, or empathically based client-centered therapy ... to move themselves out of depression" (Hubble, Duncan, & Miller, 1999, p. 95). The client's positive expectations about the effectiveness of the treatments offered probably also contribute to the effectiveness of most treatments (Arnkoff, Glass, & Shapiro, 2002).

Houston, we have a problem! In this age of evidence-based treatment where it is generally believed that some therapies have been shown to be more effective than others, and some treatments have been shown to be ineffective, how can we believe in the dodo bird verdict? We know that the average difference between various treatments for a variety of problems is minimal; however, hidden in these averages could be a significant difference in the effectiveness of particular treatments for a particular problem (Chambless, 2002; Siev & Chambless, 2007). The jury is still out; however, it looks like the effectiveness of specific techniques for specific diagnoses has been exaggerated. Yes, all treatments are not equal, and some have greater potential to harm. Yes, squeeze for premature ejaculation, Wet-Stop for enuresis, exposure as treatment for fears (Lambert & Bergin, 1992), exposure and response prevention for obsessive-compulsive disorder, CBT for panic attacks, and a few others are probably the most efficient and effective treatments. However, many treatments of choice are believed to be more effective than they really are because of the present economic and political climate, which demands evidence-based treatments but ignores the biases in the research supporting the evidence base.

As in psychotherapy outcome studies, the biases and deficits have been ignored in the research supporting the efficacy of specific drug treatments. The economic climate has so influenced research that all drug effectiveness studies must now be viewed with caution. We live in an age of "evidence-b(i)ased medicine" (Melander et al., 2003). The profit-driven pharmaceutical industry underwrites about 70% of U.S. drug research (DeAngelis, Fontanarosa, & Flanagin, 2001) and influences the outcome (Lexchin, Bero, Djulbegovic, & Clark, 2003). This influence is shown in a recent review of pharmaceutical-industry-funded research that compared the effectiveness of five new antipsychotic drugs. Heres et al. (2006) found that 90% of the studies favored the medication made by the company funding the study. To bias results the researchers used the following: (a) relatively brief trials, to avoid the expectation that three fourths of the patients would stop taking the antipsychotics because of intolerable side effects or lack of efficacy, as happened in the major NIMH-funded study of antipsychotic drug effectiveness (Lieberman et al., 2005); (b) an inadequate dose of the competitor's medication; and (c) research designs and statistical techniques that favored their drug. John Davis, MD, one of the authors in the Heres's study, estimated that "90 percent of industry sponsored studies that boast a prominent academic as the lead author are conducted by the company that later enlists a university researcher as the 'author' " (Vedantam, 2006a).

Using this biased research, the makers of brand-name drugs then employ more than 90,000 handsome and attractive "detailers" in the United States at a cost of more than $12 billion a year to influence physicians to prescribe the medication (*Wall Street Journal*, 2006). Because drug companies seem to be controlling the information physicians, consumers and insurance providers rely on to base treatment decisions, it is not surprising that the use of medication with youths is so widespread and disconnected from sound research (Weisz & Jensen, 1999). Probably 80% of all medication provided to minors is "off-label," not supported by research with the same age group, according to the American Academy of Pediatrics Committee on Drugs (1996).

The financial tentacles of the pharmaceutical industry extend to federal regulatory agencies, professional organizations, medical journals (Turner, Matthews, Linardatos, Tell, & Rosenthal, 2008),[8] continuing medical education (Steinbrook, 2008), scientific researchers, media experts, and consumer advocacy organizations (Abramson & Starfield, 2005; Antonuccio, Danton, & McClanahan, 2003).[9] Even the *DSM*, which defines the disorders, was written by authors with financial ties to the pharmaceutical industry. "Of the 170 experts who contributed to the manual … more than half had such ties, including 100 percent of the experts who served on work groups on mood disorders, such as depression, and psychotic disorders, such as schizophrenia" (Vedantam, 2006b). Fifty-nine percent of writers of clinical practice guidelines had financial relationships with the companies whose drugs were considered in the guidelines they authored (Choudhry, Stelfox, & Detsky, 2002).[10] To recap, drug makers underwrite research and treatment guidelines and then pay doctors who prescribe the drugs to lecture to other potential prescribers who are paid to attend (Campbell et al., 2007).[11]

These relationships are synergistic, as exemplified by the recent rise in the off-label use of atypical antipsychotics in the treatment of youths, according to Harris, Carey, and Roberts (2007, http//www.NYTIMES.com/2007/05/10/health/10psyche.html). They reported that psychiatrists

who took the most money from makers of atypicals tended to prescribe the drugs to children the most often, the data suggest. On average, Minnesota psychiatrists who received at least $5,000 from atypical makers from 2000 to 2005 appear to have written three times as many atypical prescriptions for children as psychiatrists who received less or no money. ...

One of the first and perhaps most influential studies [on the effectiveness of atypical antipsychotics in the treatment of bipolar disorder in youths] was financed by AstraZeneca [DelBello, Schwiers, Rosenberg, & Strakowski, 2002]. Dr. DelBello led a research team that tracked for six weeks the moods of 30 adolescents who had received diagnoses of bipolar disorder. Half of the teenagers took Depakote, an antiseizure drug used to treat epilepsy and bipolar disorder in adults. The other half took Seroquel and Depakote.

The two groups did about equally well until the last few days of the study, when those in the Seroquel group scored lower on a standard measure of mania. By then, almost half of the teenagers getting Seroquel had dropped out because they missed appointments or the drugs did not work. Just eight of them completed the trial. ... Dr. DelBello and her co-authors reported that Seroquel in combination with Depakote 'is more effective for the treatment of adolescent bipolar mania' than Depakote alone. In 2005, a committee of prominent experts from across the country examined all of the studies of treatment for pediatric bipolar disorder and decided that Dr. DelBello's was the only study involving atypicals in bipolar children that deserved its highest rating for scientific rigor. The panel concluded that doctors should consider atypicals as a first-line treatment for some children. The guidelines were published in *The Journal of the American Academy of Child and Adolescent Psychiatry*. Three of the four doctors on the panel served as speakers or consultants to makers of atypicals, according to disclosures in the guidelines. ... AstraZeneca hired Dr. DelBello ... to give sponsored talks.

Having researchers state at the end of publications whether they have ties to drug companies does not resolve this problem.

Many factors need to be considered before attempting an "evidence-based" psychotherapeutic intervention. The intervention should be tailored to the client's developmental stage. What works for adults does not necessarily work for youths. For example, young children think differently than more mature clients. They may egocentrically believe that events occurred because they caused them, that they were responsible for and deserved the consequences they received, or that events were caused by co-occurring events. They may have a shortened time frame and consider only immediate and observable consequences while ignoring intentions and long-term consequences. So when teaching anger management, a therapist should consider that someone whose level of moral development is based on the consequences he receives would not be a good candidate for an intervention to control his anger based on empathy for others. A child with an anger control problem who is a concrete thinker might need a concrete behavioral solution, such as role-plays in which instead of hitting he practices telling the teacher or counting to ten or walking away, saying, "I'm rubber you're glue. Whatever you say bounces off me and sticks to you." Or he could use the child-tested "You are." Someone who seeks immediate gratification probably requires immediate rewards. An adolescent or adult with an anger control problem who is an abstract thinker (having reached formal operations) might be able to benefit from a more cognitive insight-oriented intervention, such as realizing that when he is angry he is being like the father whose anger he disliked. The client's theory of change and Piaget's view that clients can assimilate in information that is only a little different from what they know and expect influence the choice of intervention. A major criticism of the youth outcome research is that it "is often adevelopmental" (Weisz & Hawley, 2002, p. 21).

The client's strengths and weaknesses (insight, judgment, ability to learn, social support, ability to attach and care about others, ability to observe thoughts and feelings, physical health, attention span, etc.) influence the choice and effectiveness of interventions. Past treatments can influence the treatment plan, and clients can often identify what has been helpful and what has been ineffective in their past attempts to deal with a problem. Exploring these previous efforts can shorten what is sometimes a trial-and-error process of finding the most helpful intervention.

A client's present situation and stresses and his or her family dynamics and social environment all influence the choice of intervention. For instance, because a child's needs might not be able to be met by an overwhelmed parent living in a chaotic environment, the therapist or caretaker might seek help from a grandparent, Big Brother or mentor, teacher, or after-school program to supply the routines and consistency the child needs. Maslow's hierarchy of needs helps determine priorities. A homeless or hungry client first needs shelter and food. An abused client first needs to be safe. A client's insurance, transportation, and finances can affect the choice of intervention.

With increasing frequency, I find clients are requesting specific interventions. Because I look for interventions that are compatible with the clients' motivation and theory of change, when they ask for something reasonable, such as EMDR for trauma or medication for anxiety or depression, I support their request because they are motivated and believe strongly in the intervention. Sometimes they request approaches that do not seem helpful, such as boot camp or individual therapy for their child's conduct disorder or ADHD, dietary treatment for ADHD, and marriage counseling for domestic violence. Then I provide educational arguments that support alternative approaches.

Therapy is effective. Most adult clients who stay in treatment improve (Seligman, 1995). A meta-analysis of 475 adult treatment outcome studies concluded that the average client was better off than 80% of untreated controls (Smith & Glass, 1977; Smith, Glass, & Miller, 1980). As Wampold (2007) explained, this means "the average patient receiving treatment would be better off than almost 80% of untreated patients." Converting this "to an index called the number needed to treat (NNT), the number of patients who need to receive the experimental treatment ... to achieve one success ... is equivalent to an NNT of 3 (Kraemer & Kupfer, 2006), that is, three patients need to receive psychotherapy to achieve a success relative to untreated patients" (p. 865). Research on youths shows a similar rate of improvement (Weisz, Weiss, Alicke, & Klotz, 1987; Weisz, Weiss, Han, Granger, & Morton, 1995). Many studies that compare treatment in clinical settings with control groups or waiting lists support the benefits of psychotherapy (Shadish et al., 1997). In general about 65% to 70% of selected clients respond favorably to specific treatments for specific diagnoses in controlled efficacy studies, in comparison to 31% of controls (Seligman, 1996; Wampold, 2001).

But, to recap, research has especially explored cognitive-behavioral techniques, behavior modification, and medication. Much of the proven efficacy of these approaches may actually be attributed to research design and other therapeutic factors rather than to these interventions themselves. Research has not and may not be able to separate specific treatment techniques from the context of the therapeutic relationship in which they are embedded and thereby identify decontextualized active treatments. Manuals cannot exist apart from the complex common factors in which they are imbedded. For example, when cognitive-behavioral techniques are used to treat depression, their effectiveness is related to the strength of the therapeutic relationship and the client's emotional involvement (Castonguay, Goldfried, Wiser, Raue, & Hayes, 1996). Despite all the "treatment of choice" talk, and the emphasis on techniques, they play a role in determining outcome, but a small role.

The research on the treatment of childhood depression and anxiety is characteristic of the literature on most disorders. Compton, Burns, Egger, and Robertson (2002) reviewed the studies that underlie the use of evidence-based techniques for treating children with depression and anxiety disorders. Their findings are characteristic of the present outcome literature. Almost all the research on treating childhood depression was on cognitive-behavioral or behavioral approaches. These interventions were more effective than no treatment or waiting-list controls, which are minimal criteria for effectiveness. However, when compared to "a variety of alternative treatments (e.g., relaxation training, non-focused supportive therapy) … all active treatments were effective in reducing symptoms of depression among children relative to wait-list [inactive] controls." Generally effect sizes of "6% to 14% of the variance in outcome were attributable to specific treatments." The authors concluded, "Depressed children responded similarly to most active interventions, including cognitive-behavioral therapy, attention-placebo, and nonspecific supportive interventions." They found similar results in their review of 21 studies of anxiety disorder treatments that met their criteria for adequacy of design. In these studies, (a) almost all interventions were cognitive-behavioral or behavioral, (b) educational supportive therapy and "placebo attention controls" also caused comparable improvement, and (c) treatment effectiveness was enhanced when family involvement was added to the treatment. Therefore, specific treatment techniques for specific diagnostic categories are a small contributor to change, and these techniques depend on timing and the common factors.

Because the research literature indicates that psychotherapy for adults and youths has been shown to be effective, and no particular theoretical approach is dramatically superior to another, then common factors, not specific treatment techniques, account for the preponderance of client change. Building on the pioneering work of Rosenzweig (1936), Jerome Frank (1971, p. 350) identified factors common to all psychotherapies that could contribute to their success. His research indicated, "Common to all psychotherapies are an emotionally charged, confiding relationship; a therapeutic rationale accepted by patient and therapist; provision of new information by precept, example and self-discovery; strengthening of the patient's expectation of help; providing him with success experiences; and facilitation of emotional arousal."

Seven common factors have been extensively resear⌐
acteristics, the therapeutic alliance, therapist charactei.
processes present in most techniques, extratherapeutic forces, ⌐
related factors, and placebo effects can influence and determine outᵤ
This research is helpful in informing the therapist's artful selection anᴅ
timing of interventions.

2. Client Characteristics

Client characteristics are a major contributor to outcome. "One of the
most overlooked factors in psychotherapy research [is] the contribution
of the patient to the therapeutic process. Most observations of distinc-
tions between treatments tend to focus only on the therapists' behaviors,
interventions, and adherence to prescribed techniques in isolation from
the larger context in which they occur. However, the nature of therapeutic
process is inherently transactional. Patients are always coauthors and co-
constructors of the treatment process" (Ablon & Marci, 2004, p. 9). We
share with the client the responsibility for the outcome of treatment.

Power

Not all clients or all clients with the same diagnosis have the same potential to change. Each client enters treatment with a fairly fixed capacity to
form relationships, a capacity that correlates with outcome. Clients who
have demonstrated an ability to form relationships by beginning treatment
with social support improve more than those that are unsupported and
isolated (Kazdin & Whitley, 2006). Socially involved clients might have a
better treatment outcome because they are more able to attach to people,
form stronger therapeutic alliances, and use their relationship with others
and the therapist to reduce anxieties generated in treatment that interfere
with motivation and engagement.

The capacity to form relationships is rooted in genetics, early attachment
patterns, and the history of subsequent relationships. Genetics contributed
boundaries to introversion, extraversion, and resilience. These partially
inherited abilities affect the client's and therapist's capacity to form relationships, cope with stress, and obtain social support. Analogous to early
attachment behavior patterns, clients with social support might be able to
explore more deeply and take more risks in treatment because social support
might be a marker for having the capacity to use a secure interpersonal base
to which they can return and calm down. The avoidant client that is more
anxious with intimacy might not have social support, fear engagement,
and avoid or take inappropriate risks in treatment, thus limiting his or her
progress. Highly resilient clients can benefit from almost any intervention.

The client's early attachment patterns may influence core personality
variables and the therapeutic relationship. A frequent focus of psychotherapy involves attempts to correct faulty affect regulation. The template

for dysfunctional affect regulation has been theorized to originate in the rupture and repair patterns of the mother–infant attachment. Early attachment can be seen as a process by which the brain is formatted to modulate affect. "Schore (1996, 1997) has written about the developing brain as experience-dependent. He suggested that the infant's early affect is changed from despair to joy by the repair process. This change in affect is associated with the secretion of dopamine and endogenous opiates, which then prompt synaptic growth in the prefrontolimbic regions of the right brain. These are the regions involved in the infant's capacity for self-regulation. Failure to achieve repair in a reasonably consistent manner leads to structural changes in the brain that Schore believes form the biological substrate of later psychiatric disorders (Lewis, 2000)." The evidence that infant and childhood patterns of attachment are consistent enough to strongly influence adult interpersonal relationships must come not from the concordance of client self-report measures, but from longitudinal and experimental research that is only recently becoming available.

There is evidence from the attachment literature to support the connections between adult attachment style, quality of social support, therapeutic alliance, and treatment outcome. These connections have generated research on supplying different treatments for clients with different attachment patterns. For example, Mallinckrodt, Porter, and Kivlighan (2005) suggested that therapists could improve outcome by, for instance, regulating the level of emotional distance in therapy to gently alter the client's dysfunctional attachment pattern (e.g., by creating a slightly closer relationship than the avoidant client is comfortable with, or a more distant relationship than a client with high attachment needs might desire). However, they noted that the American Psychological Association Division 29 Task Force on Psychotherapy Relationships concluded that there is not yet sufficient research evidence that improved outcomes can be obtained by tailoring interventions to the client's pattern of attachment (Ackerman et al., 2001).

Client characteristics, such as participation in treatment, have been shown to influence outcome (Adelman, Kaser-Boyd, & Taylor, 1984; Mussell et al., 2000). Child involvement (defined as initiating discussion, engaging with treatment material, showing absence of withdrawal and avoidance, demonstrating self-disclosure and enthusiasm prior to exposure in the treatment of anxiety) has been related to improved outcome (Chu & Kendall, 2004). Child involvement has been estimated to account for about 16% of the variance in the outcome of developing self-control in impulse-disordered youths treated with CBT interventions (Braswell, Kendall, Braith, Carey, & Vye, 1985). Outcomes vary with the client's expectation of success and failure (Drew & Bickman, 2005; Joyce,

Ogrodniczuk, Piper, & McCallum, 2003; Lambert, 1992) and the client's deficits and strengths, such as the capacity to provide a narrative and the client's depth of pathology.

Positive outcomes are facilitated by client pretherapy characteristics of psychological mindedness ("the ability to understand people and their problems in psychological terms") and the quality of object relations—the client's lifelong pattern of regulating affect, forming mature "equitable" relationships characterized by love, tenderness, and concern ... [with] a capacity to mourn and tolerate unobtainable relationships [as opposed to reacting] to perceived separation ... loss ... disapproval or rejection ... with intense anxiety and affect" (Piper, Joyce, McCallum, & Azim, 1998, p. 561). Pretherapy client characteristics of being self-critical, guilty, and perfectionistic prior to treatment have been shown to be related to the poorest outcome and the least ability to accept and develop social support in and out of therapy (Blatt & Zuroff, 2005; Shahar, Blatt, Zuroff, & Pilkonis, 2003). These pretreatment characteristics influence the transference, which is a major contributor to the therapeutic alliance and to outcome. The nature of the client's *self-reported* early relationships has been shown to directly determine outcome, irrespective of the treatment offered (Hilliard, Henry, & Strupp, 2000). But memory is constructed and strongly affected by the client's present emotional state and needs. For instance, depressed clients often recall depressing events from their past, but when they become happier they report more favorable memories. When clients describe past relationships, they may be offering clues to their present concerns and desires about the relationship they want and fear with the therapist. We do not know the validity of self-reported recollections.

Client characteristics, such as diagnosis, coping style, and emotional reaction to treatment techniques, can determine the effectiveness of therapist interventions (Norcross, 1997). The youths' and caretakers' level of motivation to change is related to outcome and typically not adequately focused on by the therapist. In their meta-analysis of 114 adolescent treatment outcome studies, Weisz and Hawley (2002) found 4 that assessed the youths' motivation for treatment before starting. In only 39 studies did the therapists "report at least one procedure designed to support or enhance motivation for treatment (e.g., giving rewards for participation in therapy, identifying and working toward goals the youth identified as important)" (p. 28).

Furthermore, the client's age and gender might influence outcome. For youths, females may improve more than males, and adolescents may improve more than children (Michael & Crowley, 2002; Weisz et al., 1995); however, these differences might be an artifact of the outcome studies' dependence on cognitive-behavioral treatments. With youths, age, and therefore cognitive maturity, is related to improvement when cognitive-behavioral treatments are used (Durlack, Fuhrman, & Lampman, 1991). Children do not have a well-developed capacity to observe and discuss their cognitive processes, and females may be more adept than males at using introspective techniques. Females are also more frequently treated for internalizing disorders, whereas males have possibly more resistant acting-out diagnoses.

Assessing and supporting client characteristics that promote favorable outcomes needs to be an early focus of treatment. For instance, because clients who expect success form better therapeutic alliances that are related to greater improvement, therapists can stimulate the clients' early expectation of success by making hope-inspiring statements and indicating that others with similar problems have benefited from the type of treatment being proposed (Constantino, Arnow, Blasey, & Argras, 2005). Perhaps the clients' expectation of success can be stimulated by sharing case examples, the theoretical and empirical bases for the treatment, the usual success rates, and by displaying confidence in the treatment. When interventions make sense because they match the clients' theory of change and beliefs about the causes of their problems, and when clients anticipate that an intervention will benefit them, they are more prone to form a stronger alliance and stay in treatment (Elkin et al., 1999; Iacoviello et al., 2007). Introducing treatment techniques may not be appropriate when the client does not anticipate success.

The client contributes to each of the eight sources of change, is active and pivotal in the change process, and shares responsibility for the pace and direction of treatment. The choice of a particular intervention must consider the client's ability and readiness to use the technique. It is insufficient to automatically choose an intervention solely because the technique has been shown to be powerful. Because clients can mold techniques offered by the therapist "to fit their own aims and goals … therapy largely works by clients operating on therapy procedures, rather than vice versa" (Bohart, 2007, p. 125). Therefore, techniques are useful to the extent that they are acceptable to the client's needs and theory of change and to the extent that the client can attend to and accommodate new information and experiences. Clients' beliefs influence their receptivity to information. They tend to avoid information that contradicts their beliefs and attend to information that supports their beliefs. And when in a highly emotional state they are particularly resistant to incorporating information that might seem threatening. This pattern can be augmented by living in a post-fact society (Manjoo, 2008) in which information is subordinate to beliefs and ones' senses cannot be trusted, because what we see and hear has been distorted and photoshopped for political and economic reasons. The therapist predominantly offers interventions from which clients extract what they can use to go in the direction they want to go.

3. The Therapeutic Alliance

The therapeutic alliance is probably the most powerful contributor to change, with an effect size of about 5% to 7% of the variance in outcome (Messer & Wampold, 2002). The therapeutic alliance may account for more than half of the beneficial effects of psychotherapy (Horvath, 2001). The degree of agreement between client and therapist on goals (Creed & Kendall, 2005; Tyron & Winograd, 2002)[12] and methods to accomplish them, and the affective bond between therapist and client, all compose the therapeutic alliance and correlate with outcome ($r = .22$) in adults (Martin, Graske, & Davis, 2000) and youths (Shirk & Karver, 2003). The alliance more strongly predicts outcome than treatment techniques or the therapist's theoretical orientation (Barber, 2000; Klein, Schwartz, Santiago, Vivian, & Vocisano, 2003; Messer & Wampold, 2002; Vocisano et al., 2004; Zuroff & Blatt, 2006).

As a reaction to the domination of the medical model that relies on a particular treatment for a specific diagnosis, John Norcross, as president of the APA Division of Psychotherapy, launched a task force to identify empirically supported aspects of the therapeutic relationship that resulted in change. The task force results were published in *Psychotherapy Relationships That Work: Therapist Contributions and Responsiveness to Patient Needs,* edited by Norcross (2002a) and summarized by Norcross (2002b), who indicated that after reviewing the adult outcome research, the task force identified common factors that affect outcome. They found that effectiveness of treatment was facilitated by mutual agreement on goals and collaboration, cohesion in group therapy, and therapist empathy (emotional attunement). The task force concluded, "The therapy relationship makes substantial and consistent contributions to psychotherapy outcome independent of the specific type of treatment. Efforts to promulgate practice guidelines or evidence-based lists of effective psychotherapy without including the therapy relationship are seriously incomplete and potentially misleading on both clinical and empirical grounds. The therapy relationship acts in concert with discrete interventions, patient characteristics, and clinician qualities in determining treatment effectiveness" (p. 6).

We can expect that the more the client and therapist believe in each other's abilities, the stronger will be the therapeutic alliance and the client's motivation to tolerate the frustrations of treatment. The depth of the relationship with the therapist from engagement to therapeutic alliance through termination covaries with outcome. The relationship can foster hope, provide support to attempt and persist at change, and allow the client to experience a healthy relationship. Rather than treatment techniques and the therapist's theoretical orientation, the importance of the therapeutic relationship was dramatically demonstrated by the finding that supportive college professors were as effective as experienced therapists in treating randomly assigned adult clients in the Vanderbilt I study

(Henry & Strupp, 1994; Strupp & Hadley, 1979). As the client feels cared about by an idealized authority figure, and worthy of care, he or she may realize that others could also care and help.

The capacity of the alliance to rebound from damage is associated with client improvement (Stiles et al., 2004). Ruptures in the therapeutic relationship can occur when the therapist confirms the client's dysfunctional interpersonal expectations by flunking the client's transference tests. These tests repeat a "core conflictual relational theme" involving an expected response from the therapist and an expected response to the therapist from the client (Luborsky & Crits-Cristoph, 1990). For example, a client who expected to be hurt or rejected by others tried to be so pleasing to me that I became annoyed, which caused her to feel rejected. Therapists can contribute to ruptures when countertransference takes over or when they are poorly emotionally attuned and fail to mirror adequately, mistime an interpretation or intervention, or present values and beliefs that challenge the beliefs that are central to the client's identity. The process of rupture and repair can be a major contributor to creating change in adult therapy (Safran & Muran, 1996). However, ruptures in the therapeutic relationship with youths may be more difficult to repair (DiGiuseppe, Linscott, & Jilton, 1996). To avoid failing transference tests, I try not to treat a youth in the same way that parents treat him or her if I suspect that being seen as an extension of the parent could cause the client to reject me. With court-ordered clients, the therapist's appearing to be authoritarian can cause the therapist to seem to be an extension of the court, causing resistance in the client.

The therapeutic alliance is best developed when the therapist's actions and interventions are appropriate to the youth's developmental level. For instance respecting an autonomy-striving adolescent by emphasizing confidentiality and collaboration can improve his or her involvement (Church, 1994). Adolescents are particularly prone to worry that the therapist will not keep confidentiality (Kuhl, Jarkon-Horlick, & Morrissey, 1997) and that sharing personal information will be too uncomfortable (Pavuluri, Luk, & McGee, 1996).

In treating youths, the therapist's forming a therapeutic alliance with the caregiver(s) is moderately related to the youth's outcome (Karver, Handelsman, Fields, & Bickman, 2006). These researchers found .26 to be a minimal estimate of the average effect size between parent participation in treatment and youth outcome. At the least, caretakers are needed for transportation, history and ongoing information, and support of the treatment process. Usually their collaboration with and encouragement of the youth affects attendance and outcome. When parents are not supporting treatment, the prognosis is diminished. When they are not part of the solution, they are part of the problem, and a significant potential for change is lost. Barriers to treatment (such as finances, family scheduling difficulties, and parental pathology), parents' unrealistic expectations about the youths' treatment, parents' misperceptions about their role in remediation, parents' anticipating being blamed for the youths' problem, and parents' lacking hope or being angry at the youths are frequent problems that must be identified early and addressed to facilitate engagement.

Often the reasons that parents do not engage are the same factors that contribute to the youth's presenting problems. Parents may treat the therapist in a way analogous to how they treat their child. For instance, a parent who is too overwhelmed to participate in treatment may be contributing to the youth's problems by being unavailable or inconsistent. A parent who is critical of or has unrealistically high expectations for the therapist might also be easily disappointed in the child. In addition, previous therapy experiences color caretaker's willingness to engage. These researchers found that when parents felt respected by a previous therapist, they expected a more positive outcome in subsequent treatment (Kerkorian, McKay, & Bannon, 2006). "Parental engagement in the treatment process is influenced by parents' beliefs about the cause of their children's problems, perceptions about their ability to handle such problems, and expectations about the ability of therapy to help them. ... [These] parental attributions and expectations influence three aspects of treatment: help seeking, engagement and retention, and outcome" (Morrissey-Kane & Prinz, 1999, p. 183).

When Carl Rogers emphasized the healing effects of the therapeutic relationship, he described one type of relationship, based on unconditional positive regard, that he felt was beneficial to all clients. Different clients may require different types of therapeutic alliances. Alliances can be viewed as composed of nurturing, insight-oriented, and collaborative components (Bachelor, 1995) or personal (warmth, self-disclosing) and professional (helpful, confronting, and collaborative) aspects (Mohr & Woodhouse, 2001). The "one size fits all" approach is not applicable to diverse populations. As Arnold Lazarus stated, "Effective practitioners need to be aware that *relationships of choice* ... are necessary for salubrious outcomes" (Norcross & Goldfried, 2005, p. 402).

It is important to note that the client can perceive the therapist's interpretations and techniques as influencing the therapeutic alliance rather than solely affecting symptoms, as therapists generally assume. When clients experience an interpretation as helpful, the therapeutic alliance can be improved, whereas inappropriate interpretations and ineffective interventions harm the alliance (Luborsky, 1976). In one population of adult clients, 73% indicated that their therapist's clinical interventions were "critical in the development of their alliance" (Bedi, Davis, & Williams, 2005, p. 320).

Building and maintaining the therapeutic alliance is crucial to treatment, but if it is the central activity and discussion topic during treatment, then outcome is threatened. When therapists become excessively focused on offering interpretations about the relationship and talking about the nuances of the transference and alliance, clients can become upset and feel criticized by the therapists' statements concerning their interactions and the quality of their bond (Piper et al., 1991). As Kozart (2002) theorized from the Vanderbilt II and subsequent research, when the alliance is the "primary theme or topic of clinical contemplation, the therapeutic alliance may be undermined, [in contrast to focusing on] goals drawn from other spheres of the patient's life and the tasks necessary to achieve those goals. ... The therapeutic alliance is generally fostered by the therapist's ability to sustain conversation that is explicitly oriented to ... goals and topics rather than the actual quality of the patient–therapist bond" (p. 221). He speculated, "The clinical relationship is not merely a means to define clinical goals and implement tasks; rather, the goals and tasks are the means to strengthen a relationship that has an intrinsically therapeutic effect" (p. 220). In other words, we need to have something to do and talk about while the relationship is developing, and talking about the relationship can be counterproductive in building the relationship. In fact without discussing it, the therapeutic relationship can be built, maintained, and therapeutic.

The alliance can be therapeutic because it provides or facilitates a *corrective emotional experience* that challenges the client's transference expectations. Such an experience is created when the therapist reacts differently than the client anticipates and thereby challenges the client to develop new patterns of understanding, expectations, and relating. When clients are confronted with the disparity between what they expect and how the therapist responds, clients can feel angry or confused and withdraw from the relationship. Probably the common factors contribute to the clients being able to tolerate and benefit from having their expectations disconfirmed. For instance, when clients are motivated and trust the therapist, they may be more able to disclose feelings about the therapist, question habitual patterns that they had taken for granted (appeasing, intimidating, controlling, appreciating, criticizing, lecturing, etc.), and assimilate the therapist's unexpected response. The research literature provides theoretical and empirical support for this therapeutic process. However, Bernier and Dozier (2002) suggested caution in depending on client–therapist differences to create the corrective emotional experience. They believe that some similarity in the client–therapist match of beliefs, demographic variables, and values is needed to facilitate the alliance. The dissimilarities that create the corrective emotional experience can subvert or facilitate a positive outcome, depending on "a host of reasons ... including the rigidity and extremity of the client's maladaptive relational style and the sensitivity, experience, and clinical skills of the therapist ... and the security of each partner's attachment status." They suggested, "Just as clients may vary in their receptivity to challenges to their current style of functioning, therapists may also vary in their ability to provide the trust and security that are necessary for a corrective emotional experience to take place" (p. 41).

4. Therapist Characteristics

Therapist characteristics make a significant contribution to outcome, independent of treatment techniques as shown in therapist-within-treatment effects. In a study of nearly 1,200 patients and 60 therapists in a managed-care treatment setting, "approximately 8% of the total variance and approximately 17% of the variance in rates of patient improvement could be attributed to the therapists" (Lutz, Leon, Martinovich, Lyons, & Stiles, 2007, p. 32). In clinical practice in a sample of 6,146 adult managed-care clients and 581 therapists, the therapist on average contributed about 5% to the variance in outcome of therapy when measured by client self-report of global functioning (Wampold & Brown, 2005). This estimate was lower than the 8.6% of overall outcome variance attributed to therapists in an analysis of 27 studies (Crits-Christoph & Mintz, 1991) and the average of 8% found in the reanalysis of the NIMH Treatment of Depression Collaborative Research Program where therapy was manualized and patients had similar diagnoses (Kim, Wampold, & Bolt, 2006).

Five percent to 8% of outcome variance, a seemingly small amount, is actually quite significant. As Dr. Wampold explained,

> There is a statistic called Number Needed to Treat (NNT). It is the number of patients who need to receive a particular treatment (versus the alternative) to achieve a success. For example, the NNT for chronic heart failure for beta-blockers v. placebo is 24. That is, 24 patients are needed to be treated with beta-blockers to achieve one success relative to what would be achieved by the administration of a placebo (outcome here is hospitalizations). That is, if 24 patients are treated with beta-blockers, one fewer patient will be hospitalized than with placebos.
>
> [In regard to the 5% of outcome variance due to the therapist, in comparing a] better therapist with poorer therapist, regardless of treatment, the NNT equals 4. Now, this is quite convincing. First, psychotherapy is dramatically more effective than many accepted medical practices. Second, getting a better therapist is almost as important as whether one gets treatment or not.[13] It makes little difference which psychotherapeutic treatment the patient gets. Thus, we should be focusing on getting patients to the better therapists and not worry about the particular treatment delivered. (Bruce Wampold, personal communication, February 25, 2007)

Therapist characteristics of friendliness (Samstag, Batchelder, Muran, Safran, & Winston, 1998), warmth and genuineness (Truax, Altmarm, Wright, & Mitchell, 1973),[14] positive regard, empathy (Miller & Baca, 1983; Rogers, 1957),[15] and support (Keijsers, Schaap, & Hoogduin, 2000), as well as the therapist's faith in the client and the treatment plan, have been shown to predict outcome (Luborsky, McLellan, Diguer, Woody, & Seligman, 1997).

The view that therapist characteristics of empathy, positive regard, and genuineness cause treatment outcome has been out of favor since the behaviorists and cognitive behaviorists have dominated psychotherapy. Their views (as represented in the work of Beck, Rush, Shaw, & Emery, 1979) and many others who support evidence-based treatment contend that the therapeutic relationship might facilitate the effectiveness of some techniques, but the relationship itself is not a change agent. However, the relationship alone has been shown to be related to outcome more strongly than treatment techniques or the therapist's theoretical orientation. It is not clear how the therapist characteristics that contribute to forming the relationship actually influence outcome. They could be therapeutic in themselves, as Carl Rogers contended, because they counteract "conditions of worth," thus enabling clients to develop their own identities. These therapist characteristics also could improve outcome because they increase the therapist's influence and the client's compliance, as suggested by Strong (1968). These therapist characteristics could facilitate the emulation of the therapist or encourage the client to experience an emotionally corrective relationship.

When therapists show warmth, flexibility, honesty, interest, respect, openness, reflection, and support; facilitate the expression of affect; and provide interpretations that the client accepts, they create an emotional connection, a mutual appreciation, that contributes to treatment outcome (Ackerman & Hilsenroth, 2003).[16] The therapist's contribution to outcome largely varies with his or her capacity to engage the client, which depends, in part, on the therapist's personality and interpersonal abilities. Therapists who report having social support and being less self-critical and more comfortable with interpersonal closeness seem to form stronger alliances (Dunkle & Friedlander, 1996).

The client's perception of therapist empathy is strongly related to outcome. When clients describe the therapist as empathetic, treatment outcome is positive (Orlinsky, Grawe, & Parks, 1994); and when clients describe the therapist as lacking empathy, the outcome is poor (Mohr, 1995). Empathy has been shown to have physiological components. Clients' perceptions of moments of high empathy in psychotherapy have been shown to coincide with moments of synchronous galvanic skin responses

(Marci, Ham, Moran, & Orr, 2007), synchronicity of client and therapist neurological mechanisms (Carr, Iacoboni, Dubeau, Mazziotta, & Lenzi, 2003; Siegel, 2001), and observer ratings of behaviors reflecting solidarity (raising the other's status, giving help or rewards) and positive regard (showing pleasure and satisfaction) (Marci et al., 2007).

Different demographics respond to different therapist characteristics. When a sample of middle-aged White female clients with a median of 15.5 sessions were asked to describe what contributed to their fairly strong alliances, they reported such therapist behaviors as teaching useful techniques, showing nonverbal attention, showing interest, being caring and understanding, soliciting and respecting client choices, smiling, giving warm and personal greetings and farewells, paraphrasing, identifying client feelings, encouraging the client, and referring to material in previous sessions (Bedi et al., 2005). They also reported that the alliance was strengthened when therapists made understanding and normalizing comments, did what they said they would do, admitted to not having all the answers, and explained confidentiality and how therapy would work. This particular population further indicated that having books in the office on the client's issues, being well groomed, serving tea and snacks, laughing together, showing concern by giving a tissue when the client cried, and showing care by accompanying the client somewhere after the session all strengthened the alliance.

It is surprising that the therapist's gender, type of academic degree, years of training (Berman & Norton, 1985), and theoretical orientation do not appear related to outcome (Okiishi, Lambert, Nielsen, & Ogles, 2003; Okiishi et al., 2006). When asked about the therapist's theoretical orientation, John Norcross responded, "The therapist's theory is essentially a set of value statements that may be transmitted to patients to help them make sense of their condition, generate a sense of universality, and provide reassurance. Beyond these, however, the therapist's theory is largely independent of the empirically informed principles that direct the selection of interventions and relationships" (Norcross & Goldfried, 2005, p. 435). In the same roundtable discussion, commenting on the usefulness of psychological theory to guide the choice of technique, Miller, Duncan, and Hubble concluded, "The field should abandon theory of any direction like a blind date with a 'born to lose' tattoo" (p. 435).

The alliance and outcome are enhanced when therapists (a) engage the client by showing accurate affective attunement, speaking with clarity, demonstrating caring and understanding, providing an acceptable rationale for treatment, and instilling trust, hope, and belief in the therapist's competence; (b) try to develop agreement on goals and a mutually acceptable treatment plan; (c) generate the expectation of change;

(d) supply interventions appropriate to the client's theory of change, cognitive and developmental level, and present state of motivation and anxiety; and (e) identify and override barriers to change and continuing treatment. It seems that everything the clinician does, including managing the sessions, sharing personal values, developing goals, managing transference and countertransference, and so on, should be considered in relation to its effect on the therapeutic alliance.

5. Common Processes Present in Most Techniques

Common processes present in most techniques contribute to outcome. They might include learning principles (desensitization, operant conditioning, modeling, etc.), disconfirming irrational and pathological beliefs (Weiss, 1993), being listened to by a caring person, shifting the client's attention (e.g., from affect to cognitions, from self to others, from present to past, etc.), focusing on an acknowledged problem or a problem that the client has been told that he or she has, and activating client self-observation (Beitman & Soth, 2006; Korotitsch & Nelson-Gray, 1999). Keeping track of problem behaviors can be an effective treatment in some situations (Latner & Wilson, 2002). In most treatments the client receives encouragement and support to change. Focusing the client's attention to therapeutic activities between sessions is essential in cognitive-behavioral and behavioral treatments and increasingly common in other forms of therapy and might be considered as another common factor (Kazantzis & Ronan, 2006).

Another element found in most treatments is an explanation of the client's problem that (a) replaces the pessimistic way the client has constructed his or her condition and (b) allows the client to pursue more healthy responses. As Wampold (2007) described in his acceptance address to the American Psychological Association upon receiving the Award for Distinguished Professional Contribution to Applied Research, "A commonality of all psychotherapies is that they are based on particularly compelling explanatory systems, at least to their adherents. ... The power of the treatment rests on the patient accepting the explanation. What is critical to psychotherapy is understanding the patient's explanation (i.e., the patient's folk psychology) and modifying it to be more adaptive. ... The acceptability of the explanation depends on the proximity of the explanation to the attitudes and values of the patient" (pp. 862–864). Soliciting client feedback can also enhance the effectiveness of most treatments.

Adjusting Treatment to Client Feedback Can Improve Outcome   When I am aware that clients are not getting what they want from treatment, that therapy is not containing the factors needed for a positive outcome, I try to identify and correct the defects. But often I do not know that there is a problem, and the client does not tell me, for instance, that there were issues the client wanted to talk about but did not or that the client did not feel understood. Helping to repair or form the alliance is often difficult to accomplish if the client feels injured and just withdraws a little and the therapist does not notice.

Clients may be better judges of their progress than therapists, because therapists' ratings of the strength of the alliance do not correlate with outcome as well as clients' ratings do (Bachelor & Horvath, 1999; Horvath & Symonds, 1991). Furthermore, therapists can be poor judges of what clients are thinking or feeling, because clients and therapists only somewhat agree about the strength of the therapeutic alliance (Hersoug, Hoglend, Monsen, & Havik, 2001).[17] It has been known for some time that therapist' clinical judgment cannot be trusted, because statistical and base-rate predictions are superior to clinical intuition (Grove, Zald, Lebow, Snitz, & Nelson, 2000; Meehl, 1954). Therefore, obtaining the client's perspective is particularly important, because therapists may not make accurate assessments of the client's satisfaction with the course and expected outcome of the treatment.

Outside of the cognitive and cognitive-behavioral traditions, therapists have been reluctant to formally monitor process and outcome during treatment and then adjust their approach to the feedback. In fact, in one study therapists were asked how they would handle failing cases, and 41% reported they would continue the same treatment, and 30% reported they would refer to someone else. Only 26% said they would change their treatment (Kendall, Kipnis, & Otto-Salaj, 1992). It is easy to speculate why therapists may be anxious and resistant to solicit client feedback and subsequently change their approach. The feedback may be critical of the therapist and the therapist's belief in progress. Our treatment beliefs become a part of our identity and are difficult to abandon. Responding to client feedback requires altering the therapist-friendly paradigm that lack of progress is a function of client resistance rather than of treatment and therapist factors. Likewise, for many clients, confronting the therapist with dissatisfactions may be extremely difficult, because of their fear of authority, lack of assertiveness, and need for the therapist's positive regard. Their difficulty sharing can limit the validity and usefulness of any attempts to elicit client feedback.

It is and it is not amazing that only recently the field of psychotherapy appears to be beginning to value directly asking clients during sessions how they are feeling about their treatment. After all the research showing the significance of client characteristics and the alliance, it seems obvious that customer satisfaction is relevant to generating a positive outcome. It should be mentioned that client satisfaction is related to, but not synonymous with, improvement in the form of symptom reduction. For instance, depressed clients can resolve target problems and still report they are just as depressed.

An obese client can lose weight and still feel fat. A hysterical mother with a "wandering concern" can be just as upset after her child or adolescent changes and say, "Oh, yes, he is doing his homework [avoiding homework dramatically upset her the previous session] but he keeps his room such a mess." Clients can report satisfaction because their transference needs were met or their defenses supported. Therefore, they could feel better because they feel liked or aligned with but not show symptomatic improvements.

I regularly ask clients about problems in the alliance and if they feel counseling is being helpful. A structured method can be useful to elicit client perceptions and give therapists feedback about the alliance and progress. Sometimes I use the assessment instruments that Miller, Duncan, and Johnson developed for this purpose.[18] The Session Rating Scale asks just four questions that can give the therapist an idea of how the client feels about some factors that relate to outcome. Clients are asked to rate how they viewed the therapist in regard to his or her being respectful, empathetic, and collaborative by placing a mark on a continuum describing how they felt during the session. To tap the appropriateness of the goals and the client's ability to control the direction of sessions, therapists also ask clients to rate the degree to which the session was devoted to topics they wanted to work on. The degree to which the therapist's contribution matches the client's expectations and theory of change is measured by asking whether the therapist's approach was a good fit for the client. The last question asks for an overall reaction to whether the session was right for the client. The Outcome Rating Scale of four questions measures the clients' rating of progress toward their desired outcome.

I am frequently surprised by the client's feedback. For example, I had been seeing an anxious parent for child guidance for more than 6 months and was quite pleased with our progress. Because of her anxiety I kept our conversation going and frequently brought up issues when the conversation stopped and she did not initiate another topic. Probably because I expected positive responses, I administered the rating scales at the end of a session. She placed checks at the positive extremes of all the continuums, except she indicated that there were issues that she wanted to talk about but did not have the opportunity. I began the next session by asking what issues we had skipped in the past session, and she listed two. This feedback changed my treatment approach. We were able to identify our contributions to the problem (her anxiety and lack of assertiveness and my controlling the session) and concluded that we needed to more equally share responsibility for generating topics for discussion.

Giving therapists early feedback about the client's sense of progress in therapy and disappointments with the therapeutic alliance has been shown to be helpful in improving treatment outcome (Duncan, Miller, & Sparks,

2004; Miller, Duncan, & Hubble, 2004). Just giving therapists feedback that clients are not progressing can improve attendance as well as outcome (Whipple et al., 2003). Furthermore, when clients are not progressing and their therapists receive feedback that they are not progressing and have additional information that there are problems in the therapeutic alliance, the client's stage of readiness to change, and/or the client's social support, then these clients remain longer in treatment and have better outcomes than clients whose therapists receive only feedback of poor progress or no feedback. The clients who were not benefiting from treatment and had therapists who did not receive any feedback had the poorest outcomes (Hawkins, Lambert, Vermeersch, Slade, & Tuttle, 2004; Lambert et al., 2003). These researchers found that feedback to clinicians that clients were not responding reduced the percentage of clients who deteriorated from 21% to 13% and increased clinically significant improvement rates from 21% to 35%.

Regularly Monitoring the Client's View of Treatment Can Improve Outcome There are longer and more complex instruments that have been used to obtain feedback from clients. Luborsky's Helping Alliance Questionnaire (Luborsky et al., 1996)[19] has been used to improve outcome (Whipple et al., 2003). The scale asks clients to rate 19 statements about the therapist on a 6-point scale. The statements depict client's perceptions of the therapist being trustworthy, collaborative, understanding, likeable, experienced, and so on.

Another measure, the Evaluation of Therapy Session,[20] asks clients to rate 20 questions on a 5-point scale and then describe what they liked most and least about the session. The client is asked about the expression of warmth, understanding, and caring by the therapist; the helpfulness of the session (how easily the client could talk about problems and how helpful the therapist's contributions were); the client's commitment to treatment (willingness to do homework and apply what was learned in session); negative feelings during session (disagreeing with the therapist, feeling misunderstood and uncomfortable); and difficulties talking openly and honestly. Another instrument is the Peabody Treatment Progress Battery for youths ages 11 to 18, developed by Leonard Bickman. It includes measures of clients' sense of hopefulness, their relationship with the therapist, their expectations of treatment, and their satisfaction with services.[21]

6. Extratherapeutic Forces

Extratherapeutic forces can affect treatment efficacy. After Jay Haley helped develop family therapy and propel it to be the orientation of choice for many therapists, he shocked everyone by writing a somewhat satirical paper extolling the benefits of individual therapy for children (Montalvo & Haley, 1973). He identified many powerful aspects of individual therapy, but it is surprising that none of them were a part of the actual treatment. They were all extratherapeutic processes. He noted the benefits of the child having individual time with the parent while they were coming and going to treatment, the pressure on family members to change their behavior to look good to the professional to whom the youth was reporting about their behavior, the competition parents might feel if they worried that the child was becoming too fond of the therapist (an outsider), the need to organize the family to keep regular appointments, the parents' need to set more limits on their child who might have been given subtle permission to act out by being treated by a therapist who was permissive in the service of encouraging the child to express himself or herself, the elevation of play as a means of relating to the child, and the parents tendency to rely on the therapist thus altering patterns and boundaries with other family members.

Treatment can be derailed by problems with child care, transportation, employment, and affordability. Especially for clients who are ambivalent about therapy, the response to their changes and the encouragement or discouragement to seek and continue treatment that they receive from family, friends, coworkers, schoolmates, teachers, and their religious community can influence whether clients remain in and benefit from treatment. Appropriate aftercare, social support (Mallinckrodt, 1996), and changes in the school and work environments can influence outcome. Especially for youths, the coordination of services provided by the adults in their life creates and reinforces change. Treatment is facilitated when all the adults, including professionals, provide similar expectations and consequences. I have lost clients and seen treatment sabotaged when one adult in the youth's life is working at cross-purposes to the treatment plan. For instance, one family made little progress until I discovered by accident that a powerful grandmother was critical of the new parenting that was being instituted, and the parents were unable to question her authority. Now I ask clients what others think of the changes they are trying to institute, and I look for life-space factors that can frustrate or facilitate change.

Encouraging access to community resources has been pejoratively viewed as "case management, not therapy." However, referring to services and integrating community and greater family resources into the client's life can meet basic needs and increase opportunities for change. Facilitating exposure to new experiences in the client's daily life offers the opportunity to generalize newly acquired skills from therapy into the life space and can generate material to process in therapy from the client's concurrent life. Usually clients need to make progress in therapy before they can benefit from engaging community resources. When the client has progressed to be able to benefit, then progress can be enhanced by engaging such extratherapeutic forces as joining a community; risking different styles of relating and new recreational activities; adopting alternative home and work patterns to reduce exposure to abuse, violence, and neglect; facilitating the use of self-help resources including bibliotherapy and support groups; and accessing appropriate, success-oriented educational programs.

7. Problem-Related Factors

Problem-related factors are associated with change. They might include how many, how chronic, and how severe (Garfield, 1994; Lueck, 2004) the client's or parent's problems are, as well as the client's diagnosis and its related prognosis. The potential to change varies with diagnosis and characteristics within diagnoses. Perhaps the more biologically based disorders (schizophrenia, pervasive developmental disorders, obsessive-compulsive disorder, paranoia, biologically driven depression, ADHD, etc.) are less amenable to psychotherapy than more environmentally caused disorders (adjustment disorders, PTSD, stress-related depression, etc.). Disorders that interfere with forming an alliance are particularly resistant to psychotherapy and more amenable to medication and environmental adaptations. Within each diagnostic category is a range of severity that is negatively correlated to prognosis, which is often related to how severe the trauma and how chronic the problem have been. Chronic problems may be supported by a longer reinforcement history (a stronger root system) and an early onset, which can alter further development. For instance, a reactive attachment disorder may be resistant to change because many aspects of normal development have been missed and distorted. Also, when onset is preverbal, traumas can be nonverbally coded into the brain, which can make them difficult to access through language-based interventions.

8. Placebo Effects

Placebo effects contribute to client improvement. Estimates from randomized clinical trials indicate that in medicine, the "placebo effects are robust and approach the treatment effect. [In psychotherapy] placebos are as effective as accepted psychotherapies" (Wampold, Minami, Tierney, Baskin, & Bhati, 2005). This explanation of change emphasizes the client's desire, readiness, and trust in the therapist and the treatment. The power of trust, hope, and expectations is illustrated by the effectiveness of faith healers and the popularity of commercial products, such as bracelets that cure illnesses. The successes of shamanistic and folk healing practices demonstrate that the acceptability of the healing ritual to a person seeking relief can be more critical to outcome than the scientific validity of the treatment approach.

The placebo effect is a huge contributor to change. Probably 50% of clients respond well to placebo drugs or therapies (Seligman, 2002b, p. 6). Lambert (1992) estimated that clients' expectations of success and failure, including hope and placebo effects, account for 15% of the variance in treatment outcome.

The placebo effect accompanying medication is surprisingly powerful. For instance, the research on the effectiveness of antidepressant medication indicates that at least 75% of the effectiveness of antidepressants may be due to placebo effects. Kirsch, Moore, Scoboria, and Nicholls (2002) presented a meta-analysis of 19 double-blind studies in which depressed patients were randomly assigned to an inactive placebo or to drug treatment groups. The patients who received the inactive placebo showed 75% as much improvement as the drug recipients. The authors estimated that most of the 25% of the improvement that could be considered to be caused by the active drug treatment was also a placebo response because just as great an improvement was found in subjects who received other medications that were not anti-depressants. The authors considered these medications to be active placebo treatments in which subjects experienced physical side effects that led them to believe they were receiving a potent medication. Moncrieff, Wessely, and Hardy (2004) also reported that when antidepressants were compared to active placebo controls, small or nonsignificant outcome differences were found. Therefore, believing that one is receiving a potent drug, rather than the drug's chemical action, could have accounted for its effectiveness.

As stated earlier, the research on psychotherapy indicates that active treatments, when compared to placebo treatments that are provided by equally trained therapists who provide a similar number of sessions of similar length, do not have outcomes that significantly differ from the outcomes of placebo treatments. The research on placebos supports a corollary of the dodo bird's verdict that indicates that the relationship between diagnosis and treatment is complex and not as helpful in determining outcome in psychotherapy as it is with physical problems.

The psychotherapy research leads to the conclusion that client, therapist, problem, treatment relationship, and institutional and environmental variables form the center of the therapeutic process, and the importance of evidence-based treatment techniques and the theoretical orientation of the therapist need to be de-emphasized. With some motivated and resourceful clients, our role might be to keep out of their way and provide a holding environment as they solve their problems. Some clients have the ability to use whatever interventions we offer them to change themselves, and our role is to appreciate and mirror their strengths and motivation. Others may require a great deal of guidance to acknowledge problems, reconstruct their personal view and worldview, and overcome their problems.

The verdict that treatments have similar effectiveness should not be interpreted to mean that all treatments will have the same effect on all clients. The dodo bird verdict is based on research and meta-analyses that compare average changes in treatment groups rather than changes in individual cases. Hiding in the averages, theoretical approaches may be more helpful creating change in the domains in which they operate. Cognitive approaches may change client's cognitions, affect-targeting interventions may alter affects, and behavioral or relationship-oriented approaches may affect behaviors or relational abilities. Individual clients might benefit from a particular treatment technique at a particular time in therapy. For instance, therapists frequently have to decide whether to support or confront a client. As expected from the dodo bird hypothesis, treatment groups exposed to interpretive treatments versus supportive treatments appear to have similar outcomes for clients who complete treatment. But more clients can be expected to drop out of interpretive or confrontive treatments (Hellerstein et al., 1998; Piper et al., 1998). Therefore, confrontive therapies might be used more effectively with clients with certain characteristics, such as stronger therapeutic alliances or better capacities to handle frustration. This thinking leads to basing the choice and timing of interventions on the common factors rather than just on the diagnosis.

Many of these common factors are so interdependent and interrelated that it is artificial to view them as distinct entities. For instance the more faith the therapist has in the treatment plan, the more faith the client will probably have. Client characteristics, such as motivation, level of anxiety, and trust in the therapist, can be a function of therapist behaviors. The impact of therapist behaviors is dependent on how they are perceived and valued by the client. For instance, clients with a high need for the therapist's caring and warmth might not listen to what the therapist has to say until they feel that the therapist cares about them.

Probably the most effective treatment involves fostering as many of these forces of change as possible into a mutually enhancing pattern. The most change can be expected when a highly motivated, socially supported client with a single circumscribed problem with a recent acute onset commits to a treatment plan that is consistent with the client's theory of change so both client and therapist expect improvement, which receives support in the client's life space. Improvement is facilitated when the client has the skills to accomplish change and has faith in the therapist and their collaboratively agreed-on goals and treatment plan, which are developed with an empathetic, supportive therapist who is seen as competent, trustworthy, and initially similar to the client.

To recap, change in psychotherapy is influenced by treatment techniques, but, more importantly, interrelated common factors, particularly

CHAPTER 3

The Therapist's Contribution to Treatment

Because the research indicates that many theoretical orientations might be appropriate for a particular client, relying on one orientation limits the range of interventions available to the therapist. The dodo bird verdict supports an eclectic approach that integrates helpful aspects found in multiple theoretical orientations. One way to integrate multiple treatment orientations involves the accumulation of useful aspects from various theories into a menu from which the therapist and sometimes the client can choose. The therapist is then presented with a difficult question. If interventions have similar effectiveness and the effectiveness itself is not that strong, then what is the role of the therapist? The answer appears to be that the role of the therapist is to maximize the impact of the eight contributors to change.

Although discussed separately, the forces of change are interrelated and only theoretically distinct entities. For instance, a treatment intervention is dramatically affected by its interaction with the common factors, particularly client characteristics and the therapeutic alliance. Successful interventions can improve the alliance, whereas unsuccessful interventions can harm it, and their usefulness to the client is influenced by the quality of the relationship. For example, clients can feel poorly understood when therapist-offered interventions seem too difficult or clash with their theories and expectations. And the client's willingness to tolerate and talk about frustrations with procedures offered by the therapist often depends on the depth of the therapeutic alliance as well as the client's readiness to change and belief in the usefulness of the intervention. Because therapist-generated strategies do not immediately result in the best-case scenarios, usually interventions require ongoing adjustments that are more liable to happen when the client is motivated and the alliance is strong. When the therapeutic alliance is weak, the client is more likely to abandon hope and treatment when an intervention does not produce immediate results. This interdependence between treatment interventions, the therapeutic alliance, and client characteristics blurs the distinction between working on the relationship and working on client issues (Richert, 2007).

Therapists Focus on Three Tasks to Promote Change

The role of the therapist centers on fostering and nurturing the forces that contribute to change. This complex role involves (1) promoting a secure treatment frame that meets legal, ethical, and institutional demands; (2) encouraging the common factors that affect change by strengthening helpful client and therapist characteristics, the therapeutic alliance, and the common processes underlying effective therapeutic approaches and fostering extratherapeutic and placebo forces that improve outcome; and (3) providing evidence-based and experience-based techniques appropriate to the clients' readiness to accept them.

When I began treating clients, I had very few ideas about what to actually do in therapy sessions. This chapter describes the menu of activities that I now rely on. Each therapist has his or her own menu. It has taken a long time to acquire these strategies and approaches and for me to feel comfortable applying them. Intuition and science are involved in choosing which approach to use. Before providing my input, I think about the client's diagnosis, our treatment goals, the particular problem we are working on, and the possible effect that my approach might have on the client's motivation and on our relationship. After using the approach, I try to be sensitive to how the client responds.

I am not sure how research could evaluate the usefulness of these therapist behaviors, because the choice and timing of each is so guided by the client's and family's particular situation. As Paul (1967) suggested, outcome research needs to answer the following question: "*What* treatment, by *whom,* is most effective for *this* individual with *that* specific problem, and under *which* set of circumstances?" (p. 111).

1. We Promote Change by Providing and Maintaining a Secure Treatment Frame

We display our license and diplomas. We negotiate financial arrangements and obtain permission to treat. We schedule convenient regular appointment times and avoid unnecessary interruptions during sessions. We obtain informed consent, so clients will know what to expect and there will be few surprises. We report suspected abuse and neglect and warn others about anticipated violence by our clients. We assess for suicidality and develop safety plans for those in danger and document that a risk assessment has been made. We meet the paperwork demands required by our professional standards and reviewers. The American Psychological Association (2007) and California law (Assembly Bill 2257. January 1, 2007) guide us to retain adult client records for 7 years from discharge and 3 to 7 years from the time a youth turns 18. However best practice in California would require keeping adult records for 10 years after discharge and youth records for 10 years following their 18th birthday, because the statue of limitations for initiating a licensing board action for alleging a sexual boundary violation is 10 years. The statue of limitations differs according to state. Also, we establish procedures to transfer clients and their records, and to protect the confidentiality of records in the event we are no longer able to provide services.

I maintain boundaries to minimize confusion, misunderstandings, distractions, and unrealistic expectations. I avoid having personal and family pictures in the office, loaning or giving money, meeting clients outside of the session (unless I take a youth somewhere with the parent's written permission), breaking confidentiality, being late, answering the phone during a session, and giving or accepting more than token gifts. At the same time I am aware that crossing these boundaries can be seen as caring and could be appropriate under some conditions.

Gift giving usually has implications for treatment boundaries, transference, and the therapeutic relationship. Client gifts highlight issues that may need to be addressed by the therapist. They can be motivated by appreciation, manipulation, or equalization and can symbolize or commemorate an event in therapy or the state of the therapeutic alliance (Knox, Hess, Nutt-Williams, & Hill, 2003). Receiving token gifts from clients can be problematic, or not. Usually I try to understand and respond to the motivation behind the gift in a way that does not harm the alliance.

Sometimes I give a gift for a youth's birthday, hard-fought accomplishment, or graduation from therapy. I try to make the gift inexpensive and therapeutic, such as a magic trick that the client can master and use to amaze others, a book that provides comfort or inspiration, a game, art or craft materials, a model, or a puzzle that might encourage family togetherness or peer interaction, a treat at a restaurant where I can also observe the client in a public environment, a journal to write in, an album to save memorabilia, a pretty rock or shell, or a plant or picture to commemorate an accomplishment or event.

I try to be aware of the stimulus value of my personal appearance and the presentation of the clinic and office to understand its contribution to clients' expectations, projections, and reactions. Appearances broadcast (mis)information about friendliness, warmth, compatibility, age, spirituality, sexuality, professionalism, social status, concern about orderliness and mess, and so on. Sometimes personal appearance triggers feelings because clients are reminded of other people whom the therapist resembles. Sometimes the behavior and appearance of other clients in the waiting room has an effect on a client. During the course of therapy, changes in therapist appearance can cause strong reactions in clients. Because lasting opinions about others are formed in the initial few minutes, the first impressions of the therapist and setting may have an effect on the formation of the therapeutic alliance. Presentation is particularly difficult for the child therapist who has to appeal to and not offend the complex sensibilities of children, adolescents, parents, grandparents and other professionals, all from a variety of social classes and cultures.

I write a progress note for each session and document cancellations, failed appointments, informed consent, and "medical necessity."[1] Each note contains the date, the time spent, and who was involved. To capture the goal-oriented focus of the contact, my notes identify problems worked on, interventions and their effects. I carefully document client statements and my response to safety issues, such as abuse, suicidality, and acts and threats of violence. To jog my memory, I record names and events that I need to keep track of and that show my caring and involvement (e.g., Grandma's surgery, new friend, job interview, soccer coach, etc.). I also document the conclusions of phone calls and consultations with professionals.

Therapists provide a routine that clients can expect. Especially to youths we offer snacks, drinks, and objects to fiddle with, hold, and hide behind. We provide 24/7 crisis care through reviewing safety procedures in session and through phone answering-machine messages that refer clients to backup services (911, on-call colleagues, crisis lines, and other resources). We protect the client's confidentiality and explain its limits.

I make referrals and monitor their helpfulness. When the client is able to benefit, I might facilitate access to resources in the community, such as mentoring programs, Big Brothers or Big Sisters, housing agencies, psychiatrists, mental hospitals, drug treatment, vocational counseling and training, summer job programs, college admission offices, phone help lines, tutoring, support groups, day care, homework help, legal services, food and clothes closets, primary care physicians, and so on. I advocate for clients and support their advocating for services, especially getting educational evaluations and obtaining medical care and basic necessities. With a client's understanding and permission, we change his or her environment by making suggestions to teachers, parents, or spouses; writing letters to courts, probation officers, gatekeepers, or physicians; and obtaining services for significant others who may be contributing to our clients' problems or could aid in solving them.

I prepare parents by explaining how the type of treatment is expected to help the child. For instance I might explain how play is used in therapy, so parents can value my efforts instead of thinking that I am "just playing with their child." I might explain to parents of youths in peer group therapy that the group therapists use problems between group members as an opportunity to teach skills to resolve interpersonal difficulties so parents can be less fearful when their child tells them about the bad behavior they were exposed to in their group therapy. I might prepare parents for their child's resistance to participate in treatment and elicit the parent's help.

Adhere to Personal, Legal, and Professional Ethical Boundaries   Each of the therapy professions has a code of ethics designed to protect the client and therapist. These codes provide guidelines of conduct we are expected to follow as the standard of care. They are helpful, and there can be severe consequences for not adhering to them. Psychologists are particularly cautioned to protect our client's rights; do no harm; respect privacy, confidentiality, and self-determination; not exploit or discriminate; and avoid dual relationships (American Psychological Association, 2002). How these general warnings are related to specific behaviors is often unclear, creating a great deal of anxiety for clinicians.

It appears that the vagueness in applying our general ethical standards to particular clinical situations is being dealt with by erring on the side of avoiding the risk of being sued. We live in a time that is reacting to the discovery that many clinicians have had illicit relationships with their clients. Now behaviors are being avoided that could be seen as grooming the client for sexual contact. Because we deal with vulnerable people in a dependent role, our actions and opinions can be highly influential and easily misinterpreted and lead to unintended consequences. Therapists must be cautious in touching, hugging, holding a client's hand, being too friendly, giving or receiving other than token gifts, having contact outside the office, self-disclosing personal information, telling a client you like him or her, lending a client money, employing or arranging a job for a client or family member, allowing clients to run up an onerous bill, assuming a posttherapy parental role with a former minor client, and personally providing food, clothing, shelter, medicine, child care, or companionship. David Jensen's (2005) review of behaviors that caused therapists to be brought before their licensing boards in California included these behaviors. All of these behaviors can be viewed as caring, at times, and can be therapeutic under certain circumstances.

Therapist activities that can be seen as crossing ethical boundaries can be experienced by the client as enhancing the therapeutic alliance and dramatically affect outcome. Clients can interpret boundary crossings as extraordinary caring. Clients reported that such behaviors as "meeting with the client after hours, the psychotherapist walking with the client to get food before parting ways, the psychotherapist hugging the client, or the psychotherapist giving out his or her home phone number" made a significant contribution to the therapeutic alliance (Bedi, Davis, & Williams, 2005, p. 320).

Activities at the boundaries can make the client feel truly special and cared about, but these activities are potentially perilous, because it is not the therapist's intention but the client's perception of them, sometimes fueled by pathological and irrational thinking, that can result in unrealistic hopes and fears, disappointments, and misinterpretations. Clients and society can view well-intentioned behaviors as manipulating the client down the slippery slope toward exploitation and/or subversion of client autonomy.

Sometimes we cannot trust our reasoning. We may think that certain boundaries are not needed and that the end justifies the means. We may think that particular ethical standards are needed to guide the average therapist in a typical situation or are needed to protect the defective therapist from doing harm but that in this unique instance, in which we are presently involved, these rules restrict our ability to help our client. Such reasoning could be valid, or it might be evidence that we are intelligent enough to rationalize and justify to ourselves almost anything we want to do. If a boundary crossing is being considered, I am cautious and consider seeking and documenting consultation so that the crossing does not lead to misunderstandings or change the focus of therapy from the client's needs to the therapist's. We should especially not stray from a risk-management orientation if a deviation from our professional standards must be made in secret, cannot be written openly in the progress notes, is made without informed consent and the client's permission, might cause further deviations from boundaries, and does not have the potential for significant benefit to the client with minimal risk to the therapeutic work and relationship.

We try to avoid dual relationships and approach them with trepidation because of their potential to harm the therapeutic relationship. A dual relationship involves the therapist being in two or more roles with a client. However, some dual relationships are unavoidable because the therapist is usually in multiple, potentially conflicting roles, such as an employee (of the parent, third-party payer, and/or clinic providing services) and therapist of the youth. In working with youths, we are particularly prone to dual relationships because multiple modalities may be provided (individual, family, peer group, conjoint, child guidance), so different types of relationships and expectations are being juggled concurrently. Several family members may be involved in treatment, and the therapist may be in different roles with different stakeholders. Furthermore, the therapist may struggle with conflicting roles when relating to other institutions with which the youth is involved, such as school, court, Children's Protective Services, probation, and so on. Especially in residential treatment and in working with youths who lack stable parent figures, the role between parent surrogate and therapist can become blurred, because the therapist may be the longest-term parent figure available to the youth.

Often a harmful dual relationship evolves when the therapist assumes roles beyond being the therapist, such as evaluating the client for school, court, or Social Security; testifying; having a professional or other relationship with someone closely associated with the client; or having a business or social relationship with the client, parent, or their associates. These relationships can harm or exploit clients and their families by generating worries about the therapist's loyalties, breaking confidentiality, and infringing on the client's autonomy. It is difficult, if not impossible, to have a nonprofessional relationship with a client that is not influenced by the power imbalance created by the therapist's role. Such relationships can damage the therapeutic relationship or, if with a former client, his or her willingness to return for further treatment.

The more immature, resistant, unmotivated, and mentally and emotionally incapable the youths are, the greater is the need to ally with the caretakers and compromise the youths' confidentiality and autonomy. These youths may not be able to give informed consent, because children have compromised capacities to understand psychotherapy and to give consent to or reject treatment. In many respects, therapists of youths march to a more complex ethical beat than do therapists for adults.

Our professional code of ethics is one of four value systems that guide our decisions. *Personal values and beliefs* (our personal shoulds), *legal requirements* (reporting laws, the Health Insurance Portability and Accountability Act [HIPAA], subpoenas), and *organizational demands* of employers and third-party payers (who can dictate who receives treatment, the type and length of services, and the type of resources available) combine with our *professional ethics*. It is our responsibility to try to resolve the conflict when these strange bedfellows conflict.

In an ideal world, our code of ethics should trump organizational demands that are based on the bottom line or corporate pathology. It is our responsibility to identify these conflicts and resolve them by helping the organization become more ethical or, at least, helping the client understand and cope with the situation, as when an organization places unreasonable obstacles in the client's path to securing treatment, when needed treatment is unjustly delayed or denied by third-party payers, or when there are hidden detrimental costs to treatment decisions.

Our code of ethics clearly states that we must give an accurate diagnosis, whereas our ethics demand that we try to do no harm. Clients must receive a diagnosis to be covered by insurance, and a diagnosis could be detrimental to them. For instance, a client might be informed that although his or her parity diagnosis may allow for more sessions and a lower copayment, later it might prevent the client from obtaining life insurance. Having to give a diagnosis can block life goals, as Senator

Thomas Eagleton confronted when he had to resign as a vice presidential candidate because he was once treated for depression or as many clients discover when they later seek employment, try to enter the military, or apply for a peace-officer position. The stigma of receiving a diagnosis can also contribute to decreased self-esteem as well as deter clients from seeking treatment (Link & Phelan, 2001). I am frequently faced with the dilemma of giving a youth a behavioral diagnosis (oppositional defiant disorder or conduct disorder) that would make him or her ineligible for special education services or giving a diagnosis of post-traumatic stress disorder (PTSD), anxiety, or depression, which would allow the student to receive these services. I also face the conflict of giving a diagnosis (e.g., a high Global Assessment of Functioning (GAF) scale score an Axis II, pathological gambling, or a V code) or recommending a treatment modality (e.g., marriage counseling) that is not covered by insurance.

Personal beliefs can conflict with the legal and ethical demands. I have struggled with such clinical questions as the following: How should I respond to the client's prejudice, criminal activity, or hurtful behavior? How should I deal with this pregnant 14-year-old? How should I respond to this subpoena? What should I do with this HIV-positive client who refuses to protect his unsuspecting partner(s)? I try to be sensitive to how my personal beliefs inform my dealing with clients who believe they have sinned or have failed to meet impossibly high standards imposed by their religious leader or who want to go to heaven to be with a loved one or impose intolerable moral standards on their family members? Should I accept and support the client's personal or religious values? Can I avoid having my personal values influence my interventions?

In some situations I might even have to ask myself if I would go to jail or lose a job or profession for my personal beliefs. Legal requirements generally trump everything. When threatened with imprisonment, fines, and loss of license, we probably need to comply with the law or be willing to accept the consequences. There is a tension between protecting our clients and protecting society. On a long-term basis, when the law is unjust we can advocate for change. For instance Section 215 of the USA PATRIOT Act[2] (Public Law 107-56) as presently written (February 2006) allows federal agents access to client records without a strong reason or significant oversight. At the same time, the therapist can face criminal charges if he or she informs the client that the records have been taken. I have known clients (including an 8-year-old) that were investigated by Homeland Security for the flimsiest of reasons. Although these investigations did not advance to my having to break confidentiality, if they had, I would have been placed in a difficult situation.

In our day-to-day practice, well-intentioned laws require us to make difficult judgments that we may not have the expertise to make. For instance, sometimes we have to decide what constitutes a serious threat of harm or suspected abuse or neglect and then report at the expense of possibly alienating the client or causing the family to be broken up. We may have to decide if a client is, or will be, a danger to himself or herself or others or if a client should be hospitalized against his or her will or if we should report a client's dangerous intent to the police and the client's target. These judgment calls could protect the client and society, lead to disrupting the client's life, and/or damage the therapeutic relationship.

Proceed With Caution When Changing the Therapeutic Frame   Meeting more or less often, switching treatment modalities (e.g., from individual to conjoint, group or family and vice versa), changing fees or meeting times, and taking breaks (for vacations or other priorities) can be easily misunderstood. For instance, increasing the length of a session because caring and concern was perceived by a client as my viewing her as unusually disturbed and fragile. Changing from individual to group, couple's, or family therapy could be viewed as a rejection or failure if not adequately discussed. Changes in the therapy frame can reverberate on many levels. Little changes in the frame can be narcissistically wounding and derail treatment. Such a narcissistic injury ended therapy for a 19-year-old client whom I practically raised for 5 years, during which time he went into residential treatment, rejected and then made a tenuous peace with his parents, discovered he was gay, learned a trade, and became employed. He angrily dropped out when the receptionist requested a $5 copay that his insurance company started to require. Nothing I could do or say would change his mind.

Use the Phone for Case Management, Not Treatment   Clients occasionally call when they are upset and want advice. I prefer to schedule an appointment rather than try to resolve the issue on the phone. Trying to do therapy over the phone is difficult because we cannot see each other's body language and emotional reactions and because there are usually significant time limitations so we can be rushed to find a solution. I have had successful phone sessions when clients could not come in for an appointment, and we were able to set aside enough time. Repeated client calls need to be discussed in therapy.

I might ask or encourage clients to call or e-mail me between sessions to leave a message about issues we have been dealing with. I might ask them to contact me after they have begun a new medication, gone to the AA meeting, attended the individualized educational program at school (IEP), tried an intervention, had a job interview or medical appointment, attempted something we anticipated might be risky, or attempted something about which they were anxious. I might call a client when I am anxious about his or her safety. I expect that the between-session contact will motivate the client, show caring, and allow for my input, if needed. But if extended contact is needed, I try to schedule an appointment.

Pay Close Attention to Starting the Therapy Hour   Before meeting with clients, I review the progress notes to refresh my memory about goals we were working on, recent events and the names of important people we might talk about. I observe the clients in the waiting room and on the way to my office in hopes of seeing how they feel. Dealing with their initial feelings often launches the session. I prefer them to start the session, so I offer them the opportunity to take control and begin. I have a starting ritual with almost every client to help him or her feel comfortable and choose the direction we might take. I offer adults something to drink and might add a snack or activity for youths. With some youths I structure the session with the expectation that we will talk half the time and have an activity the second half. The start of the session is particularly revealing of the client's motivational stage, because it provides an opportunity for the client to report his or her problems and efforts to change during the week between sessions. If the client does not begin or bring up significant material, I might ask a vague question (How are things going? What's been happening?), or I might bring up something specific (What happened with the reward system you were going to try?). I might recall our last session or focus on making the client comfortable with chitchat until he or she can take over the lead.

Prepare Clients for the End of the Hour   I try to control the pace of the hour so that the client can struggle, calm down, consolidate the gains made in the session, be ready to deal with the world, and leave with motivation to try something new and return to the next session. I look for the opportunity to transition toward ending the session by saying such things as, "Before we have to stop, would you... ." I might remind the client that we have about 10 minutes before we have to end. Sometimes we review the session to clarify and implant ideas about what we have accomplished or are working on. Some clients even write reminder notes to themselves. I may use this time to appreciate some strength the client used or to reinforce the client's intentions. I might solicit the client's feelings about the session, our relationship, and/or the progress we are making. We may have an ending ritual, such as writing a check, working out the next meeting time and giving an appointment card, or asking the same winding-down question, such as, "What do you have coming up this week?"

I have a clock available to clients so they can help pace the session and stick to the time limitations. I avoid bringing up difficult or complex issues during the last 10 to 15 minutes of a session. I use this time to summarize so they do not leave with misconceptions and emotional instability, which could result in their acting out or withdrawing into themselves between sessions. Clients need to leave in an emotional state that is good enough so they can face their challenges and responsibilities. As one client said, "I wish I could shut down to remodel, but I can't."

I am still not prepared for those who drop bombs at the end of sessions, such as the client who after a fairly unproductive session mentioned, "Oh, did I tell you my dying mother is coming to live with us?" Another ended with the doorknob comment, "I think we'll be moving to Arizona." As the door closed a mother mentioned, "My son said that he needed to talk to a therapist about something and he couldn't tell me what it was." Parents can wait until the last second to ask for advice, as the mother who said, "Elle's offender was released from prison. Should I tell her?" It is obvious that these statements needed further discussion, but not in the waiting room.

Jay Haley spoke about horizontal and vertical time in therapy. He described as horizontal the time spent doing treatment in the formal roles of patient and therapist, such as in psychoanalysis where the patient lies on the couch and is "in therapy." The vertical describes the other contact time spent in the waiting room, walking to and from the office, getting settled in the office, and preparing to leave (from couch to coach). Haley provocatively suggested that the most powerful observations and treatment actually occur during the vertical times when roles are unclear and defenses are down. Therefore I attend to waiting room and hallway behaviors, such as how a child occupies himself or herself and interrelates in the waiting room, how the parent and child separate and reunite, and how the parent supervises, prepares, monitors, accompanies, nurtures, and controls when he or she feels no one is watching. Sometimes I formally end a session several minutes early to create time for an unstructured (vertical) interaction by offering an ending statement, such as "So, I'll see you on the 20th." Then I might stall by writing a note or messing with desk and drawer stuff while the client waits for me to lead him or her out of the office. It has been during such times that clients have revealed aspects of themselves that I had not known about or have related to me in unexpected or diagnostically helpful ways. Clients can be particularly receptive to my comments during this vertical time at the end of a session because my reactions can appear more genuine and significant. Therapists and supervisors need to be aware that boundary violations tend to occur in vertical times, such as during the last five minutes of a session.

The therapeutic frame provides safety, comfort, and predictability for the client and therapist.

2. We Promote Change by Nurturing the Common Factors

A) Nurture Client Characteristics That Enhance Outcome

Help the Client Maintain a Level of Anxiety That Facilitates Change   I try to monitor the client's anxiety and keep it at a level that motivates him or her to productively participate in treatment. If clients do not have enough anxiety, they are probably not motivated to change themselves. If they are too anxious, they cannot benefit. It is difficult to judge the client's anxiety level because the signs of anxiety are often hidden and subtle. John Briere (1996) conceptualized regulating the client's anxiety in terms of keeping the client within "the therapeutic window." He described effective treatment as needing to take place within the space between (a) too much anxiety when the client's self-capacities are overwhelmed with affect so the client cannot benefit from the session and may act out or dissociate and (b) not enough anxiety so the client lacks motivation and the therapist provides support so the client does not desensitize to or process anxiety-provoking material to develop affect regulation. Briere proposed that in the best treatment, the therapist expects a little more than the client thinks he or she is capable of.

To keep clients within the window, I might need to raise their anxiety. Then I might allow silence, confront behaviors and defenses, bring up or keep the focus on difficult topics, or try to get clients to come to sessions sober so they can better access their feelings. Most frequently I need to reduce their anxiety to keep them within the window. Therefore, I might avoid silence, entertain, provide an activity, be supportive, teach visualizing a safe place to visit in their mind, or change topics and the client's focus of attention. Sometimes, particularly abused clients do not experience feelings along a continuum from mild to extreme and expect that emotions come only in extremes. They may have learned to minimize and deny feelings and/or to expect that feelings will continue to increase in intensity. They can benefit from learning to tolerate an initial emotion and experience that feelings are like waves that build, plateau, and then diminish.

If a client's anxiety is too high, I usually ask how he or she reduced anxiety in the past, and I encourage the use of those methods. At times I help clients acquire three skill sets to self-regulate stress and anxiety so they can more fully participate in therapy and daily life.

First, when clients are overwhelmed with affect, especially from past traumas, *grounding skills* can restore calmness. These skills orient the client to the present time, place, and situation and increase sensory awareness of the client, environment, and therapist. As Kepner (1995) described, grounding skills help the client separate past from present and maintain contact with the present.[3] Grounding skills are particularly effective in mastering flashbacks in which clients experience traumatic memories as if they were reoccurring in the present. I might suggest noticing that they are safe here, now, in my office where they can feel the solid floor beneath their feet and the comfortable chair they are sitting on. I might seek eye contact or ask if they would feel more comfortable holding a stuffed animal or taking a break to stretch, walk around the block, or have a snack or drink.

Second, *anxiety management skills* are complex grounding skills that are often helpful to prevent the client from being swept away by intense emotion. They include deep-muscle relaxation, controlled breathing, and guided imagery. For example, when clients feel overwhelmed with anxiety, I might use this as a teaching opportunity to learn to relax through meditation or mindfulness. Jon Kabat-Zinn (1990) developed exercises that can be taught in therapy and practiced as homework.[4] He helps clients find a comfortable position and attend to their breathing. He suggested that when the mind wanders from focusing on feeling the breath coming in and going out, the client can notice that the mind has wandered and can bring it back to feeling the breath coming in and going out. There are other breathing exercises that can be taught to reduce anxiety. They focus on breathing from the belly and/or concentrating on breathing in slowly and exhaling even more slowly.

Deep muscle relaxation can be a useful technique to control stress. It involves progressing through the muscle groups and isometrically tensing individual muscles so that the client can feel the tension build and then deeply relax and feel the tension drain from the body and experience how good it feels to relax. When deep muscle relaxation seems appropriate, it needs to be taught during several sessions. I describe it as a skill that requires practice; similar to checkers and meditation, the basics can be learned in a few minutes, but it can take a long time to fully master. Some clients find homework easier to pursue with printed guidelines they can take home or access on the Internet.[5] In managing daily life, clients may find relaxation tapes helpful. Sometimes a tape made by the therapist can be particularly soothing.

Third, *pacing skills* can help clients recognize and then control the level of stress and stimulation that they expose themselves to in life and in therapy. Often these skills are taught after grounding skills have been mastered. Clients become overwhelmed by anxiety because they might deny the impact of stress and seek even more stimulation. Such clients move from one stress to another without regard for their health. They ignore their needs and do not appropriately eat, sleep, exercise, or pace activities to their stress level. I try to teach these clients to recognize their physical and emotional needs and then respect their personal needs by controlling the level of stress to which they allow themselves to be exposed. In therapy sessions pacing skills involve the ability to choose the level of stress the client is ready to work at, and these skills are manifested by clients taking a break when feeling overwhelmed, controlling their degree of exposure to anxiety-rich topics, and leaving time at the end of sessions to prepare for reentering the world.

In addition to teaching clients to self-regulate anxiety, I foster the development of interpersonal processes to manage affect by being emotionally attuned, caring, and supportive so the client can express and desensitize to anxieties in session with me and by encouraging the client to reach out to appropriate others. Sometimes I help clients access support from social networks (e.g., family, friends, and associates with common concerns, such as neighbors, Parents Without Partners, parents of classmates, peer group therapy, and support groups for parents and youths with similar problems). For parents these efforts to tap into the village needed to raise a child can strengthen therapy, and these efforts are a powerful treatment. As Whittaker and Garbarino (1983) said, encouraging partnership with the community "is not only a desirable but a necessary condition for effective, efficient and truly humane services" (p. 43).

Promote Humor   Humor is a powerful lubricant that can entertain, build and heal the alliance, and reduce anxiety and defensiveness. For instance, I asked a frightened new client what grade she was in, and when she said she was in third grade, I said that I was too. She looked puzzled, laughed, and relaxed. Another time I was meeting with a sulking, oppositional 14-year-old who refused to talk to me throughout the intake. She remained silent through all my attempts to engage and entertain her. Then she inhaled some mucus with a loud sound, and I jokingly responded to her grossness by trying to out gross her by slowly licking my lips as if I were saying, "Mmmm, that tasted good." She instantly responded, "No thanks, I use toilet paper." I cracked up, and then she laughed, and that broke the ice. I think she realized that I appreciated her quick wit. Exaggerating consequences into the ridiculous range helped another client cope with his flaws and desensitize to fears. The anxious 17-year-old kept avoiding sitting next to a girl at lunch. I went on about how she would throw up and die and everyone would hate him and he would be thrown in jail for murder and his friends wouldn't visit him and he would have rats in his cell and so on. He laughed and role-played things to say to her while I gagged in response. The next session he said they had been eating together all week and "she only passed out a few times." Humor helped to normalize a secret worry that he was thinking about sex too much. I told him, "It's just a stage. People outgrow that by the time they are 87. Guys have the ability to think about girls every 3 seconds, devote 98% of their brain to sex, and still answer the teacher's questions and chew gum." He said he thought about sex only every 5 seconds, so he was probably retarded. Through bantering back and forth he was able to bring up concerns he had been worrying about and receive support. As T. S. Eliot remarked, "Humor is also a way of saying something serious." I look for opportunities to inject humor into sessions, and I try to be sure that my joking is not a disguised expression of my frustrations and needs.

Avoid Silence   The use of silence in psychotherapy has been a favorite technique since Freud used it to generate helpful anxiety, reflection, and the projection of transference feelings onto the therapist. However, it can be disruptive with youths and more disturbed clients who rarely need to feel more anxious in sessions.

I try to notice when silence generates unproductive anxiety, misconceptions that the client cannot talk about, or projections onto the therapist of alliance-harming transference feelings and thoughts that cannot be processed helpfully. To avoid these problems, Ladany, Hill, Thompson, and O'Brien (2004) explained to higher functioning adult clients how the therapist might use silence in sessions. They might say, "Sometimes I may be silent to give you time to problem solve and experience or reflect on your feelings. At times my silence might make you uncomfortable, and you might make assumptions about what I am thinking or feeling. It is usually helpful to discuss these feelings and assumptions with me." Silence is embedded in the therapist's concurrent nonverbal communication, which influences how the silence is interpreted.

Silence can be helpful in therapy when there is a strong alliance with higher functioning clients who demonstrate that they can use it effectively to problem solve, think productively about issues, and understand the helpful intentions of the therapist.

Pay Close Attention to the Client's Level of Motivation   Prochaska and DiClemente's work on matching the intervention to the client's level of motivation to change provides useful guidelines to selecting and timing interventions (DiClemente, Schlundt, & Gemmell, 2004). They described substance-abusing clients as progressing through five stages of change that can be applied to psychotherapy clients: precontemplation, contemplation, preparation, action, and maintenance.

Precontemplation: In this stage clients may be unaware that they have a problem. They may assume that things are not that bad or that change is not possible. They may want someone else to change. They may have been coerced into coming to therapy by parents, school attendance officers, judges, physicians, and so on. At this stage of motivation to change, treatment might focus on psychoeducation, providing nurturing and support, consciousness raising, outreach, and engagement. The techniques of motivational interviewing might be most helpful during the first two stages of change. It emphasizes (a) promoting engagement and expressing empathy through active listening, (b) developing discrepancies by pointing out differences between the client's behavior and his or her greater goals and values (such as noting that the client values having a close family but is working long hours, is buying the kids lots of stuff, and is too tired to do things with them), (c) "rolling with resistance" by avoiding confrontation of the resistances through stating arguments for and against change, and (d) promoting the client's efficacy by increasing hope, commitment, and belief in the ability to change.

Motivational interviewing is a treatment-enhancing procedure as well as a treatment in itself. It evolved from Rogerian therapy, and its techniques have been shown to be as effective as other active techniques. Burke, Arkowitz, and Menchola (2003) concluded from their analysis of 30 studies that 51% of subjects who received a motivational interviewing intervention improved at follow-up compared to 37% of those who received no treatment or treatment as usual. Hettema, Steele, and Miller's (2005) meta-analysis of 72 studies supported its usefulness to reduce dropouts and increase adherence to treatment.

This technique has been used successfully almost exclusively with alcohol, drug, diet, and eating problems but has not been well explored as an adjunct to treatments for other disorders. However, it may have potential to boost the effectiveness of any active treatment by evoking and exploring the client's values and reasons for change and then supporting the client's arguments for change with active listening. This process appears to increase the client's motivation to change and elicits commitment statements that correlate with outcome. Amrhein, Miller, Yahne, Palmer, and Fulcher (2003) found the strength of the client's commitment statements at the end of motivational interviewing predicted behavioral change. Commitment statements can indicate that the client is moving from contemplation to preparation.

Nock and Kazdin (2005, p. 873) showed that using motivational interviewing with parents generated "greater treatment motivation, attendance and adherence to treatment." This was accomplished by offering three 5- to 15-minute doses of "providing parents with information about the importance of attendance and adherence, eliciting motivational statements about attending and adhering to treatment, and helping parents to identify and overcome barriers to treatment" (e.g., lack of transportation, belief that treatment is irrelevant, poor relationship with therapist).

Contemplation: Clients in this stage are aware that they have a problem but are not ready to take action. They may say they will take action in the next 6 months. Clients can remain at this stage for a long time.

In comparison to clients in precontemplation, they can be more aware of other feelings than shame and are more open to new ideas and relationships. At this stage therapy probably needs to focus on raising awareness of the negative consequences of problem behaviors and developing supportive relationships. For instance, a parent at this stage generated a list of serious losses she would endure if she stopped drinking, including having no easy way to unwind after a tense day at work and giving up long-held friendships with fellow heavy drinkers. She wondered if she would ever again feel relaxed and have fun. However, weighing this against her worsening health problems and the fear that she was harming her son through alcohol-fueled anger outbursts and modeling excessive drinking, she decided to quit. She said that a first step might involve attending an AA meeting to develop new friendships with nondrinkers. Remembering that she had successfully abstained from drinking for 2 years at an earlier time in her life helped her to move quickly through this stage.

Preparation: Clients at this stage are thinking about taking action or have tried something and failed. They are motivated to act and state goals but lack the abilities to succeed. Clients may want their pain removed without having to give up their defenses or behaviors. As one client said, "I want to get better grades, but homework is against my religion. That's my video-game time." For clients preparing to take action, therapy often focuses on practical problem solving, planning, mirroring, and containing unproductive emotions.

Action: At this stage clients are doing something about their problems. They have had some success with change and are working hard to change. This and the next stage are the most suitable for suggestions, advice, and cognitive-behavioral and behavioral interventions including skill training, although increased therapist support is often needed. For example, a parent, mostly in the action stage, recognized that his placating behavior and his too rigidly held nice-guy persona left him feeling depleted and frustrated because his own needs were being ignored. As he was beginning to change his parenting and set more limits, he found useful the advice to postpone answering his teenagers' constant requests for help or money by saying, "I'll let you know, later." This gave him the time to evaluate, and he discovered that he could honor their requests, offer other solutions, or just say "no." He then looked at his fears about saying no, and they became less powerful. He concluded that his continual acquiescence was creating children who were takers who had developed too great a sense of entitlement that caused them to be angry when he and others did not cater to their demands. He also realized that his relationships with adults were characterized by too much giving and that he needed to work on setting limits and allowing himself to receive from others.

Maintenance: Clients in this stage are trying to maintain the changes they have made and avoid regressing. Relapse prevention strategies might be useful at this stage as well as reviewing progress and the benefits of their new situation. Preparing for termination is usually a focus of treatment at this time.

The stage that clients are in when they enter therapy affects whether they continue (precontemplaters are the most prone to drop out) and how much progress they make (the higher the stage at entry, the more progress). These stages are not always mutually exclusive and do not necessarily follow each other in a sequential order (Littrell & Girvin, 2002). The client's readiness to change is not necessarily predictive of treatment outcome. One reason that recognizing there is a problem, wanting to change, believing one can change, and already having made attempts to change might not be related to improvement is that these motivational factors can be correlated with problem severity and emotional disturbance (Gossop, Stewart, & Marsden, 2007). Thus, the more severe the problem and complicated by comorbid conditions, the more motivated but, unfortunately, the more resistant to change the problems may be.

Building and maintaining client motivation to change is a crucial focus of treatment. I try to monitor and increase the client's motivation to change by

- highlighting the client's previous successes and the successes of others with similar problems;
- minimizing the difficulties in the journey toward accomplishing goals (unless the client shows an ability to respond to challenges with tenacity);
- pointing out the difference in trajectory between the clients' values and ideals and where their present pattern is taking them;
- gently sensitizing clients to the negative consequences of their behaviors while elaborating and fantasizing about the positive consequences that might accompany change;
- collaboratively identifying a path toward improvement that is clear, reasonable, and accomplishable;
- providing support and appreciation for the client's willingness to struggle with bettering him or herself;
- building self-esteem and the alliance; and
- avoiding confrontation and ruptures while normalizing and depathologizing the client's struggle.

Often Therapy Needs to Start With What the Client Is Ready to Work On Engagement precedes supplying treatment techniques. Connecting with clients often requires relying on active listening (which demonstrates understanding and the willingness to stay attuned to clients while they are having pleasant and unpleasant feelings), being interested in their interests, and mirroring their strengths. Connecting with youths can involve appreciating their video-game skills, visiting their favorite Internet sites such as MySpace, encouraging them to bring in their favorite activities, and providing activities they can look forward to doing. The more resistant, sensitive to confrontations of defenses, and disturbed the client, the more treatment needs to be supportive and focused on reducing present stresses (rather than uncovering and confronting) and the more the engagement process is therapeutic in itself rather than a means to making techniques more palatable and effective.

My career has involved creeping along the continuum from therapist-directed treatment toward parent- and youth-directed treatment. Now I try to share responsibility for the direction of therapy. Rather than starting treatment with my assessment of the problems and my solutions, as much as possible I focus on soliciting the client's concerns, goals, and ideas about how to accomplish them. I ask clients if they can identify strategies they found helpful when they struggled with similar problems in the past. The greater the client's contribution to identifying the problems, formulating the goals, and developing the treatment plan, in which youth and parent describe what they can contribute to reaching the goals, the more successful I expect we will be.

For instance, I saw Pearson and his single-parent mother when he was 14. His school and probation officer referred him because he had been charged with tagging, was not passing any classes, and had more than 100 citations for arguing with staff at school and occasionally fighting with peers. The mother and son had one goal: to take the court-ordered graffiti program and get off probation. The mother talked, and Pearson smiled. They were not ready to work on school behavior, and they colluded to blame and threaten to sue the school for racism. The mother's solution had been to keep Pearson in his room so he could not misbehave at school or in the community. She demanded that he silently accept her discipline and became outraged if he voiced any objections.

After a few weeks of trying to get them to agree to my goal that he needed to change his behavior in school, I said that I guessed he was angry at school for telling him what to do. The mother responded that he obeyed her and was not angry at home and that school authorities didn't understand how to treat Black males. Then she demanded a letter stating that he should be allowed to take the graffiti course to get off probation. When I said that I could not yet write the letter because I did not know Pearson, because he had not talked during our five sessions, they stopped keeping appointments.

When he was 16 he returned to therapy, and we started to identify problems and goals. He still gave only minimal responses, but this time

I kept placing responsibility for establishing goals on Pearson, and after three sessions he identified two goals that he was willing to work on. He wanted to get off probation and graduate. As we struggled to identify ways to accomplish his goals, he acknowledged that he would need to control his temper so he would not get suspended or violate probation, and he would need to complete assignments. We then focused on how his mother could contribute, and she said she would help him with homework and would work on controlling her temper, too. I offered to help them learn to use self-talk and calming techniques instead of getting angry, and they did not object. I then said that another way of controlling anger was to express angry feelings in calm words, but the mother would not allow this at home. We worked on self-talk and other anger management techniques but did not deal with the mother's parenting or Pearson's displaced anger.

Our work together formed a base from which we could focus on the mother's overcontrolling and harsh discipline and their colluding to project blame and responsibility for his behavior problems. Eventually the mother allowed him to voice his feelings if he did it respectfully. During their first contact when I tried to focus on her parenting and the need for Pearson to stop getting citations, they felt misunderstood and avoided the next few sessions. When my offerings were in the service of their goals, my input was easier to tolerate. I do not think there was anything I could have said when we first met that would have engaged them. They wanted support for their defenses and behaviors. They were more motivated at our second contact, possibly because they changed during the hiatus from therapy. The mother started to think Pearson had a problem and thought about her contribution to his anger at school. She was concerned that Pearson was still on probation, had not accumulated many credits, and was closer to emancipation. We were able to progress as long as I did not blame or correct them. As she became less controlling, he became less angry and more caring of her. He got off probation and attended night school to make up credits. We were able to move on to talking about how to be a man. His role models were Homer Simpson (alcoholic), "gangsta rappers" (violent), and Michael Jordan (unobtainable).

In Choosing Where to Focus Treatment, Try to Be Attuned to the Societal, Biological, Interpersonal, Behavioral, Emotional, Imaginary, Sensate, and Cognitive Characteristics of the Client That Contribute to Problems By attending to all these aspects, we can identify and treat those parts that maintain problems. Extending the BASK (behavior, affect, sensation, and knowledge) model (Braun, 1988), Lazarus (1989) developed the mnemonic BASIC-ID (behavior, affect, sensation, imagery, cognition, interpersonal, and drugs/biology) to sensitize therapists to seven aspects of problems that need to be identified, because each can maintain the problem and each may require interventions. He emphasized that change may be temporary if all the contributing facets of the problem are not treated. Sometimes the most significant of these aspects of the problem is withheld by the client, and I try to invite the missing pieces into the session for examination.

Lazarus (obviously a proponent of brief, cognitive-behavioral, and behavioral therapy) provided an example of how he uses the BASIC-ID to dissect a problem into seven parts and then treat each part with a brief intervention.[6] He worked with a client whose presenting complaint was that he was worried about losing his job. Lazarus asked questions to identify each aspect of the problem:

Behavior: What are you doing when you are worrying? Where are you? It doesn't happen when I am busy. It's when I'm in bed. It stops me from sleeping.

Affect: How does the worrying make you feel? Depressed and like a loser.

Sensation: How does the worry make your body feel? Tense. I grind my teeth and toss and turn.

Images: What pictures come to your mind when you think of yourself as a loser? I see myself as a bum, like a bag lady. It's like when my father used to tell me I would end up in the poorhouse. I see him yelling at me.

Cognitions: If you lost your job, would you end up in the poorhouse? I know I wouldn't. It would be difficult, but I'd manage.

Interpersonal: Does the worry happen around certain people? The boss's son really bugs me. He's always mad at me. I have to report to him, and he is the golden boy. Talking to him makes me so anxious.

Drugs/body: When you can't sleep, do you resort to drugs or alcohol? My doctor prescribed .5 mg Xanax.

Following this rapid assessment, Lazarus began treatment with one intervention for each aspect of the problem. *Behavior:* He suggested periods of time or places to worry, instead of in bed at night. He also suggested the client leave the bedroom when he could not sleep and snap a rubber band worn on the wrist when the worry began, to punish the cognition. *Affect:* He suggested a self-assuring mantra ("I will be able to survive") to replace the worry. *Sensation:* He taught the client deep muscle relaxation focusing on the mouth and jaw. *Images:* He helped the client install a clear vision of his dealing successfully with the boss, his father, and unemployment. *Cognitions:* He taught the client to alter faulty cognitions by correcting his catastrophic thinking. The client was encouraged to think, "I'm just unemployed, not reprehensible." For the *interpersonal* realm, he recommended social skills training to deal more effectively with the boss's son. In regard to *drugs/body,* he taught relaxation techniques that focused on breathing exercises to promote sleep.

To control a client's level of anxiety and keep him or her functioning within the therapeutic window, I might shift the client's focus between behavior, cognitions, imagery, feelings, and knowledge. For instance, Ella became emotionally overwhelmed with anxiety while talking about her husband's abuse of her and her daughter. I shifted her attention from feeling and describing the affect to describing where the incident took place (knowledge). Rather than having to stop, she continued to talk and desensitize herself to other aspects of the trauma. When she calmed I asked more about affect, and she returned to feeling more anxiety. Shifting between attending to happier situations and anxiety-provoking situations helped her daughter continue to talk about the domestic violence. She was able to fully describe a frightening incident in which her father hit her mother by alternating between describing the incident and drawing a picture of a happy time the family had flying kites at the beach. Another time she alternated between describing and crying about the domestic violence (affect) and drawing the incident (imagery).

Moving between the past, present, and future can be another method to control anxiety while keeping the client focused on treatment issues. For instance, a teen client displayed a pattern of acting out to avoid feelings generated by her sadistic father. Treatment focused on exposure and desensitization to her early traumas to reduce the avoidance and escape responses that were her presenting complaints. It was anxiety producing to face past affects and to acquire skills to cope with affects in her present life, but she was motivated by a desire to be successful in social relationships in her future. She had a goal of eventually having a group of friends and feeling comfortable with them. Processing family-of-origin situations generated anxiety that limited her ability to continue talking. Shifting her attention to social skills acquisition (the present) reduced the anxiety, whereas focusing on her future goal of being socially successful renewed her motivation to expose herself to more early trauma. She was able to desensitize to the trauma, correct misconceptions, and work on making friends through shifting between past, present, and future. Therapy that shifts between times and/or elements of the BASIC-ID to maintain working levels of anxiety may appear chaotic, but working in many areas at the same time can be efficient and goal directed.

Another schema for directing the therapist's attention involves the acronym STAIRCaSE (situation, thoughts, affect, intentions, responses, consequences, and self-evaluations), which can "help the therapist formulate the problem at hand and also assess ongoing client progress in becoming aware of the interrelationship among these different aspects of their functioning" (Goldfried, 2004, p. 99). The clinician is urged to attend to the client's STAIRCaSE. Changes in these factors often account for progress in treatment. I also try to be aware of both content and process and shift from one to the other when the client moves out of the therapeutic window.

These acronyms can be used to guide the two main functions of the therapist: assessment and treatment. Placing a client's behavior problems in the context of its antecedents and consequences can contribute to a more complete understanding of the client's problems and a more detailed treatment plan (Ellis, 1984). For example, if a client presents with an anger control problem, we can look at the ABCs of the problem (antecedents, behaviors, and consequences) and examine each in regard to the aspects described previously in the acronyms. This process might begin with finding antecedents by examining when the anger began to be a problem in his life. We might identify antecedent situational triggers and help the client become aware of and observe bodily sensations (e.g., clenching fists or teeth, tensing muscles, sweating, feeling cold, rapidly breathing). We might identify situations that precede anger, such as teasing or roughhousing that starts as fun and turns serious, particular tender spots such as insults about weight, comments about mother or intelligence, or aggression that erupts before dinner when structure and blood sugar levels are low. We might learn that anger occurs more frequently when stresses are compounded, such as when visitors disrupt routines or when the family is on the way to the airport. Identifying the antecedents can ssuggest interventions that alter the situations. We might try to install behaviors by teaching the client to count to 100, write in a journal, walk away, take a shower, or pound a pillow. We might try to alter images by exploring how family-of-origin members expressed anger and how the client responded to this modeling. We might try to impact the affect by relaxation techniques and use self-talk cognitions to calm down. We might intervene by altering cognitions through teaching assertiveness techniques including "I messages." Self-talk is a major part of most anger management. Clients learn to tell themselves such things as "If I blow up, I'll get in trouble," "I'll show them. I won't let them know it bothers me," "They don't even know my Mom. They are just saying that to get me upset," "This guy is a jerk. Who is around that I can hang out with instead," or "I'm going to calm down and win by using humor or coming up with the best argument. I won't try to win by using force." We might look for biological contributors, such as ADHD and prescription drugs, that could influence control, as well as substances that the client might be using that influence expressions of anger. We might identify images that motivate the client to be aggressive, such as identifying with the parent or bully who treated him violently. We might focus on changing the pattern of consequences that support aggression by teaching caretakers to use contingency management to offer rewards and punishments and model nonaggressive responses. Identifying the ABCs of the aspects of the problems described by the acronyms often allows clients to make informed contributions to treatment strategies.

Ask About Previous Treatment and Reactions to Former Therapists, Especially About What Was Helpful and How and Why Treatment Ended   I anticipate that the client's description of previous therapy will foreshadow our relationship. Complaints and reasons for having terminated are admonitions to heed. When clients describe a previous therapist's strengths and deficits, they may be describing what they want and do not want in therapy. Usually earlier success is a good prognostic indicator, and I may try to reunite these clients with their previous therapist, if that is at all possible. However, a successful previous treatment may foreshadow future disappointment with me for not being like the idealized prior therapist, especially because it can be time-consuming and annoying to retell everything to bring the new therapist and relationship up to speed. Generally I follow the admired parts of the previous therapist's path.

B) Nurture the Therapeutic Relationship and Therapist Characteristics That Promote Change
In the service of engagement and forming a therapeutic alliance, I try to identify and pass the client's often unconscious tests, such as the following: Are you going to abuse me? Do you care? Are you going to be like my parent [or spouse or previous therapist]? Will you reject me? Will you think I'm stupid or crazy? Do you like me? Pointing out these interpersonal expectations and making interpretations about how they were helpful in the past, but now cause problems, is usually insufficient to pass transference tests, especially at the start of treatment. I anticipate that clients may need to repeatedly experience a comforting answer throughout treatment. For example, clients who feel that no one will care about them might question their negative assumptions when the therapist shows caring by noticing their needs or remembering the details of their narrative or phoning when they miss an appointment. For clients who fear being seen as dumb, asking them for their opinion or respecting their advice might contribute to correcting their expectations. Clients who feel unlikable might be less self-effacing when they experience the

therapist's enjoying and appreciating them. Even such repeated experiences might not be enough to counteract transference expectations and might be met with "It's your job to act that way." These client expectations can be well entrenched, and correcting them can be a central theme throughout treatment.

Some clients cannot fully use techniques rooted in language and the conscious processing of information to feel comfortable, engage, and experience a therapeutic relationship. Particularly young children, clients who have been traumatized and/or never had a healthy attachment, and those who are stressed and in a highly emotional state may have difficulty using left-hemisphere processes to self-regulate their emotions and form a relationship. Allan Schore (2003) focused on how the therapist can facilitate a therapeutic alliance with such clients. He described the alliance as being similar to infant attachment, a process that takes place without language, in which the emotionally attuned therapist's unconscious capacities respond to the client's unconscious, emotional communications to cocreate the holding relationship. He emphasized the empathy, calming, and trust that can develop from the feelings communicated by postural shifts, facial expressions, tone and volume of voice, respiration, gestures, eye movements and contact, nonverbal utterances, physical distance, and touch.

Generate Hope   I try to convey to the client that together we will identify problems and what to do about them, that I have worked with others with similar problems, and that I would like to help and think I can help. Part of motivating clients to continue to engage and pursue treatment goals involves helping them believe that the goals are attainable. Patients who expect to be successful form a stronger therapeutic alliance and improve more (Irving et al., 2004); furthermore therapists' optimistic expectations also predict outcome (Meyer et al., 2002). Generating hope is one of our most powerful therapeutic tools (Snyder, Ilardi, Michael, & Cheavens, 2000). These authors described hope as a future-oriented cognitive process involving (a) defining a goal; (b) identifying a pathway, a strategy, to reach the goal; and (c) the belief that one can accomplish the strategy.

I am careful what I communicate to clients about their treatment and its expected outcome. The power of suggestion is potent and can cause change. For example one study showed that when college student volunteers were told they would receive a mild electric shock that could cause a headache, two thirds reported pain, even though no shock was administered. Even when they were told that they had not received a shock, all of the subjects insisted that the pain was real (Wade, 1996). Our belief in our effectiveness and our expectation that our clients will change can reduce their anxiety, help them believe that treatment will be productive, and motivate them to trust us and commit to the therapy process. Our lack of faith can sabotage treatment, because for all participants therapy is a faith-based enterprise.

A Good Therapist Is Often Like a Good Parent   I try to stay connected, keep communication going, and continue caring even when I have little power or control over what the client does. It is challenging to care about someone who continues to repeat harmful patterns or is less motivated than I am. I encourage some clients to idealize and incorporate parts of me to draw on between sessions and use throughout their lives. As the therapeutic relationship develops, often clients form internal representations of their therapist in "auditory, visual and felt presence forms" that support continuing to process the therapy session, encourage "self-guidance," and provide a "source of support, comfort or soothing" (Knox, Goldberg, Woodhouse, & Hill, 1999).

Perhaps the good therapist embodies Freud's view of a good parent, who is able to "hold them tight and let them go." Just as many parents discover, emancipation from family and therapy can involve an option to return before leaving again. As a good parent does, I mirror and soothe. I model more adaptive approaches to problems. I try to develop a holding environment where the client can feel safe to explore and express feelings. I foster a relationship with me and/or others that can compensate for missed and dysfunctional parenting. For instance, a client with a dominating and controlling parent might benefit from a relationship that supports the client's decision making and learning to participate in an equal relationship where his or her needs are expressed and considered. I try to provide such clients with opportunities to have "a voice and a choice" (Haim Ginott). A young client with externalizing problems who lacks parental attention and appropriate consequences might benefit from contingent consequences and supervision, whereas an abused youth with internalizing problems might need nurturing and a supportive relationship.

Similar to parenting, our goal as therapist is to be "good enough" (D. W. Winnecott) rather than perfect, and we hope the client can learn to accept us with our shortcomings, which can make expectations for other relationships more realistic. We cannot meet all the client's needs and expectations. There are limits to our attunement and availability, just as there are limits to everyone else with whom the client will have to deal. I try to provide the appropriate amount of caring. Too much caring can make clients care so much about the therapist that they withhold information for fear that they will lose the therapist's approval. Sometimes too much therapist caring can be experienced as being controlling or engulfing. It is natural that too little caring can be seen as being distant, unattuned, or insensitive and harm the therapeutic relationship.

Mistakes and ruptures in the therapeutic alliance can be therapeutic if they can be repaired. In fact, "rupture and repair" is an integral part of deepening the therapeutic alliance and possibly promoting the internalization of the therapist as the client copes with the fear of losing the therapist. In the mother–infant bond, friendships, marital relationships, and the patient–therapist alliance, the internalization of the idealized other "occurs as a result of participation in relationships in which strong affective bonds are established and their inevitable ruptures repaired. The affective bond process of establish/rupture/repair is understood as the underlying dynamic of internalization" (Lewis, 2000, p. 137). Repairs in the therapeutic relationship can lead to moments when the client realizes that the therapist really cares and to corrections in the client's core transference feelings that he or she projects onto others.

Ruptures can be identified when clients disagree with the therapist or emotionally withdraw from the therapy process or relationship. Safran, Muran, Samstag, and Stevens (2002) identified two types of alliance ruptures: withdrawal ruptures and confrontation ruptures. To resolve withdrawal ruptures, the therapist is urged to explore and foster the expression of the underlying needs the client is unable to verbalize. In confrontation ruptures, the therapist is urged to resolve the rupture by "exploring the fears and self-criticisms that interfere with the expression of underlying needs" (p. 514). The therapist is urged to assume responsibility for his or her contribution to the rupture, empathize with the client's feelings, and explore the unmet needs behind the client's confrontations.

Ruptures can be triggered by the therapist's emotional misattunement that can be repaired most economically by recognizing and validating the client's feelings and then apologizing for the therapist's error. With this in mind, I try to identify and admit my mistakes. For instance, I might fail to mirror properly or be unable to stay connected to clients when they express emotions that trigger my personal, nontherapeutic reactions. To avoid feeling the client's pain, I might give advice I later regret, or I might offer an intervention before the client is ready, which disrupts the therapeutic alliance. One type of rupture is generated by the client's transference. In such instances, clients believe their realistic or unrealistic or conscious or unconscious expectations are confirmed, and they may experience the familiar, painful feelings that accompany the relationship ruptures in their daily lives. They may feel unsafe, afraid, rejected, blamed, tricked, disappointed, cheated, put down, judged, uncared for, and so on. Later in treatment with older clients, helping these clients identify these feelings, explore the misconceptions underlying them, and/or realize that these feelings or conclusions have been unrealistically generalized from past situations can repair these ruptures. These understandings can help restore the alliance as well as sensitize the client to how these assumptions need to be monitored because they can sabotage therapy and other relationships. However, pursuing these goals at the low ebb of the relationship can be difficult, because discussing these inappropriate projections can cause the client to feel judged, blamed, and misunderstood. Sometimes therapists find themselves in a situation where they may need to just validate the client's feelings in hopes of more thoroughly addressing the situation at a later time, after the relationship has been rebuilt.

An example of a rupture that was due to my error and the client's distortions recently occurred in my practice. An emancipating college student who attended therapy once a month had not resumed treatment after the winter holidays. As we both were planning to be away, it was difficult to schedule her next session in advance. She finally called to reschedule 3 months later. Toward the end of our next session, she admitted feeling quite wounded that I had not gotten in touch with her to reschedule, saying that she had thought I must not care about her or that her problems were not important enough to warrant my time. I sincerely apologized for not calling, explaining that I forgot that I had stated that I would initiate contact, as I thought that I had left it up to her to call. I acknowledged how pleased I was that she called and then told me her concerns, and that I was very sorry she had to endure several months of hurt feelings because of my lapse. I also told her that I had been wondering about her but assumed she was doing well and that her busy schedule of full-time work plus classes was the cause of her not resuming treatment, and that I had expected her to call when her schedule permitted. After I inquired about several important areas of her life, she seemed to relax into the rhythm of our usual treatment relationship.

At the next session I revisited this issue. I said that I thought that my mistake of not calling had led her to fall into her old assumptions that she tended to resort to when people disappointed her. She was insightful and recognized that my behavior mirrored her parents' painful ignoring of her, as the lion's share of their attention went to her two troubled brothers. We talked about how my lapse was acutely painful to her because of her history. She admitted that she had seriously considered never calling me, thus leaving therapy with the belief that one more person in her life whom she had grown to trust had disappointed her, because she was not a very interesting, appealing person. This rupture deepened our discussions about how this dynamic played out in her daily life, including its contribution to her perfectionism, her codependent relationships, and her tendency to run away from relationships when she felt ignored. More importantly, this rupture and repair deepened our relationship.

Encourage Reasonable Goals   Helping a client to formulate realistic goals and the process of mutually agreeing on and changing goals can be a central focus of therapy for some older clients. To formulate goals I frequently ask clients what some have called "the miracle question": What would you be like and what would you then be able to do if your problem(s) no longer existed? The more specific the answer is, the more useful it is. For instance, wanting to be less depressed is not as helpful as "If the depression evaporated I could be more social. I could go to the gym, talk to people I now avoid, pay my bills instead of procrastinating."

Agreeing on what can be achieved and accepting what we cannot accomplish are core principals of AA and productive ongoing focuses of psychotherapy. How therapists and clients feel about therapy depends partly on expectations. If expectations are too high, we fail. If they are too low, we provide inadequate treatment. Realistic expectations for therapy contribute to developing realistic expectations in many areas of the client's life (e.g., relationships, child development, parenting, achievement, family life, health, success, and happiness).

Sometimes parents want to change too many of their child's behaviors, and we need to work on one or two things at a time. I might tell such parents, "The longest journey starts with the first step," or I might ask them, "Do you know how to eat an elephant? One bite at a time." Sometimes I have to tell myself the same things when I generate too many goals for a client or when the client's initial goals differ from mine.

Some clients do not have a goal, or they have a goal that is a reflection of their pathology or resistance ("I want to be alone, quit coming here, drop out of school, get more sex and drugs, not have any goals"). These responses may show how hopeless and unmotivated the client feels. I try to avoid immediately stepping in with my empirical and experiential knowledge or taking responsibility by suggesting goals for the client to reject. I prefer to try to more fully understand the client's situation and expect that reasonable goals will surface as we explore his or her thinking from different perspectives.

Keep It Simple   When I ask clients what had been helpful about therapy, they surprise me with simplistic answers: "You cared," "I didn't know I was so angry [or depressed]," "You didn't get mad when I … ," "You helped me tell him how I felt," "You were thinking about me after I left," and "I knew you cared when you came out to the car." People are often ruled by core issues that are not very complicated, such as being afraid of abandonment and rejection, incorrectly blaming themselves for things that were not their fault, or having unrealistic expectations for themselves and others. I try to avoid complex explanations, express things in the simplest way, and keep the focus of treatment to a few core issues.

Often therapists are helpful in unintentional ways, because our listening and typical reactions contrast so dramatically with what our clients have come to expect from others. We may be doing something very powerful when we do not criticize, abuse, or get angry; when we treat clients respectfully or ask for their ideas and listen to them; and when we set a limit or fall from a pedestal and are still likeable.

Do No Harm I aspire to avoid blaming, bossing, keeping secrets, ordering, degrading, abandoning, being distracted, turning to clients to meet my needs, believing everything clients say, sharing personal information that is not therapeutically helpful, boasting, and lying. I try to avoid working with clients I do not like or with whom I do not feel safe, being seductive or sarcastic, and sending a client out of the office in a dangerous state. I try not to give preferential treatment to clients based on their socioeconomic status, attractiveness, or ability to pay, and I try not to give in to the temptation to allow treatment decisions to be influenced by the amount of paperwork and personal inconvenience they generate.

C) Nurture Extratherapeutic Forces of Change

Help Clients Realize That They Are Not the Only One With These Problems and That Societal Forces Have Contributed to Their Problems Clients may have a problem that they keep secret because of shame and self-blame, thus missing the opportunity to learn that many others share their difficulty. Clients might feel they are the only one with their problem until they learn how ubiquitous the problem is. Realizing they are not alone can reduce their shame and allow them to share their experience with others and reach out for help. For instance I have known many clients who participated in domestic violence or molest groups who reported that the most beneficial aspect was the realization that there were so many others with the same problem.

While we may not want to "globalize" problems by projecting blame and responsibility on to societal forces, at the cost of ignoring the clients' personal contribution to problems, it is increasingly common for therapists to educate clients about the connection between their problems and the societal forces that perpetuate them. Some problems are highly intertwined with societal forces, as exemplified by the culture-bound syndromes that appear in the appendix of the *DSM-IV* (American Psychiatric Association, 1994, pp. 844–849). For some problems the connection is not evident to clients who may believe that their personal inadequacies are the main cause of their difficulties. It may be a parent with an aggressive child to become sensitive to the influence of violent media; a client with an eating disorder (possibly a culture-bound syndrome)[7] to explore how her exposure to advertising models and pop culture has affected her; a battered woman to therapeutic for a how living in a patriarchal society has contributed to her situation; a single mother worried about financial problems to understand the connections between her depression and her former partner's lack of support and participation as well as the impact of reduced government spending for medical care, job training, and child care. And an overwhelmed grandmother who has to raise her traumatized grandchildren might be less self-blaming when she learns that she and so many others are collateral damage from the wave of methamphetamine addiction sweeping the western United States, which has made so many parents incapable of parenting their children. Understanding the political and economic contributions to personal problems often depersonalizes and depathologizes the problems and reduces shame and self-blame.

Many of my clients' problems are partly caused and/or made worse by societal factors that require superhuman abilities to overcome. Probably 70% of my clients are poor (on Medi-Cal). Many live in drug-infested, violent, postliterate (Jameson, 1991), and antieducation neighborhoods where having expensive, flashy things (bling) is equated with self-worth. These families are busy trying to be safe and surviving with decreasing governmental help.

The demographics of my caseload clearly indict fathers as one of the contributors to my clients' problems. Of all my youth clients, only one fourth have biological fathers living in the home. Of these fathers living in the home, only 40% can be seen as functional (employed, caring, able to contribute positively to their child's treatment). Sixty percent are dysfunctional (addicted, chronically ill, rigid or authoritarian, a detriment to their child's progress in treatment). Approximately 50% of my clients come from single-parent households without any father present in their lives.[8] The biological fathers and subsequent father figures are absent because of molest, domestic violence, or drug-related problems; they were never or only briefly involved; or they are highly dysfunctional for other reasons. Therefore, probably 1 in 10 of my clients could claim a functional father who lives in the home and can be an ally with the therapist to help the client. When I have moments of withdrawal from my addiction to being nonjudgmental, I blame fathers. Of course this feeling is countertransference. My hostility evaporates when I treat perpetrators, abandoning fathers, batterers, drug addicts, and dysfunctional men, as I learn about their histories and dynamics. Their life stories and struggles are similar to those of the youths I treat. Acorns do not fall far from the tree.

Absent fathers are a national problem. In the United States in 2004, 36% of all births were to single mothers. Twenty-five percent of Caucasian children, 46% of Hispanic children, and 69% of African American children were born to unmarried mothers (Hamilton et al., 2005).

Upon the birth of their child, about two thirds of unwed parents say they strongly intend to marry, but within the next year and a half, only 13% do marry (Popenoe & Whitehead, 2003). We are raising a generation that has turned to the media for images of a male role model. These models are not based on academic achievement or concern for others and our planet.

The mothers, grandparents, relatives, and other caretakers who are raising my young clients are typically burdened with emotional problems and unrealistic expectations about parenting, the missing parent, and the child they are raising. Often these single-parent households emotionally center on the missing parent. These families are generally characterized by shame, guilt, father or sometimes mother hunger, the idealizing and demonizing of the absent parent, and anger at his or her abuse and lack of adequate financial help. In situations where the uninvolved parent has periodic contact, family members go on an emotional roller coaster caused by the unfulfilled promises of the uninvolved parent, which result in repeatedly raising hopes followed by crushing disappointments. Many of the mothers and grandmothers who take over parenting remain emotionally attached, financially dependent, and legally embattled with the missing parent. Some continue to be involved with them in a codependent relationship that exploits the caretaker and drains the family's resources. These caretakers require treatment so that their children can improve. The youths could more easily adjust to their dysfunctional, absent parent if their caretaker could protect them and model successful coping strategies.

Sometimes understanding powerful societal forces and their connections to personal problems can result in trying to impact the problem on both a personal level and a societal level, such as the client who was able to obtain a home loan by challenging her bank's policy of redlining her neighborhood, and the client who challenged and changed an institution's admission policy to obtain services for her son with Asperger's syndrome. Many abuse treatments describe the final stage of recovery as pursuing a survivor mission where clients help themselves by helping others with similar problems (Herman, 1992). Graduating to be a counselor or sponsor in addiction treatment programs is another common example of how a client can mend through helping others who have the same problems the client once struggled with.

3. We Promote Change by Providing Evidence-Based and Experience-Based Techniques and Activities That Foster Treatment Goals

In selecting and offering an intervention, I try to consider the following: Is this approach productive in progressing toward our treatment goals?

What are the costs and benefits of this intervention? Is the intervention compatible with the client's beliefs? What is the client's reaction to it? How does this intervention affect the therapeutic relationship?

Teach a Variety of Skills   Therapists may teach specific skills such as behavior modification, anger management, budgeting, making friends, communication skills, parenting, empathy, assertiveness, and problem solving. Sometimes acquiring skills can generate others and an avalanche of positive change.

Teaching these skills often requires breaking down larger goals (e.g., making friends) into discrete parts that can be modeled, shaped, and reinforced as opportunities arise in the therapeutic relationship, activities, and role-plays during sessions and by helping adults in the youth's life teach and reinforce the skills in daily life. For instance in training social skills, we might identify and teach skills the youth lacks, such as establishing and maintaining eye contact, greeting, showing interest, actively listening, asking questions to keep up the conversation, giving and receiving compliments, setting limits, or politely disengaging. Some clients may need to remediate or learn to cope with barriers to making friends, such as difficulty tolerating teasing or losing; lacking marketable peer skills or common interests; being overly sensitive to touch; cheating, lying, stealing, or not sharing or taking turns; violating others' personal space; having inadequate affect modulation or anger control; having unrealistic fears (afraid of being harmed, rejected, criticized, or abandoned); being aloof, self-centered, smothering, attention seeking, bossy, or controlling; choosing inappropriate friends; or obsessing about real or exaggerated problems. For some clients challenging and correcting their cognitive distortions might need to be a focus, such as using all-or-none reasoning, having self-critical thoughts, expecting the worst, or projecting blame and responsibility.

Part of the art of psychotherapy involves balancing (a) focusing on problems and teaching new skills (a process that can be perceived as criticism) and (b) appreciating and reflecting the client's strengths. Focusing on skill acquisition can damage the relationship by making the client feel unaccepted, especially if the client is not motivated to change. Motivated clients are more likely to appreciate the therapist's focus on skill development. Sometimes when I focus on skill acquisition, I think I have lost opportunities to build the relationship, and when I focus on appreciating and accepting the client, I wonder if I should have focused more on skill development.

The ease of acquiring skills is interwoven with client characteristics and the treatment relationship. For instance, Tam had emotional outbursts and obsessed over being threatened and retaliating. He never trusted me enough to allow me to teach him relaxation techniques. In contrast, Cameron was 3 months into a new school term, and when I asked him to draw his classroom he drew the desks, the whiteboard, and several animal cages. He could not name any classmates. In an effort to bring the social scene into the foreground, I suggested that part of making friends involved learning names, and I wanted to know who his classmates were. The next week he entered the session and spontaneously asked for the drawing he had made the previous week. He proudly wrote everyone's name over their desks and told me something about each classmate. He wanted to please me and give me a gift.

Using "establishing and maintaining eye contact" as an example of a skill that might need to be taught, the therapist might select strategies that depend on the client's motivation, ability to tolerate frustration, and level of cognitive development. When clients are motivated to learn a new skill, they may be more willing to tolerate the stress involved in examining the validity of the thoughts and feelings that motivate avoiding eye contact and in trying on new behaviors and cognitions.

When clients are not motivated or are too young to observe their own feelings and cognitions, then less stressful approaches are needed that do not threaten engagement. For instance, I might try to use our interactions to model, shape, and reinforce eye contact and then work on generalizing the skill to the client's life space. When avoidance is anxiety driven, as the relationship deepens and session routines become established, risking eye contact can naturally increase and be appreciated. I might directly address the issue by offering feedback about how I am frustrated by the lack of eye contact ("I'm not sure you are listening" or "I'm wondering if you are think-ing about something else"), teaching the skill through games and activities (mirroring and copying games, making funny faces when the client looks away so he or she will keep eye contact to avoid missing something), and sensitizing the client to possible consequences ("Kids might think you are stuck-up or don't want to be friends"). I might harness parent and teacher resources and coach them to focus on eliciting and appreciating the client's eye contact.

In addition to directly teaching skills, I look for opportunities to teach a process for acquiring skills that the client can continue to use when other needs surface. For instance, Andrew was brought to the clinic by his foster mother because he had been repeatedly suspended from fifth grade for making sexualized comments and not being able to keep quiet in class. He had been raised by an unemployable single parent who was frequently homeless and lived in places for less than a year. Andrew missed 2 years of formal schooling by fourth grade but was close to grade level in academics.

He may have been molested, missed years of socialization, and never had a best friend. He apparently did not know what a friend was or how to get one. He settled for acting sexual to make classmates laugh and to feel connected to them. When I asked him what he wanted from peers after he got their laughter, he said, "Then they are my friend." He clearly needed to learn more appropriate socialization skills, but he needed to develop many other abilities before he could tolerate the closeness and frustrations involved in relationships. I was able to get him interested in watching peers to see what friends were doing with each other. In the process he observed his classmates making friends, and he started to copy the approaches that he admired. Just teaching him to be funny in a nonsexual way would not have generated as much progress. He discovered a process to acquire skills that he could use in the future. He learned to watch those who were successful and adapt their methods to his purposes. A few sessions later he described how he was working on handling teasing by responding with humor, as a peer did on the bus.

Supply a Variety of Approaches to Change Cognitions, Feelings, and Behaviors
I attend carefully to client's words and nonverbal communications. At the same time, I pay attention to my feelings, the process (the overall pattern of what is happening in the session), treatment goals, possible solutions, and obstacles to accomplishing them. I may need to offer limits and boundaries and confront unproductive behaviors and defenses while making calculated judgments about the benefits and possible harm to the therapeutic alliance that these confrontations could generate.

I correct misconceptions, which are often based on negative conclusions that clients have made about themselves during childhood or in times of crisis. For example, for abused clients the most typical harmful misconception is self-blame. Especially for youths much of trauma work involves correcting this misconception. That is why it has been described as "INMF" work: "it's not my fault" work. I am fond of asking the question posed in eye movement desensitization and reprocessing (EMDR) treatment: "What did that experience cause you to think about yourself?" When clients are able to answer, their response can focus treatment on the misconception they drew from their trauma that could underlie many of their problems.

I normalize ("Anyone would feel frustrated and depressed caring for a dying parent," "I know you thought it was rare, but more than one third of women are molested"), depathologize ("Lots of 4-year-olds have nightmares; it's a peak time for fears;" "His ADHD is an inherited, neurological disorder that is not caused by parenting"), and provide other efforts to reframe problems.

Reframing is a powerful technique from cognitive-behavioral therapy that helps the client understand his or her situation in a new way. For example, reframing can dramatically change a relationship if an injured party can, instead of feeling rejected, see another's anger as an attempt to gain attention or as bravado replacing anxiety, or as a sign of feeling rejected and wanting more love, as if the anger were a way of saying, "I hate you because I'm not getting enough of you." Reframing helped a father who was often angry at his son for using foul language and calling him a bitch. The father usually reacted with punishment and a lecture about respect. I agreed with the parent that his son's behavior was inappropriate and then reframed the teen's offensive language as progress in comparison to the temper tantrums he used to have. I explained that he was progressing along a continuum from out-of-control behavior to out-of-control words to in-control words and that when he got angry, we were presented with an opportunity to help him move further along the continuum to where we eventually wanted him to be: using in-control words. I suggested that instead of getting upset at the words, he could say that he understood that his son was angry, but he wasn't sure what was causing the upset. The father used future upsets to help his son verbalize his anger in a calmer way and then problem solve. Instead of seeing disrespect, the father saw progress and opportunity. In another example of reframing, a parent complained about how she resented all the chauffeuring she was doing for her 16-year-old and her friends. I reframed the trips as an opportunity to talk with her daughter, learn about her friends, and see them interact. The mother now looks forward to these times.

A familiar reframe involves helping clients focus on finding the lesson or growth opportunity in the problem they are having. For instance, unemployment, academic problems, a divorce, or an affair can motivate the client to identify his or her contribution to creating the problem. The client then might be better able to avoid repeating the pattern. Often I see parents who ineffectively nag their children to do chores or homework until the youths resent the parents. Reframing the nagging as begging the child to "please, please do your homework so I will not have to give a consequence" has motivated some parents to start using contingent rewards, such as "no electronics until homework is checked."

Normalizing and reframing a teen's behavior helped his mother see the normal and healthy aspects of his behavior and then abandon her hostility. She was angry with Chris for being "so vacuous." Chris had learning disabilities, and after years of frustration with school and making friends, he isolated himself in the house and would accept only home schooling from 7th to 10th grade. He played video games, smoked pot, and related infrequently to peers over the Internet. He began conjoint therapy (mother and son) in April, and the goals the mother and I (but not Chris) agreed to included getting him educationally evaluated by the school and then returning to school. By September he had started 11th grade, but by October his mother complained, "All he wants to do is meet with a small group of peers and talk about who likes whom and who broke up." This was upsetting for the mother until she realized that Chris had missed 4 years of social development and was more like a junior high student than a junior in high school who might be expected to have developed interests and some degree of loyalty and intimacy with a peer group. The mother became more understanding and supportive of Chris's peer group involvement and appreciative that the peers were going to school and not using drugs. As in these examples, many interventions benefit the client by ultimately facilitating improved relationships.

Sometimes I help clients to externalize the problem, which involves placing the blame or cause of the problem outside the client or the client's volition and then mobilizing the client's resources against the problem. Externalizing can help clients realize that the problem is not a defect in them but an indication of a force outside of their identity that they can challenge so that it does not influence them to react with a problem behavior. For instance a patriarchal society could be viewed as fomenting a couple's marital problem, and they could be motivated to battle the roles they have been taught and adopted. A client's panic attacks could be viewed as caused by his or her body's faulty flight-or-fight response, and the client could be taught to manage the reaction. As Michael White (1988–1989) suggested, a child's encopresis could be viewed as an anthropomorphic character, "Sneaky Poo," whom the child could trick and conquer.

I foster insight for clients when useful by asking questions that lead to awareness. Therapists generally value understanding and promote the clients' understanding of themselves and others. For instance, I asked a client who repeatedly complained about her husband if she was comparing her husband to someone else in her life. This led her to realize that she had been unfavorably comparing her husband to an idealized childhood image of her father instead of seeing her husband realistically. She reported, "Since I stopped comparing, I appreciate him more and am not so angry at him."

I help clients identify, label, and express feelings in words so these feelings can be understood and managed symbolically rather than held in or acted out in unproductive behaviors. Some therapists describe three skills they consider central to the effective treatment of adolescent and adult clients. They foster the abilities of mentalizing (thinking about feelings while having those feelings), metacognition (thinking about one's cognitions), and meta-awareness (being aware of one's awareness). I help clients face and master thoughts, feelings, and memories they have avoided. I help them mourn losses and repeatedly expose themselves to pain until it does not hurt anymore or hurts less. I listen to confessions and give absolution. Sometimes I avoid past pain and problems and focus on learning new skills, identifying and following passions, mirroring accomplishments, and developing hopes and goals. I notice, help create, and celebrate successes and teach clients to savor them. I identify and mirror strengths and help clients use them as resources so they can move on to the next developmental stage. I try to make up for missing or defective parenting and relationships by providing and/or steering clients to compensatory, corrective emotional experiences.

Sometimes I help clients identify life scripts and deconstruct narratives. One of the biggest changes I have seen in a client involved correcting her lifelong belief that she was dumb. She was viewed as the stupid child in her family of origin where she was kept home to care for the babies. As she went to school infrequently, she had no friends and could not keep up with the academics. She eventually dropped out of school to work, and she married an abusive man who kidnapped their son and told him that his mother was dead. She came to one session with several huge binders of letters that she had written to officials and organizations across the country in her effort to find her son. Surprisingly she succeeded when the child saw his picture on a milk carton in New York and started asking questions. Her writing and the strategies she employed impressed me. I thought she was very smart, so I gave her an IQ test. She scored 127, which is the 96th percentile. From then on I teasingly called her "One-twenty-seven," and her self-esteem improved dramatically as she understood why she had failed in school. She began to expect more of herself, her new husband, and her son, which resulted in all of them having more successes.

Many cognitive-behavioral interventions involve teaching clients to use self-talk to self-soothe; to distract from anger, anxiety, guilt, and depression; and to facilitate desensitization and affect modulation. However, it should not be surprising that self-talk is not a silver bullet that can be relied on to produce change, because it is an intervention aimed primarily at cognitions while problems are manifested in multiple domains. Furthermore, self-talk is difficult to use when the client is highly emotional, when the client is unable to observe himself or herself, and when the self-talk is not believable. Perhaps people can attend to only one thing at a time, so when clients focus on self-talk, they are thinking instead of behaving or emoting. One form of self-talk, repeating a mantra, helped some clients cope with anxiety and facilitate change. For example, an obsessive client was able to tolerate postponing and then eventually stopping her excessive Xeroxing and shopping by chanting, "Less is more" and then talking to herself about how she was so overwhelmed with possessions that she could not find her things when she needed them. Afraid of not being able to find important documents, she made four copies of everything and was so buried in papers that she had not filed her taxes in 4 years. Another client found that singing the refrain "Gotta let go. Gotta let go" from a Holly Near song allowed her to bind her anxiety and tolerate the frustration of not being able to micromanage her emancipating adolescent son.

Sometimes self-talk can be combined with learning to be an observer of a greater process. Recognizing a problem situation and then thinking about consequences or questioning the reasons behind one's actions are self-thoughts that are often a part of anger and anxiety management. Challenging obsessive thoughts and arguing against their validity is part of many cognitive-behavioral approaches and can be incorporated into treating obsessive-compulsive disorder (OCD). Schwartz (1996) developed a treatment for OCD that relies heavily on self-talk and reframing. He teaches clients to control obsessions and compulsions through developing their ability to use the four Rs: First, *relabel* the thought. The client is encouraged to tell himself or herself that the belief that stimulates the obsession or compulsion is not real: "It is only a thought." Second, *reattribute* the thought to being a result of a chemical imbalance in the brain rather than the client's personal belief. Third, *refocus*. Instead of acting on the urge or impulse, the client is encouraged to substitute other behaviors and thoughts with the hope that over time the urge will extinguish. Fourth, *revalue*. Tell oneself that the OCD thoughts are not that important and can be tolerated, ignored, and viewed as background noise. This approach attempts to empower the client to overcome urges by strength of will and treats failure as a weakness in motivation and commitment. Sometimes clients find this process more palatable if they are taking medication and given permission to engage in their ritual thinking or behaviors one or two times before they begin to challenge the obsessions and compulsions.

Sometimes clients who are bipolar are able to modulate feelings by telling themselves that they cannot trust their thinking when they are at the depressive or energetic extremes of their emotional continuums. They learn to observe their behaviors and emotions and then tell themselves, "It's the chemicals in my brain that create these feelings and thoughts, and I can't trust them." Similarly, clients who are socially anxious have been able to challenge their assumptions that, for instance, others are thinking negative things about them by telling themselves that they cannot trust their thinking in certain situations, such as when they assume others are thinking about them. Self-talk is a major component of most cognitive-behavioral treatments for depression and habit control.

Therapeutic self-talk is more easily assimilated when the content is created by the client rather than prescribed by the therapist. Usually clients can identify previous situations when they used self-talk to cope successfully. EMDR provides a process for identifying self-talk that clients may be motivated to adopt. In EMDR, after identifying the client's problematic thoughts, clients are asked what they would rather think. Then they are encouraged to adopt those thoughts instead. For example, a client kept thinking, "There must have been something I did to cause my son to be gay. Maybe I didn't give him enough love as a baby." She also had the competing thought that being gay was not caused by her treatment of him. After psychoeducation and discussion, she became more able to tell herself that his sexual preference had nothing to do with her parenting. When she thought that, she was able to be more loving to him.

I may validate and witness clients' stories and point out connections between thoughts, feelings, actions, and events. I facilitate awareness of the consequences of choices and behaviors. I help clients generate and explore choices, develop priorities, and refocus attention and energy. Sometimes I focus on creating awareness of the feelings that generated behaviors. For instance, a divorced father once boasted that after his son mentioned that he didn't want to visit him for the weekend because of opportunities to be with friends, the father angrily told his son, "You don't have to visit me if you don't want to." This led the son to feel rejected and avoid visiting the father for several months. When the father became aware of the hurt and anger behind his comment to his son, then he could understand his son's feelings of rejection. The father was then motivated to apologize, which restarted the weekend contacts. Therapists often encourage clients to take responsibility for what they are responsible for and reject responsibility for that which they are not responsible. This is a constant theme with conduct-disordered clients who typically do not see their contribution to problems with others, and with neurotic clients who tend to overestimate and misinterpret their contribution to problems.

I help clients, especially youths, talk about their life, express feelings, learn skills, and work out problems by providing art supplies, sand tray figures, puppets, and other media. Many clients choose and enjoy expressing conscious and unconscious feelings, thoughts, memories, and fantasies through such materials. I provide board games, activities that can be generalized to peers (pool, ping-pong, basketball, tetherball, wall ball, four square, catch), and craft projects (constructing with a hot-glue gun, making beaded necklaces or friendship bracelets, making models and rockets) that build rapport, foster engagement, teach frustration tolerance and acceptance of rules, and provide opportunities for skill development, successes, and creativity. Play therapy can be an effective treatment (Bratton, Ray, Rhine, & Jones, 2005) that can be even more powerful when the parent is included or taught to provide the therapy. On the other hand, these activities can also be used by a client to avoid the therapist and dealing with uncomfortable content.

With art, sand trays, and puppetlike materials, I might allow client-directed free expression, which the early play therapists thought was therapeutic in itself, but necessarily I introduce more structure, because the effects of trauma are not necessarily remediated by just repeatedly reenacting the trauma in play without input from the therapist. This was demonstrated by the Chowchilla children, who were kidnapped from their school bus and hidden underground yet continued to have PTSD and foreshortened expectations for the future 4 years after they escaped the ordeal, even though they repeatedly reenacted the traumatic events in their play (Terr, 1983). To provide structure I appreciate Richard Gardner's (1971) "mutual story telling technique," which encourages youths to express a story and offers the therapist the opportunity to retell the story and insert therapeutic information, alternative behaviors, thoughts, and endings that may correct irrational beliefs that underlie the client's problems. For instance, a child might tell a story in which the parent hits the annoying baby who cries too much. The therapist could then comfort the parent or infant and offer alternative perspectives, motivations, solutions, and endings.

I might provide structured activities, such as developing a lifeline from birth into the future on a huge piece of butcher paper. Sometimes several sessions are needed, and the parent(s) might be invited to provide information and correct and clarify the child's story. For some clients this activity can progress into the future to explore long-term goals. For older clients the lifeline has extended to death and identifying last words to friends and family members, writing an obituary, or designing a tombstone. The activity allowed a confused 12-year-old with a chaotic history, with the help of her mother, to develop a coherent life story and feel more like a hero than a victim. Once an 8-year-old insisted that she start her time line at a point before she was born instead of at birth, where I had asked her to start. As I got to know her I understood the importance of her needing to draw herself in her mother's womb. She was adopted at birth and had been wondering about and missing an idealized mother. This longing helped fuel her behavior problems.

In the service of developing family cohesion, I might suggest that a family draw a family shield that depicts relevant family events, values, or characteristics, or I might encourage clients to draw their family showing each member doing his or her usual or favorite activity or showing the family in a situation that has meaning for the client. Just seeing whom the client chooses to include in the pictures often significant. Sometimes clients are more open to talk when they are occupied with a task. Sometimes the task itself generates conversation. I might ask clients to draw themselves on an island with what they think they might need to be happy. Making collages from magazine pictures or from Internet sites, such as Google Images, can be less threatening than drawing. Teenagers usually enjoy making collages about themselves, leading to discussions about their past traumas, identity, values, or future. Google Earth is an Internet site that I frequent with clients, who give me a tour of the neighborhoods in their life.

When they contribute to problems, I might identify and challenge unproductive and irrational thinking (all-or-none reasoning; catastrophic thinking; minimizing; denying facts, feelings, awareness, consequences, and responsibility; projecting blame, feelings, thoughts, and responsibility; etc.) as well as expectations and behavioral patterns (sex-role stereotypes, perfectionism, procrastination, codependency, etc.). I seek clarification when I am confused. I repeat, use active listening, and summarize. I take an active stance against harming self and others. I try to enjoy each client and try to keep him or her safe.

Drawing from Gestalt therapy, I try to create experiences instead of talk about them. For instance I might ask the client to pretend he is talking directly to a person instead of talking about the person. I might role-play an upcoming job interview, a new assertive behavior, or how to handle a bully, ignore teasing, respond to a threatening spouse, ask someone out on a date, set limits, or control anger in a provocative situation. When parents are unable to follow through with contacting an organization such as Big Brothers or connecting with a teacher, I might encourage them to make the call during the session while I support the parent.

I use role-reversal role-plays to help clients understand their effect on others and communicate their impression of others. Having family members act out situations or acting out a situation with a client and then reversing characters can be helpful but require therapist-imposed structure so that participants do not become malicious. Doubling is another technique (developed by Moreno, the founder of psychodrama and the sociogram) that has been shown to be effective (Kipper & Ritchie, 2003). Doubling involves a role enactment in which one person portrays himself or herself and another person acts alongside as a double and expresses or guesses what the actor is thinking or intending. The double serves as an auxiliary ego and model for the client and mirrors the client's feelings, doubts, and fears, thus providing support to verbalize feelings (Goldstein, 1971, p. 156).

Therapists generally encourage moderation. I help reduce or increase goals, feelings, and behaviors. Albert Ellis once said that mental illness was "taking things too seriously." He was trying to be provocative, but many of the problems clients present with are about too much or too little of something. Clients often suffer from too much or not enough thinking about themselves, thinking about others, feeling, thinking, worrying, playing, working, cleaning, anger, virtue, vice, caution, immediate gratification, buying, using substances, exercising, eating, and so on. One day in back-to-back sessions, I had a client who wanted to work on being able to have sex without caring so much about her partner's experience so she could focus on her own sensations, and then a client who wanted to have more awareness of her partner's feelings during sex.

To reduce stress and strengthen identities and families, I encourage individual and shared routines and rituals (such as having morning and bedtime routines, singing and playing games in the car, celebrating events, eating meals together, having family council meetings, having family night). As with all interventions, just adding them to the family may not be therapeutic, because they can be transformed by the family system, so that celebrating a birthday or eating together could provide just another opportunity for more of the same dysfunctional relating. Rituals and routines can contribute to improved family functioning but usually require several therapy sessions of preparing, adjusting, and problem solving to become helpful.

Some clients find emotional relief through inventing a healing ceremony or adopting a religious or spiritual practice. Shredding, burning, or burying papers with worries or fears written on them; celebrating a divorce with a party; telling a "worry doll" a problem and leaving it in the office; going to confession; scattering ashes; creating a cleansing ceremony; attaching hopes and worries to a helium balloon and watching it float away; calming oneself by drinking tea while taking a bath surrounded by candles; imagining a safe place and mentally going there to relax and find nurturing; and writing a letter and burning it are rituals that clients have created and found helpful. Some rituals help the client process feelings, whereas others celebrate and display to themselves and others what they have accomplished.

I note medication use, effectiveness, and compliance. Problems with medication are a frequent theme. According to Breen and Thornhill (1998), the sources of noncompliance can be attributed to three factors: medication, client, and provider. Side effects are the most frequent reason for noncompliance. Weight gain, loss of appetite, headaches and stomachaches, tiredness, insomnia, and wired or weird feelings are common complaints. Particularly with young children, taste and difficulty swallowing pills can be problems. The complexity of the medication regime may be bothersome when multiple administrations are required at inconvenient times. The medication may be ineffective or seen as ineffective, and problems with insurance coverage and cost can deter use. Client factors that often interfere with compliance include alternative healing practices, memory deficits, financial stress, psychopathology, substance abuse, and cultural and religious attitudes that foster shame and beliefs that needing medication is a sign of lack of will power and inadequate self-discipline. Without the caretakers' support, medication regimes for youths cannot be initiated or maintained. Youths can feel embarrassed about friends knowing they are taking medication, so they may resist taking medications at school. Administration can lead to power struggles with youths who are not accepting of the need to take medication because of minimizing or denying their problems. Therapist and health care provider factors influence compliance. Compliance can be related to the client's belief in the effectiveness of the medication and the therapist's ability to involve the client in the decision-making process and proactively facilitate ongoing communication about side effects, effectiveness, and worries. Sometimes clients stop taking medication without mentioning it, so the therapist needs to ask periodically about medication use and problems.

I encourage family council meetings to provide a structure to promote sharing feelings, solving problems, showing appreciation, and planning family activities. For some families the meeting may be the only time during the week that they are all together. Usually three or four office visits are required to teach a family to conduct these meetings. The meeting follows a structured format divided into five parts: (a) review minutes of last meeting and evaluate solutions, (b) identify gripes, (c) acknowledge appreciations, (d) do plan and schedule, and (e) enjoy an ending activity. The meeting begins by appointing a secretary to take notes and a chairperson to facilitate. Then, except for the initial meeting, the family's first task is to review and evaluate the solutions they agreed to try during the week to solve the problems they had identified during the previous meeting. The secretary reads the log of the last meeting and might say, "Has our idea of waking earlier helped us to have a less rushed, smoother running morning?" "Has Mom fixed the flat tire on Bill's bike?" "Is the chore schedule working out?" or "Is the alarm clock helping Susan get up in the morning?" Sometimes the devil is in the details: By what time will the dishwasher be loaded? Who takes a shower first? Does cleaning the kitchen include wiping off the counter?

The second segment, gripes, encourages each participant to identify a problem or voice a complaint in a nonblameful way, such as "I'm not getting to work on time and need help in the morning to leave earlier," "I'm feeling frustrated at having to do so much cleaning up after dinner," or "Robert keeps the light on, and I can't get to sleep." Then all members are asked to brainstorm solutions and select one to be tried during the coming week. Just identifying a problem frequently mobilizes everyone to act differently. Only one or two problems should be worked on in a meeting.

The third section, appreciations, provides a time to acknowledge specific helpful acts and accomplishments. Members might say such things as, "I would like to congratulate Jeremiah for learning the four table," "Thank you for fixing my window," or "I want to thank Gloria for helping me in the kitchen last night."

The fourth section is devoted to planning and scheduling. Families are so busy they need time to coordinate activities, events, appointments, lessons, transportation, child care, and so on. This section involves writing on a calendar the coming week's events so all are aware of everyone's activities. Future activities can also be mentioned and planned, such as trips, graduations, performances, holidays, and vacations.

The final section involves agreeing on an ending activity, such as singing, cooking, going for ice cream, playing a game, making popcorn, telling stories and jokes, watching a favorite TV show, exercising, dancing, showing off, eating, or doing whatever fits the family's desires.

The meeting should not take more than 1 hour but should be much shorter with younger children. Meetings are best when everyone is encouraged to contribute and no one dominates the discussion. It is necessary to choose a regular weekly time, such as before dinner on Sunday or before a favorite TV show. Everyone in the household might be invited. If people refuse to attend, they may join later, once they see the benefits of attendance. The secretary's notes can be kept as a journal to document the family's history and growth.

I might recommend and discuss books, TV shows, popular music, or movies and offer videos and handouts to teach lessons. Bibliotherapy, Internet-based treatment, and self-help groups can be nearly as effective as therapist-led treatment (Norcross, 2006). It is difficult to discuss the effectiveness of self-help books in general, because there are so many (more than 3,500 new titles in 2003 alone), with different levels of quality. The research has indicated (at least with well-educated, older, depressed, or anxious Caucasian women) that self-help books are more effective than no treatment, but they produce lower levels of improvement than therapist-directed interventions (Menchola, Arkowitz, & Burke, 2007).

I present and discuss parables, *cuentos* (Costantino, Malgady, & Rogler, 1986), and metaphors to teach in a way that sidesteps defenses, such as the story of the knights described later in the conclusion of this book. I am fond of another metaphor with the same theme for helping some resistant clients change. It is the story about letting go of the log:

> There was a swimmer who was about to drown when a log came floating by. By clinging to the log he was able to be safe. But the river pushed the log downstream so that he could not get to shore. Often the thing that helps you get through one situation becomes the obstacle to dealing with the next situation. The more you cling to the log the more you are prevented from getting to shore. When you are ready, you have to let go of the log to get to safety.

A useful metaphor for reducing the stigma of ADHD comes from Thom Hartmann (1997), who presented ADHD as "a collection of skills and predilections necessary for the success and survival of a good hunter" (p. 27) who now has to learn to function in what has become a farmer society that values the skills of a cultivator who is "slow, careful, methodical, and, sometimes, boring" (p. 30). He believed that a problem for these individuals is that schools and jobs require a farmer mentality. His solution: Society needs to adapt schools to hunters, and hunters need to find hunter jobs, such as police officers, trial lawyers, executives, and entrepreneurs. He described Edison, Franklin, and Hemingway as successful examples of how ADHD can be associated with creativity, high achievement, and unique gifts.

Despite the general prohibition against giving advice, therapists frequently give advice directly or in the form of education. For instance, I might recommend that clients face fears or express feelings assertively instead of ignoring them, or I might suggest avoiding being alone when they confront an abuser or feel suicidal. I recently told a client that I did not think it was a good idea to keep bringing her young children to visit their dying grandmother in intensive care. I told parents of young children to turn off their televisions during 9/11. *Teaching* a client to use time-out instead of physical punishment is not that different from *advising* them to use this technique. I generally am reluctant to give advice. Usually by the time the client has explained his or her situation fully enough for me to offer an opinion about what he or she should do, the client is able to come up with a different approach. I try to ask the best questions to help clients find the knowledge within themselves rather than to tell them "the" solutions. When problem solving, I often rely on White's narrative therapy technique of asking clients to generate an example from their past when they successfully dealt with the problem we are talking about, and then I help them adapt their solutions to the present problem. When they come up with past successes, they are often motivated to overcome what now seems to be a not-so-insurmountable problem.

I make direct and hypnotic suggestions. Hypnotic suggestions were beautifully developed by Milton Erickson (Haley, 1973), who, for example, said to an anxious new client, "I bet before this meeting, you were anxious." He was implanting the idea that the client's anxiety was in the past and she was already much less anxious. Once I told a presently calm but volatile client whom I intended to confront, "I want to say something, but I'm concerned you'll get angry and walk out; so we won't be able to finish talking about it until next time." By this statement I wanted this previously violent client to control his aggression by observing his reaction instead of just reacting, and I wanted to implant the idea that if he got angry he could walk out instead of hit the therapist, which he had done with a previous therapist. I also wanted to imply that if he left, we would still continue counseling next time. I try to be aware of what my statements suggest.

I am particularly sensitive to how influential comments can be that are made in subordinate clauses, in jokes, and in asides, because they might slip in under the defenses. I frequently say the most significant thought in a subordinate clause, such as "It's hard going to a new school, even for someone as approachable as you are." Comments directed to a third person about a client can powerfully affect the client. I might, for instance, try to build the client's self-concept by mentioning his or her strengths or a newly developed skill to a family member so the description can be overheard.

A related technique is negative labeling, which gives a pejorative name to something so it is seen by the client as unfavorable. For example, I used negative labeling in combination with boundary setting and the "freeze-frame" technique (Wexler, 1991) to help an adolescent control his anger. I negatively labeled a threat he made as a "temper tantrum," hoping he would want to be seen as more mature. I explained that I was worried we could not continue therapy if he could not control his behavior, because both of us had to be able to feel safe for us to get along. He could think, feel, and say almost anything in session, but there were limits on behavior. He could not threaten or act in a threatening manner. He said he would not do that again and reluctantly agreed to explore the causes of his rage. His threat had been motivated by my refusing to do what he wanted, which he experienced as a rejection. He discovered these underlying feelings when we replayed what preceded his anger by pretending what happened was on videotape. Then we viewed it in slow motion and could start and stop the tape to figure out what we were feeling.

Clients Help Teach Us How to Do Therapy   Providing psychotherapy has helped teach me what I need to research and what to expect. Clients have shown me mistakes that I need to avoid repeating and instincts I can trust.

Clients constantly show the roads to pain, and at the same time they help me see how these paths could have been avoided. From hearing their stories I am more able to anticipate problems and identify issues to discuss and have a wider repertoire of possible solutions to suggest. They have exposed me to so much.

One of the lessons I have learned is to say less, more often. I used to be so excited when I understood a connection between behaviors, feelings and behaviors, or the past and present that I would rush to make the interpretation and feel competent and impressive. Now I am more cautious and do not reveal about 70% of what I am thinking. First I wonder if what I have to say is appropriate to the client's goals, the strength of our therapeutic alliance, and his or her level of motivation and developmental stage. I also think of Piaget's research on assimilation and accommodation and remember that clients can take in information that is only just a little different from what they know. This thinking leads to taking smaller steps and adjusting treatment to the client's state. For instance when the client is not able to process my verbal input because of intense emotion or dissociation, I might adopt a "watch, wait, and wonder" stance and try to communicate nonverbally.

Explore, Rather Than Challenge, Resistances   I have learned not to keep pushing clients when they are resistant to try new behaviors that I think they are ready to perform. The therapist rarely wins when the process becomes a power struggle. For instance, rather than pressure a shy client to talk to a new person or try to persuade a client to trust me and reveal more in a session, I might explore the client's reasons for being reluctant. Often, as clients explain, they desensitize themselves to their fears and display irrational thinking patterns that can be identified and corrected. Some clients can be motivated to try new behaviors by reviewing past successes when they risked healthier behaviors and were proud of the effort and by anticipating positive consequences that change might engender.

Sometimes a client presents a resistance or decision with such conviction that the client seems 100% sure of his or her intentions. However, these choices might be ambivalent expressions that can be framed in terms of an intrapsychic debate in which part of the client believes in avoiding the challenge and part believes in trying the new behavior. Sometimes I try to facilitate reasonable risk taking by identifying these alternative or "possible selves" (Oyserman, Bybee, & Terry, 2006) and helping the client argue against the resistances. I might ask the client who insists he or she cannot do something, "Is there a part of you that feels differently?" "What would that part urge you to do?" "What could derail those efforts?" or "How could that part of you deal with those obstacles?" This approach is similar to working toward integration of different personality states in clients with a dissociative identity disorder.

Parents or Other Caretakers Can Be a Valuable Resource   Usually the treatment of youths is dependent on engaging their caretakers. The process of engaging the caretaker(s) is similar to engaging most adult clients with the addition of being able to harness their motivation to help their child. Adults who will not collaborate with a therapist for their own benefit often will be cooperative when their child's welfare is at stake. For example, it is not unusual for a battered woman to tolerate her abuse until she fears her child will be harmed. However, parents may be difficult to collaborate with because they may feel guilty and fear being blamed (Tarico, Low, Trupin, & Forsyth-Stephens, 1989) or minimize or deny the seriousness of the youth's problems. They may not value therapy or they may be unwilling or unable to make the sacrifices that the youth's treatment and the parents' involvement require. They may present with pathology, beliefs, unrealistic expectations, and parenting deficits that cause, contribute to, or maintain the youth's problems. For example, fearful youths often have fearful parents, whose anxiety further contributes to maintaining the youth's fears. These parents might model anxious responses and protect the child from being exposed to feared situations so the youth cannot desensitize to the fears. Conduct-disordered youth may have parents who often collude with the youth and blame others for the youth's misbehavior, minimize and deny the youth's contribution to problems, and parent without supplying consistent, contingent consequences or adequate supervision.

Work with parents is a major part of treatment, especially when young clients are not able to engage in the therapeutic relationship or to generalize what they learn in sessions to their environments. Conduct-disordered youths typically tell only their side of the story, so for the therapist to be adequately informed about the youth's behaviors and contribution to problems, a great deal of contact with the caretakers is needed. Treating youths with behavior problems also usually involves the confrontation of their behavior and defenses, a process that they want to avoid. So parents are needed to ensure attendance. Continuing parent participation is needed in treating conduct-disordered, impulse-ridden, ADHD, and other youths who need behavior modification. These youths generally lack internal controls and the maturation to respond to techniques based on the therapeutic relationship, empathy for others, or the observation of their own cognitions and behaviors. Therefore, almost the entire burden of supplying external controls falls on the caretakers.

Beyond the benefits of the therapeutic relationship, it can be difficult to develop specific techniques that match youths' needs and level of developmental maturity. When I figure out interventions that can be potentially helpful, I often teach them to the parents and help the parents implement them with their child. For many clients changes in the environment seem needed. School advocacy, morning and bedtime routines, help with homework, teaching social skills, supervised play dates, behavior modification charts, family council meetings, and so on clearly depend on parental involvement.

Parents often need to be a focus of treatment because they can sabotage treatment, cause premature termination, support the youth's cooperation and attendance, help repair or increase ruptures in the relationship with the therapist, reinforce or challenge the youth's behaviors and defenses, model and reinforce curative behaviors, and provide an emotionally healing relationship. In fact, parents may be able to do pretty much what the therapist can do, only with greater influence and frequency.

When Treatment Stalls, Enlist Additional Resources and Look for Secrets   Treatments for youths and adults can be enhanced by involving significant others in the treatment plan (Fernandez, Begley, & Marlatt, 2006). Turning to family, peers, professionals, and community resources can be helpful to provide support, therapeutic activities, modeling, and consequences for motivated and resistant clients. Drawing from this model, I treated Shane, age 14 years, who was so resistant he refused to meet with me. He had learning disabilities and failing grades, but because he tested on grade level, his school would not supply additional services for him. He was athletic but could not participate in sports because of his poor grades. Since his parents' divorce, he shifted between households where parents were absorbed in work and caring for other children. He spent afternoons getting into trouble with mildly delinquent peers. Weekly meetings with the adults in his life (mother, father, stepparents, and grandparents) led to pooling their resources to provide after-school supervised activities, agreeing on consistent consequences and expectations, which dramatically changed Shane's attitude and grades, and supporting each other in the face of Shane's initial resistance. The village came together to raise him. Their caring for Shane motivated their cooperation, which replaced their triangulating him in their battles with each other. When I closed the case, Shane was on the basketball team and told his father, "See, I told you I didn't need counseling."

I search for family members and professionals who can assist in treatment. For instance, increasing consequences provided by a probation officer dramatically influenced a behavior-disordered youth who had not received consistent supervision, routines, and consequences from the adults at home or at school. Months of being threatened by his parent, teacher, and therapist had no effect. Andy continued to steal from stores, hurt his sister, refuse to do schoolwork, and inconsistently take his ADHD medication. Having conjoint sessions with his probation officer changed these behaviors. After Andy was arrested a second time for shoplifting, his probation officer took him to court, and the judge gave him an ankle monitor and threatened him with out-of-home placement. Once Andy's behavior improved, Andy's parent became more consistent with providing supervision, activities, and consequences. His teacher was also able to become a mentor, and Andy's favorite part of school became helping his teacher after school.

Another example involved a 17-year-old boy who decided to stop treatment, claiming that I kept bringing up gay issues and asking him if he were gay. I was pleased that he could confront me with his frustrations, but my efforts to apologize, promise to change, and be more attuned to his feelings had no effect. Marty was from a very religious family that believed that being gay was a sin and totally unacceptable. He was obsessed with conflicts over being gay and entered each session with a report of whom he thought was gay and whom he knew was not. One session began, "I had an awful trip. This gay kid sat next to me and wouldn't stop talking to me." I asked why that was so bad, and he said, "Everyone on the bus would think I was gay, like that kid." Marty controlled every session with dramatic stories, and I was relegated to the role of appreciative audience. He treated peers in a similar manner, which led to his being teased and isolated. He told his father that I was gay and that he wanted another therapist.

I told Marty I needed to meet with his father to make plans. I explained to his father that therapy with Marty was in jeopardy and asked for his help to repair our relationship. I explained that Marty seemed to be treating me the same way he treated peers and that if he could resolve his problem with me then he might be more successful with peers. I thought that he feared being seen as gay and was controlling and seeking attention to prevent rejection. I said that I had not been bringing up gay issues; Marty had. Marty's father wanted him to be more successful with peers and agreed to support treatment after he asked me if I was gay and I assured him that I was not. We explored what the father could say to Marty, and he agreed to explain that part of being a man involved being able to work out interpersonal problems and learn to get along with peers and me. Marty returned to therapy to please his father. We reached an understanding that I would not bring up gay topics, and we would focus on dealing with teasing, making friends, and passing classes. He continued to block discussions of his feelings by controlling the session with a flood of dramatic stories. Held hostage by an issue we could not discuss, his treatment focused more on developing skills and promoting successes. Marty's father became more involved in his life by encouraging peer contact and homework routines. A more ideal treatment would have been to help the father develop a tolerance or acceptance of homosexuals and then convey this to his son, but that was not feasible.

In another situation I saved therapy by involving the parent. I called Carla's mother to help us resolve a problem that was subverting treatment. Carla, an anxious, unassertive 15-year-old who related in a seductive, passive way, wanted to leave therapy. I encouraged her to tell me her reasons for wanting to quit, but she could not. Her fear of expressing herself had resulted in academic failure and control by boyfriends. The same social anxiety that contributed to her presenting problems was threatening to end treatment. I hoped that if she could be assertive with me, the skill would more easily generalize to her daily life. I anticipated she would refuse to return to therapy and would not tell her mother why. I asked Carla's mother to help her express her gripes about therapy and then practice telling them to me. The mother did, and Carla did. Then I had the opportunity to reward her assertiveness and use her confronting me as an example of how well she could speak her mind. Similarly in another situation a spouse accompanied and spoke for a client, allowing us to repair our ruptured alliance and continue therapy.

When there is a lack of movement in therapy, I wonder if there is a secret that has not been revealed. I worked with a family for more than a year in which the adolescent continued to act out despite regular attendance and seeming cooperation from his mother. It was only by bringing the grandmother into family meetings that the mother's drinking was disclosed. It appeared that the mother worked hard every day and came home to isolate herself in her room and drink herself to sleep every night. Once this secret was revealed, the family made changes. I have seen secrets and lies about homework, sneaky efforts to see boy- or girlfriends, molest, domestic violence, substance use, and paternity subvert treatment until they were disclosed and could become a focus of therapy. Furthermore, when therapy is stalled, I might explore the possible contribution of biological, nutritional, and toxic causes of mental problems. One of the greatest sins a therapist can commit is to overlook biological causes and treat a medical problem as an emotional problem.

Chores Can Be a Useful Focus for Family Sessions   Parents are often motivated to talk about chores. Chores can be a microcosm for identifying and treating family and intrapsychic problems. Most families struggle with chore completion problems that eventually often reveal underlying dynamics that contribute to the identified patient's presenting complaints. Several themes account for problems with chores, and each leads to a treatment focus. Parents may not provide contingent rewards or punishments sometimes because they feel guilty. They may blame themselves for having been an inadequate parent in the past and/or feel sorry for the child. Some may repeatedly nag the youth and then do the chore themselves, as if they were saying, "Either you put your dirty clothes in the hamper or I will." The youth naturally elects the latter. Sometimes parents fear that if they give consequences, the youth will get angry at, ignore, reject, harm, or abandon them. This pattern is particularly seen in parents who have been victims of abuse and domestic violence. Some parents are too scattered and disorganized to develop regular chore routines. Some have unrealistic expectations that ignore the youth's limitations and/or developmental level (e.g., a child with ADHD might need repeated visual and verbal reminders).

Some parents elevate chores to a central issue because they are unable to relate to their children in a developmentally appropriate, emotionally rewarding way or because they value compliance over camaraderie. They may mistakenly believe that youths do not learn to do chores, they will never learn responsibility as adults. Sometimes parents view chore compliance as a code for the health of the parent–child relationship and mistakenly think that obedience equals love or respect, and if the youths resist the chore, then they do not love or respect the parents. Sometimes chores do not get done because the youth is being triangulated in the parent's conflicts. The youth may receive conflicting messages from the parents who undercut each other's authority. Sometimes the chores are seen as the mother's responsibility, and the father does not contribute. This modeling, and the friction this imbalance can cause, can influence the child to resist chores or to assume too many responsibilities.

Sometimes a child seems to be carrying the major burden of household work. Some parents do not ask enough of their children, keeping them dependent. Some parents resent the lack of appreciation they receive and feel like a martyr. Sometimes parents act similar to, or the opposite of, the way their parents treated them. They may resent the way their parents made them do chores and refuse to be like their parents. Some parents require many chores to foster independence, because they have tired of the youth being dependent on them.

Usually solutions involve changing the parent, the children, and the family system. Sometimes just getting the parents to present a unified front elicits cooperation from the children. It may take time to help the parents agree on reasonable expectations (that place chores into perspective and promote developmentally appropriate autonomy) and establish routines and consequences. Just teaching behavior modification can fail to address underlying problems; however, sometimes underlying issues are ameliorated by instituting this powerful parenting technique. For instance one mother stopped nagging once she discovered that a reward system would motivate her children to do chores. She became happier with her children, and their relationship improved dramatically.

There are many creative ways that families can attack recurrent chore problems:

- Racing a timer can motivate everyone to rush to complete the chores before the timer goes off.
- Assigning each chore a number, then having family members role the dice to see which chore they "won."
- Interest in chores can be stimulated by having parents pay for chores with play money that can be used to buy control of the TV or purchase phone or computer time, a later bedtime, or treats and privileges.
- It can be fun to have a "10-second tidy," where everyone runs around cleaning and straightening up before the next activity can start.
- A job wheel can rotate chores.
- A job jar can make a game out of an unpleasant obligation. It might be fun to custom design behavioral or chore charts, awards and certificates at http://www.dltk-cards.com/chart/.

Usually, no one likes to do chores. Adding loud peppy music and setting a time limit can be motivating. Solutions may last only a few weeks. When family members lose interest, changing the routine may be helpful.

It is sad to see so much of a family's interactions center on power struggles over chores. When I ask a form of the miracle question ("What would you do if you had a maid do all the chores?"), family members often have few alternatives to offer and need help to develop more family communication and mutual interests. I often ask the parents what family activities they enjoyed when they were the ages of their children. The answers can spark energy to share these activities and relive these experiences. When parents have no memories of family fun times, then developing pleasurable family activities can be a challenge.

Battles over chores can be part of a pervasive pattern of parental overcontrol. Some parents may try to control too many of their child's behaviors, sometimes because they worry too much that their child's behaviors negatively reflect on them, so they anticipate that others will judge them for their child's behavior and appearance. Such parents may try to control many aspects of their child's life, such as the youth's hair, room, dress, closet, bed making, posture, table manners, food, music, homework, peer relationships, language, fingernails, and so on. Once I treated a mother who was upset at her daughter because she would not keep her closet hangers in the same direction so they could be more conveniently put on and taken off the pole. This parent was trying to protect herself and her adolescent from consequences and found herself micromanaging and clashing with an emancipating, resentful adolescent. Such a pattern of overcontrol often harms the parent–youth relationship and generates passive compliance or rebellion.

Thomas Gordon (2000) proposed a way of classifying problem behaviors to help over- and undercontrolling parents decide which behaviors need parental involvement. Gordon divided child and adolescent behaviors into categories according to who experiences the consequences. For example, if a child comes home and throws his books, coat, and shoes on the floor in his room, the consequences (if any) flow to the child. If he throws his stuff on the living room floor, the consequences flow to the parent, who has to step over the mess. The person who experiences the consequences may be the most motivated to solve the problem. For instance, the person whose room is a mess might be motivated to clean it to find his or her things or avoid embarrassment when peers are invited into the home. When the problems generate consequences for the youth, Gordon suggests parents should model good solutions and be a supportive consultant if the youth asks for help. Parents can improve their relationship with their youth when they prioritize their change efforts to focus on those problems where they, the parents, experience the consequences.

When parents experience the consequences, Gordon recommended that the parent confront the youth with "I messages" to stimulate change. An "I message" differs from a "you message," such as "*You* slob, you drive me nuts; clean up your mess." "I messages" have three parts: (a) your feelings other than anger that the problem creates for you, (b) a nonblaming description of the problem, and (c) the reason why it is a problem for you. An example of an "I message" might be, "I feel frustrated because I spent an hour cleaning this room, and I look around and it's messy again. It's as if I wasted my time." The "I message" allows the youth to think of a solution for the parent's problem and does not generate as much resistance and defensiveness as do "you messages."

Gordon did not recommend using behavior modification because it teaches the youth to do things because of rewards, punishments, and the power of the parent rather than because of caring about other family members' feelings. There is evidence that supports Rogers' (1957) and Gordon's belief that withholding love and using other forms of parenting that rely on behavior modification and similar forms of contingent, or conditional, parental regard may create behavioral conformity but at the possible cost of other-directedness, resentment, and disregulation of emotions (Roth, Assor, Niemiec, Ryan, & Deci, 2007). I tend to facilitate change by encouraging parents to use contingent consequences in combination with "I messages" to motivate the youth.

Teach Parents to Use Behavior Modification   Many problems can be corrected by teaching parents behavior modification. This usually involves helping the parents identify and prioritize behaviors they want from their youth, identifying rewards that the youth wants, and establishing a system to motivate the youth to produce the behaviors and earn the rewards. Using stickers, tokens, charts, and play money can help motivate the youth. Rewards need to be developmentally appropriate to the youth's interests and need for immediate gratification. This process stimulates parents to focus on a few behaviors and shift from being punitive, problem focused, and frustrated with the youth to having appropriate expectations and providing rewards, positive attention, and appreciation for the child's small accomplishments. Often the child earns rewards that increase mutually satisfying interactions with the parent, such as being read to, cooking, playing games, having a catch, going to the zoo, and so on, or that increase supervised peer interaction, such as having playdates or sleepovers and bringing a friend to an activity.

Contracting is a helpful component of behavior modification. Parents select one or two behaviors on which they particularly want to focus and develop a contract to motivate compliance. The contract describes in detail the behaviors desired, the time by which completion is expected, the agreed-on reward for completing the task, the bonus behavior for going beyond the task and the additional benefits that the youth will receive, mild penalty that can be added for failure to complete the contract, and the signatures of the youth and parent indicating their agreement. A contract might read as follows: "If Billy brings home the needed materials and his homework log and completes the assignments before 8:00 p.m., he earns 1 hour of computer time. If he can do this without reminders, he earns another half hour of computer time. If he does not complete the assignment by 8:00 p.m., then he has to accompany mom to the grocery store and carry all the bags to and from the car." Negotiating and clarifying the terms of the contract and writing it on a fancy form can be an enjoyable task that leaves the youths motivated to comply and earn what they want. I look for consequences that have the potential to promote the parent–youth relationship.

Provide Sex Education   Parents of younger clients often ask when they should teach their child about sex and wonder how to start. I refer them to the many books that are available. The books by Peter Mayle (1973, 1975) are my favorites. As parents search to find books they like, they learn ways to explain issues to their children.

I frequently treat teens who have been molested, are sexually active and at risk for problems, or come to treatment with presenting complaints (sometimes suicidal) related to the breakup of a relationship. These clients usually require sex education that is developmentally and culturally appropriate. Whenever possible I work with their parents (who also may have been molested) to help them provide the information to their youths, or I conjointly present the information to parents and youths so they can discuss the issues and support each other. In conjoint sessions I may start by encouraging the parents to tell about the sex education they received and the education they wished they had received. I ask about the parents' hopes for their teen in regard to his or her sexuality and the teen's reaction to these values. But family values can clash with teen desires and disrupt the process. When teens do not want their parents involved in discussions about their sexuality, I meet separately with the teen and the parent(s).

I most frequently treat highly sexualized teen girls whose behavior has been molded by earlier sexualization and compounded by failures to establish competencies in other areas. Some teens are verbal and talk about sexuality without anxiety, whereas others need support to talk about sexual issues. To be less threatening, I start with values-clarification materials, discuss teens in general, elicit comments, and, if possible, move to the personal. Rather than emphasizing an accounting of dangers and dire consequences, I present material in the context of helping them have good experiences and acquire the skills needed to enjoy themselves and be safe. A main goal is to foster enough trust so youths can ask questions that have remained hidden because of shame and embarrassment. I assume questions will remain unasked, so I introduce resources they can access anonymously in private. A favorite Web site is http://www.sexetc.org, which is a teen-to-teen platform overseen by Rutgers University. Immediate personal answers to which is manned by Boys Town with paid, experienced, crisis counselors. Questions can be found 24/7 at the National Teen Emergency Hotline, (800) 448-3000.

Sex education topics usually include the following: the family and personal values about sexuality, abstinence, and abortion; birth control methods (including the morning-after pill, Plan B, which is presently available over the counter, which most adolescents do not know about); the double standard (e.g., boys who carry a condom are cool, whereas girls who take the pill or carry a condom are promiscuous and easy); peer pressure; how to tell when one is ready for sexual activity; and the many things that a couple can do besides intercourse, including "outercourse." We also may discuss typical bodily changes, the fertility cycle, and periods. Therapists cannot assume that sexually active girls, even those who have been pregnant, know the basic facts about sexual development, periods, pregnancy, the sexual response cycle, and orgasms. We cover self-protection skills, such as protection from diseases, pregnancy, and violence and intimidation. Using videos from Planned Parenthood is invaluable, as they impart a great deal of information and model teens discussing sex in a straightforward way. I tell teens that part of enjoying sex involves first being able to eliminate worries, because "it is difficult to have a good time if you are afraid that the other person will hurt you, leave you, tell everyone, get you pregnant, or give you a disease." Such statements often lead to a discussion of self-protection skills and birth control, including discussing the various options and where and how to get them and role-playing how to deal with medical personnel. I have samples and pamphlets about various birth control methods in my office. Many teens say they rely on the withdrawal method, and they do not know that withdrawal usually provides inadequate protection from pregnancy, because "boys are like basketball players, they dribble before they shoot." I encourage them to be assertive in demanding condom use ("no glove, no love"). I suggest that if a boy does not initiate condom use, he may be saying that he does not care about the girl's safety or pleasure, and we practice "condom comebacks," which are clever responses to guys who do not want to use protection.

I encourage teen girls to have female best friends before they have boyfriends so they can learn about emotional intimacy and loyalty without the sexual pressure in the boy–girl relationship. Forming these relationships with girl peers is often a focus of therapy, because so many sexually active teen girls distrust other girls. Girlfriends can be a safety net, providing useful information about a boy's previous relationships and intentions and important emotional support when breakups occur. Girlfriends have the potential to prevent the social isolation and secrecy that accompanies abuse that may occur in one third of teen dating relationships. The abuse can include efforts to get the girl pregnant to better control her. I try to sensitize girls to the signs of abuse and help them develop a strategy to extricate themselves from such situations. Parents and girlfriends can play important roles in recovering from abusive relationships. Adolescents are bombarded by misogynistic music and a pop culture that pressures teens to have sex and idealize a body image that requires silicone, steroids, and starvation to achieve. Exploring the impact of this culture on the client's self-image can be a self-esteem-building component of sex education. I encourage them to discuss these issues with their girlfriends.

We may discuss the difficulty of assessing the true intentions of a potential boyfriend, because boys know how to say what they think the girl wants to hear, and the girl may minimize, deny, or want to fix deficits that would generate flight in higher self-esteemed girls. As one 17-year-old angrily responded to my probe about why her new boyfriend went to jail,

"I don't like people to ask about my past, so I don't ask about his." Facing emancipation, she was so desperate to have a boyfriend that she preferred not to know. I took the fallback position that I had an uncomfortable feeling about him because he repeatedly said, "gonna," as in "gonna go to college, gonna get a job, gonna stop smoking." This also made her angry, so I dropped the subject. Two sessions later she started to complain that he was a lot of hot air and not going anywhere in his life.

To enjoy sex requires communication and a close enough relationship so a girl can say such things as "No," "Not that," "Not now," "Slow down," or "You're hurting me," without fearing the boy will be angry. I present masturbation as a way to learn how the sexual response works so girls can educate their partner. "You need to know how you can be pleased before your can show others how to please you." But many girls deny that they masturbate and insist it is gross. Masturbating can help them understand their sexual response cycle and the need to have time to get excited and become lubricated so sex will feel pleasurable. Rather than communicate directly, teens may try to tell their partner what they want by doing it to the partner. If they want to be kissed a certain way, they kiss that way and hope the partner will respond in kind. I take the stance that they need to communicate more clearly, because if they don't their partner will understand and change "when money grows on trees and people live in peace" (Shania Twain). I might say that boys and girls are different. Boys get excited quickly, and girls get excited more slowly. Therefore, girls may need to tell boys how to please them, or they may find that they are just starting to get excited and the boy is having a cigarette. The concept that sex can and should be pleasurable for the girl (rather than something needed to get or keep a partner) is often a new idea that generates much discussion.

I try to eliminate unrealistic worries and correct misconceptions (everyone is having sex, a girl can't get pregnant the first time), promote informed and higher self-esteemed choices, delay intercourse until the teen is ready, develop the skills to practice safe sex to protect against unwanted pregnancies and diseases, discuss homosexual and other gender concerns, reduce embarrassment and other barriers to buying and using condoms and seeking medical consultations for STDs, increase understanding of and empathy for the opposite sex, develop an awareness of the contribution of peer pressure and pop culture to the teen's identity and sexuality, and discuss dating abuse. Because their culture does not provide male role models who value caring and healthy relationships, males often need sex education that explores what it means to be a man, father, and husband.

The male clients that I have had the most experience with have fallen on the extremes of the continuum from internalizing to externalizing.

Internalizers are empathetic, fearful of rejection, and need help to approach girls, whereas externalizers may fearlessly and aggressively pursue girls for sex in a predatory manner. One such adolescent explained, "The ones that have been molested and the fat and ugly ones are the easiest to play." I ask externalizing teens what they think about the students at Antioch College who passed a student government resolution that men must obtain verbal permission before engaging in each sexual act, even if they had done the same act previously. For instance men had to ask if it was all right to kiss even though they had kissed and even had sex on another occasion. This often leads to a valuable discussion about girls having the right to say no and boys' feelings about stopping. I try to expose them to the concept that if a girl says "no," that means "stop," and, in fact, if she says "yes, yes, yes, no," that means "stop." Externalizers may respond better to consequences, such as warnings about having to pay for the care of children for the next 18 years if they do not use condoms and going to jail if they are charged with abuse or statutory rape.

Internalizers may need education and reassurance about penis size, being a late maturer, the medical treatment for and the time-limited nature of the curse of acne, and their being normal. I have not seen teen boys who worried excessively about wet dreams or masturbation. They seem to have gotten the message that it is normal, but some fundamentalist parents are still concerned about masturbation. Breakups, the loss and repair of friendships, reputation, and self-esteem are often issues for these teens. Their identity and masculinity can feel destroyed when a relationship is terminated. Role-plays can be included that teach social skills (maintaining eye contact and reading others' reactions, approaching and making conversation, sharing interests and searching for common interests, displaying appropriate body language, etc.). Another pertinent issue involves identifying the types of relationships that teens can have (platonic friends, friends with benefits, boyfriend or girlfriend, one-night stands). This can lead to the acceptance of different relationships and the realization that one person does not have to meet all the client's needs.

Many teens are exposed to sexuality on the Web. Forty-two percent of teen Internet users ages 10 to 17 years reported visiting sexually explicit (pornographic) sites (Wolak, Mitchell, & Finkelhor, 2007). Sixty-six percent reported that the exposure was unwanted and took place while using file-sharing programs to download images. Thirty-eight percent of male and 8% of female Internet users sought out pornographic sites in the past year. I try to convey (as suggested by Jochen Peter, PhD) that what they see is only one type of sexual activity, which probably does not correspond to what most adults typically do in their sexual lives.

Trying to impose a rational decision-making process on fantasy-based, hormonally driven desire and arousal is a challenge. Teaching girls to be more assertive and boys to be more considerate is difficult in the context of a societally constructed sexuality based on male initiation and pursuit and dominance over female resistance and naïveté. Providing appropriate information, engaging community and family resources, and teaching teens to discuss sexual values, feelings, and relationships are components of treating many troubled teens.

Sometimes We Cannot See Any Solutions   I no longer panic and worry about being an incompetent therapist when I feel my clients' helplessness and hopelessness, and I cannot think of any solution to their problem. The more I care about a client, the more pain I feel. I have even come to welcome this discomfort because it usually means I am feeling the world from the client's point of view. I have walked a mile in their shoes. I understand why the client is stuck and cannot easily change. It is often from this viewpoint that I can really help. I expect that answers will come to me and that I eventually will be able to add my resources, objectivity, and problem-solving abilities to the situation.

In seemingly solutionless moments the client has rejected my solutions. Each rejection increases my understanding of the client's situation, and I may think that I cannot relieve the client's pain or budge his or her thinking. Sometimes after we acknowledge being stuck, we both continue to focus on the situation in a more informed way after the session. Over time one of us usually comes up with a useful idea. In addition, situations and priorities change. Of course if we remain stuck, I can seek consultation.

Sometimes I become stuck because I have uncritically adopted the client's assumptions. As I continue to think about the situation with more objectivity and from different perspectives, I add my ego skills and resources, and new opportunities surface. For example, Marco hated school and just wanted to work but could not get a work permit because he had poor grades and attendance. I understood why he hated school and agreed with him after meeting with his teachers. I can usually facilitate changes at schools, but I could not in this situation. We were stuck. I went home angry at school regulations and feeling that I had nothing to offer him but support, which felt inadequate. Then another client with equally severe learning disabilities told me about the new NASA and space-themed high school that he was going to attend. After talking to the admissions director, I was able to help Marco enter that program. At the same time, despite my pessimism, he went to his local pizza parlor and asked for a job. The owner told him he was too young, but Marco kept hanging around and cleaned tables, bussed dishes, and took out the garbage. After a few days the owner started to give him money. It was not long before he had a job and was surviving school.

Another time I felt hopeless about being able to help Denna. She was suicidal and had severe OCD and Tourette's syndrome, which medication, psychosurgery, and 6 months in an inpatient cognitive-behavioral treatment program could not diminish. I secretly agreed with her that suicide was an understandable course. In desperation I searched the Web for treatment ideas and found inspirational stories of athletes who had similar deficits, and I shared the printouts with her. She was not athletic, but our discussion led her to recall that once she wanted to be a singer. She could control her twitches when she sang at home, but she insisted she was too shy to ever sing in public. With the help of her parents and a sensitive music teacher at school, she started to feel successful in a singing group that performed at local nursing homes. She even got close to a boy in the group. These painful moments of being overwhelmed by a client's situation can generate opportunities.

I select from this menu of strategies and techniques to maximize the sources of change to impact outcome. I do not feel fully responsible for what the client does. I am responsible for what I do. I have the most control over my input. What clients ultimately do is multiply determined. My input is one contribution, but I rarely have the power to control their reaction.

CHAPTER 4

Using the Therapeutic Relationship
as a Treatment Tool

Whether curative or facilitative, the therapeutic relationship appears to be central in creating change. Maximizing therapist characteristics that promote engagement, the alliance, and progress requires therapists to understand their feelings during therapy and constantly monitor the usefulness of their self-disclosures.

The Therapeutic Relationship Is Not an Authentic Relationship

We are not our client's friends, business associates, lovers, or parents. What we do and say fits through the screen of helping the client. Our actions are goal directed. In therapy the intimacy is predominantly one-way.

Arnold Lazarus described himself in therapy as an Authentic Chameleon, meaning he plays a role defined by his intention to facilitate treatment. Of course this is not an ideal way to be in our personal lives. For me, being a chameleon usually does not involve acting in a fully inauthentic way. It is often a process of sorting through the many reactions I have to the client's presentation and choosing the response that seems the most therapeutic. To choose a response that the client needs can require that I do not react with an instinctive response. To thoughtfully respond to a client, sometimes I have to remind myself that the client's feelings about me are not just about me but a reflection of the client's projections and the role I adopt in the service of helping them.

It is a conceit for us to think that we are a paragon of mental health and that we can just be ourselves and reveal ourselves to heal our clients. Some clients need us to be idealized, some need to see our frailties, some need us to be assertive and set limits, and some need us to be apologetic or nurturing. Some need us to focus on the forest; some need us to focus on an individual tree. Some need us to be angry at the way they have been treated; some need us to be forgiving, calm, or sympathetic. What is helpful at one stage of treatment might be contraindicated at another time. Being authentic requires us to relate in the present, in the moment, without observing ourselves. However, being a therapist often demands that we critically observe our client, our interactions, and ourselves so we can control our biases and needs and remain focused on treatment goals.

The therapeutic relationship also differs from a real relationship in that it is paid for, follows professional ethical principles, usually takes place only at a scheduled time in an office, and is confidential and separate from daily life. For the most part clients need not worry that we will tell others their business or that they even sought contact with us. This separateness from daily life has advantages and disadvantages. Separateness and confidentiality provide additional safety to facilitate client disclosure. At the same time separateness can become a frustration to clients when they must accept the limit that the relationship cannot evolve outside of its therapy-focused boundaries. The therapeutic relationship is not an equal relationship. The clients have the problem. They are coming to us for help. Therefore we are, in part, responsible for them and what happens in the session. It is a relationship that the clients do not just experience. They have the possibility of stepping out of their role as a participant to observe, discuss, and learn from the relationship, such as when the therapist asks the client to explore his or her thoughts and feelings about what just happened between them in the session.

Sometimes aspects of an authentic relationship surface in treatment. Clients may have feelings about us that are not generated by our role as therapist, and we often care deeply and have emotional reactions to clients apart from their role as clients. However, these authentic feelings are intertwined with the part of the relationship that is focused on treatment goals, the part that is based on unconscious transference and countertransference tests and projections, and the part that is created by the therapist to repair injuries and compensate for missed experiences. For some clients I am influenced by their not having a father and that I may be a significant father or grandfather image for them. Because a major source of self-esteem, self-image, and impulse control comes from receiving approval from and incorporating an idealized other, I am sensitive to providing the approval and successes that a concerned father would have provided. Each case requires a different balance between catering to the relationship and focusing on remediating problems. The conscious and unconscious authentic relationship can be important, inconsequential, helpful, or detrimental. For some clients the authentic relationship can be an important part of therapy. On the other hand, some clients improve from acquiring and practicing techniques learned from computer-based programs or self-help books in which they are not exposed to a real personal relationship (Scogin, 2003). I try to develop the quality and intensity of the therapeutic relationship according to the client's needs and treatment goals.

Therapist Self-Disclosure Should Be Limited

Freud (1912) exemplified the confusion in the field over therapist self-disclosure. He wrote that the therapist should mirror and thus "be impenetrable to the patient" (p. 18). However, in practice he was often freewheeling in his use of self-disclosure. Widely followed guidelines for self-disclosing have not been established, possibly because the usefulness of therapist self-disclosure is so dependent on each client's particular background and situation. For example, Eda Goldstein (1994) wrote of her psychotherapy that when her therapist reluctantly disclosed that they had the same birthday, "I began to feel more positively toward Dr. C. I shared more of my inner life with her and my depression began to lift. Instead of continuing to see her as part of the mother's movement for middle-class morality, I experienced her as someone like me. Long after the termination of this treatment 25 years ago, this event still stands out in my mind more than anything else about the therapy. There have been many occasions in which the memory of our common bond soothed me and made me feel less alone" (p. 418). Later in life she became a therapist and met with a patient to whom she revealed that they had the same birthday. This disclosure was met with the client's anger and accusation that the therapist was "trying to take away her specialness," in the same way that her intrusive parents had hurt her.

Some clients do not want to know about us. Some clients want to know about us and are grateful for every tidbit of information they can find. They ask if we are married or divorced, if we have children, how much we are paid, if we would have an abortion, what car we drive, if we are a Christian, Democrat, homosexual, rocker, victim of abuse, pot smoker, duck hunter, and so on. Some particularly want to know what we think and feel about them, and they guess from the personal effects in our office, our dress and nonverbal communication, how quickly we return their calls, how long the sessions are, how much we self-disclose, and the friendliness of our greetings and farewells. I respond with caution to client inquiries. In seeking personal information, clients could be gathering data that confirm their inaccurate assumptions, such as that I could not understand them or be familiar with their issues, because I have certain values or have not personally experienced their problems. They also could be trying to create a distraction from the treatment process by avoiding the anxiety of talking about themselves by putting the focus on the therapist. They could be testing the boundaries of the professional relationship by trying to make it more equal and personal.

The question of why the client wants to know is usually more important than whether I self-disclose. For instance, if a mother asks if I have children, then she is probably asking if I have had the personal experiences to understand and help her. So if the answer is "no," then it needs to be followed with reassurance that I have other knowledge and skills that compensate for my lack of personal experience. In addition, we may need to be clarify that she may have to educate me about particular parenting issues with which I am not familiar. The parent's concern is reasonable and deserves a truthful response, especially to the extent that she is asking about my experience and expertise, in the same way that a medical patient might ask a surgeon how many similar operations he or she has performed and what the success rate has been. On another level such a question might be asking about my capacity or availability to parent her or her child. The childless woman who asks if I have children may have a different agenda that I may need to understand before answering. Immediately answering could distort this exploration. Because I do have children, I usually gain credibility, but this disclosure has led parents to want to compare their children with mine—not helpful.

There can be costs to withholding personal information. If the therapist deals with the client's personal questioning by delving into the client's motivation for asking, then not answering can be time-consuming and distracting. If we do not answer, clients could see us as aloof and distant, and they could assume their negative suspicions about us are confirmed, because we are hiding the truth. There are costs to sharing. When I answer I am careful that I am not meeting my needs instead of the client's or creating a focus on myself instead of on the client. Self-disclosure can be motivated so easily by nontherapeutic factors rather than by the client's needs. In fact distracted, inexperienced therapists may do the most self-disclosing (Williams, Polster, Grizzard, Rockenbaugh, & Judge, 2003).

The client's assumptions that a similar background or orientation ensures more understanding, familiarity, and acceptance may not be true, and similarities may inhibit the client from exploring problems and alternatives from different perspectives. So when I am asked for personal information,

I might respond by exploring what they are assuming about me and how that makes them feel. However, sometimes my willingness to disclose is more appreciated and important than the content of the disclosure and may initiate a productive discussion. A danger is that differences can become a central focus to the exclusion of work on more important issues. The client's ethnic background can influence his or her expectations for, and reactions to, therapist self-disclosures, because some groups expect more personal contact whereas others might be uncomfortable with the professional's self-disclosures.

Dissimilarities in sexual orientation and religion are particularly incendiary, and some clients cannot or do not want to work with a therapist who differs along these lines. Clients from any minority orientation might associate therapist differences with being uninformed and anticipate discrimination and/or nonacceptance. Because these similarities are so important to some clients, they often seek referrals to therapists with similar backgrounds who they expect will affirm their orientation and condone their beliefs. Insistent clients may need to know the therapist's orientation and values, even if that disclosure results in terminating the relationship. The benefit of the immediate engagement, based on the client's projections onto the similar therapist, might outweigh the potential problems by enhancing the therapist's credibility and facilitating the therapist being seen as a role model. Furthermore, similar therapists might have a more nuanced, informed understanding of the client's struggles and community.

However, selecting a like-minded therapist can have costs. Such therapists may have experienced similar problems and offer the client the solutions that the therapist found helpful, even though the situations are different. The instant comfort and immediate engagement based on similarity of religious, sexual, ethnic, and political orientation; use of substances; past traumas; or history of problems may result in the therapist's colluding with the client to avoid important issues and diverse perspectives. The client can miss the opportunity to get along with and feel accepted by dissimilar others, a process that might be central to the client's healing. Furthermore, there are good and lousy therapists of all persuasions, and no orientation is an assurance of greater wisdom, competence, or even expected agreement. Politics is a hot topic, and even when we are in agreement, I typically avoid disclosing my preferences, which can divert or disrupt the focus on the client's goals.

To recap, before answering a client's probe, I wonder if the therapeutic alliance is strong enough to handle the answer or the cost of not answering. Sometimes the relationship is damaged either way. Most of all I try to avoid giving answers that could hurt engagement and the relationship. Before disclosing I consider exploring the client's motivation behind asking. By the end of our exploration, my answer to the personal question is usually not particularly important to the client.

Possibly because self-disclosure is so rarely used by the therapist, it is so influential (Knox & Hill, 2003). For example, a third of clients in one study reported that it was critical in their forming a therapeutic alliance that the therapist shared that he or she had a problem similar to the client's (Bedi, Davis, & Williams, 2005). My answer to clients' personal questions may affect the degree to which clients see me as human, caring, involved, and having had similar life experiences. Self-disclosure can influence the validity clients ascribe to my opinions and how unusual or pathological they feel about themselves. Sometimes I initiate self-disclosures in the service of normalizing the client's situation, teaching a lesson, modeling disclosure, matching the client's level of disclosure to facilitate the discussion, or highlighting our similarities or differences. However, if disclosure is too intimate, it can make the client uncomfortable. Because self-disclosure can be viewed as a therapeutic technique, I self-disclose selectively and with caution. When I self-disclose, it is with the purpose of furthering the client's goals, not my needs.

I know that the benefits of self-disclosure can often be accomplished by means other than talking about myself. I could say, "I've worked with a lot of people who also lost someone and … ," "Usually when people have sex for the first time … ," "How do others feel when you tell them things like that?" or "My brother had insomnia, and he. …" But sometimes it has a greater impact if the response or illustration comes from my life. Sometimes I self-disclose to correct a conclusion about myself that interferes with therapy goals. Sometimes I self-disclose my thoughts and strategies for clients to incorporate. I might describe how I control my anger or how I deal with my social anxiety.

I do not want to be thought of as hiding behind my role. I want to be perceived as genuine (responding with my true feelings), honest, caring, nonjudgmental, fully present, and hopeful based on my knowledge and experience. My self-disclosures that contradict this presentation are shared only when knowing them will be helpful to the client. For instance, a client might benefit from knowing I have flaws or limits to my caring and hopefulness when I anticipate that the disclosure might lead the client to adopt more realistic expectations for himself or herself, for others, or for what can be accomplished in treatment.

A potentially useful form of self-disclosure involves the therapist's disclosing his or her immediate feelings and reactions to what is transpiring in session. Each client is different in his or her wanting to know and being able to use this information in a helpful way. This type of self-disclosure can lead to moments of authenticity in therapy that can be a powerful change agent. These moments often occur when the therapist self-discloses his or her feelings that were just generated by something the client did or said in the session, and the client's similar behavior generates similar feelings in others in his or her life. For example, I told an adolescent who was rejected by his family because he frightened them that I was also afraid when the client's rage surfaced in session. Then we were able to talk about how his anger made his parents and me feel.

I similarly described how worried I felt when a client did not show up for an appointment. This disclosure generated a powerful experience for a parent who struggled with feeling chronically uncared about and invisible. He was surprised that I had any feelings, saying that he didn't think he was important to anyone and that he had assumed I would not notice or care if he did not keep his appointment. He also said that he had not wondered how his behavior had affected me and that he rarely thought about how his behavior affected others. He then wondered if others in his life worried about him in a similar way. Understanding and correcting these patterns in session and generalizing the results to the life space were productive. He could understand that his children's lack of attention to him could in part be a reaction to his not paying attention to them. He went on to consider how pressured his life was, and that in prioritizing business and making money, he had left very little time for relationships. Although these topics had come up before, this interaction had a more powerful impact. Often it is the client's caring about the relationship with the therapist that allows such confrontations to be taken in and focused on. My self-disclosure helped this client to think about how his children felt about him and eventually to change his relationships with them.

Therapist self-disclosure can generate a powerful, authentic moment that involves the client's realizing that the therapist really cares about him or her. Some believe that such moments underlie change. They are similar to Daniel Stern et al.'s (1998) "moments of meeting," where the real relationship surfaces and reprograms the client's sense of self and expectations for relationships. I told an adolescent how excited I was and how I admired his persistence when he obtained a much-improved score on his college boards. He instantly discounted my praise and responded by saying that I was paid to say such things. Instead of processing his rich response, I got upset at him. This disclosure led to many powerful discussions about how others responded to his behavior and about his ability to tolerate closeness, but only after he saw my upset as evidence that I really cared about him.

If clients cannot discuss their reactions to the therapist's self-disclosure, then disclosing is more dangerous, because it could cause ruptures that might go undetected or be difficult to repair. Carefully assessing after disclosing is necessary to gauge the usefulness of the self-disclosure and guide further disclosures. I usually track whether my self-disclosure furthers the conversation and leads the client to self-disclose (good) or disrupts the conversation or makes it more superficial (bad). Sometimes I disclose honestly, sometimes dishonestly.

This discussion of self-disclosure and authenticity has been limited to mostly verbal therapist statements, which may be the least relevant to the therapeutic process, according to Allan Schore's orientation to treatment. He proposed that the therapist constantly reveals himself or herself to the client in nonverbal reactions before and during conscious, verbal responses. These nonlinguistic, often unconscious communications carry the most powerful information to the client. He suggested that we cannot control or hide communicating who we are and how we feel. To the extent that Schore is correct, verbal self-disclosures need to be veridical to uncensored nonverbal disclosures or else clients will notice the discrepancies. Therefore therapists would need to be personally capable of a high level of intimacy and affect tolerance to be therapeutic.

We Have to Understand Our Feelings Toward Our Clients

I believe that almost all of my feelings in session are largely influenced by countertransference. These feelings are partly unconscious, ubiquitous, and inevitable and dramatically affect what I respond to and how I respond. My judgments and feelings are constructed largely from my previous personal and therapeutic relationships. There are no normal, natural feelings that therapists should have in a session. As Anaïs Nin put it, "We don't see things as they are. We see things as we are." How we react to almost anything in session (vulnerability; dependence; noncompliance; racial, religious, cultural, social status, and gender characteristics; beauty and deformities; substance abuse; the client's diagnosis) has more to do with our countertransference, our past, than with the client's situation.

Initially viewed as just detrimental, countertransference feelings and beliefs can destroy or be an asset in treatment. I try to identify them by attending to my reactions and by exploring my fantasies about the treatment and client to make conscious my feelings of, for example, dislike, affection, confusion, optimism, incompetence, or wanting to rescue or my feeling frustrated, disappointed, controlled, afraid, rejected, ignored, envious, bored, and so on. I welcome knowing that I have these feelings. Then I can try to understand how they affect the therapeutic alliance and my efforts to ameliorate symptoms. Privately examining these fantasies usually contributes to treatment.

It is not unusual or necessarily detrimental to have feelings and fantasies about a client. The client's appreciation, trust, dependence, adulation, or idealization as well as anger, disappointment, or criticism are often creations and projections that have little to do with me as a person. In fact the client does not really know me outside of my role as therapist. My needs, family life, friendships, finances, political views and religious beliefs, life disappointments, censored thoughts, and problems have remained hidden. The client's feelings about me are mostly created by the therapy structure. Most people can be expected to be attracted to a therapist who listens, appreciates, and wants to help and form a relationship that focuses on their needs with no obligation to reciprocate or be concerned with the therapist's needs. Clients generally like me, and this attracts me to them. I might wonder what being their friend, mate, or parent would be like. When I ask myself what it would be like to have such a relationship with this client (what it would be like to adopt this youth, for example), I become aware of how the client's problems would sabotage our relationship and which problems need to be dealt with before the client can have more successful relationships. For instance, I might think this adolescent would be a great son, but I could not handle his irresponsibility or temper. Or I might think if I ran off to Bakersfield with this woman, I could not handle her neediness or inability to accept responsibility for her contribution to problems. By allowing myself to think about these countertransference fantasies, I often become sensitized to issues that need to become a focus in treatment.

Many of my mistakes come from unrecognized countertransference. I have to constantly monitor how my feelings interfere with being empathetic and accurately mirroring the client's feelings and how these feelings get expressed in my comments and goals. I want to avoid reenacting past relationships, selling clients my personal solutions to their problems, and using clients to meet my needs. For instance I may unrealistically see the client as similar to me; assume he or she has the same feelings, resources, and thoughts I have; and/or want him or her to behave the way I did or wish I had. Furthermore, especially when I do not know the other person, I tend to side with my client against his or her parent, child, or spouse. I might see my client as healthier and more reasonable than his or her spouse only to later discover that these countertransference beliefs have been detrimental to treatment, and I have been insensitive to the spouse's point of view. I have neglected to remind myself that on this planet, people usually marry others with the same degree of mental health and pathology. Ducks swim with ducks; swans fly with swans. Youths and parents both contribute to their conflicts with each other. I cannot be fully helpful if I do not see each person's contribution to problems. Furthermore, I have to avoid the tendency to minimize and deny the clients' problems so I can feel good that they are improving.

Another source of information about countertransference feelings can come from observing the client–therapist interaction. The therapist's reactions to the client can be diagnostic. I have learned to associate certain countertransference feelings that I have toward the client with particular diagnoses and treatment errors. For instance, I feel angry at hysterics, which interferes with giving clients the reassurance they may need to calm down. I typically have a particular feeling when I work with clients with conduct disorders. I start to like them and feel that they have been mistreated. Then I am drawn to taking their side and wanting to show them that all people are not going to be so unfair. Then, ding, ding, ding, a warning bell goes off, and I think, "Wait a minute. When I feel this way, it's usually with a client with a conduct disorder who probably needs more confrontation of behavior and defenses and less understanding and support." The bell helps me notice that because these clients project blame and responsibility for their contribution to problems, they have presented themselves as victims, which triggers my caring. I also may have been misinterpreting their narcissism and lack of neurotic censoring of their conversation as trusting me and an indication of a deeper engagement than really exists.

Because some of my reactions can be fairly universal, recognizing the feelings I have toward the client can lead to understanding that the client generates similar reactions in others that may contribute to the client's problems. For instance, if I feel smothered by their caring or find myself withdrawing from their neediness, or I become annoyed at their passivity, control, or unreliability, then I can imagine how their children, employer, or spouse might feel. I once told a parent that I found myself withdrawing from him because he presented feelings in such a heightened, dramatic way. He then was able to realize that his wife and child probably felt the same way when they so often seemed unresponsive. He said that when they withdrew, he would get even more dramatic to try to elicit a reaction from them. This insight did not immediately change his behavior, but it led to about 6 months of work that resulted in change. This type of self-disclosure and subsequent exploration can indicate one of the most treacherous and hoped-for situations in treatment: the client has brought a problem from his or her life into therapy where it is now a problem between the client and therapist. This presents the opportunity to understand and solve the problem between the client and therapist in session with the potential of generalizing the solution to the client's significant relationships.

A powerful opportunity for change happens when the client's problem reappears in the therapeutic relationship, as when parents treat the therapist similarly to the way they treat their child or the therapist treats the parent similarly to the way the parent treats the child. For example, I worked with a single mother who complained that her 8-year-old daughter, Tammy, was defiant, dawdled all evening at homework, and wanted to be treated like a baby. This upset the mother, who wanted her to be responsible and successful at school and in life.

The mother was born to alcoholic parents and was adopted at age 7 by abusive parents. After leaving home at age 15, she had several domestically violent relationships until she became engaged to Art, a caring boyfriend with whom she had a second child, who was 7 months old. Although she nurtured the infant, she described herself as too busy with cooking, cleaning, and child care to play with Tammy. Similar to many victims of domestic violence and children of alcoholic parents, she focused on others' needs, suppressed her feelings, and felt uncomfortable receiving affection.

Tammy's evenings and weekends were structured around homework and chores. The mother said, "By the time she finishes homework, there is no time to play. She talks back, argues, and dawdles, and I get so frustrated that I don't want to read her a story, and I just send her to bed." The mother was most proud of how she had been competent and able to succeed financially since she left her family of origin with no money. She wanted Tammy to be able to be independent, too. I explained to her that I thought that Tammy wanted her love, saw her love the baby and Art, and felt rejected by mother's pushing her to be competent. The mother disagreed and insisted that playing with and enjoying Tammy was not a priority and seemed impossible because Tammy had to get her work done first, but she never finished it. In fact the mother insisted that teaching her to achieve was the main goal of good parenting. The mother did not value affection and was proud of how she survived and flourished without having received love in childhood.

I pushed her to play with Tammy in conjoint sessions, only to increase her discomfort. I started to meet with the mother individually and challenged her defenses, argued with her, and pressured her to value playing and nurturing with the promise that Tammy would achieve once she felt her mother's love. Using catastrophic and all-or-nothing thinking, she parried, "Life is not all about play. She'll never learn responsibility. I can't just play with her all the time."

The more I pushed, the more resistant and distant the mother became. Then I noticed that we were replicating the child-rearing pattern that she and Tammy were enacting. I asked her how she was feeling about our work together. She said it made her feel as if I were critical of her and did not like her, so she did not want to come back. I asked if that was how Tammy might feel. As we discussed this, she became aware of how Tammy felt when she pushed and why she refused to comply. We both acknowledged that pushing was not working and that we needed to try another approach.

She had never played as a child and felt uncomfortable when she allowed Tammy to take the lead, as play required, but she started to value the approach. She requested that we continue conjoint sessions and dedicated herself to bonding with and enjoying Tammy and decided to try reading to Tammy for 10 minutes at bedtime, whether or not she finished her homework. We discussed how it would take time for Tammy to accept the 10-minute limit but that she would accept it once she realized that she would get more the next night. We also talked about making the reading time more of a cuddling than a teaching opportunity.

The therapeutic relationship is woven out of fantasy and reality, needs and expectations, the conscious and the unconscious. Whether background or foreground, it has the potential to be helpful or disruptive and must be constantly nurtured and monitored.

CHAPTER 5

How Can I Keep Clients in Treatment so They Can Benefit?

Duration of Treatment Depends on the Common Factors

Some clients are short term, and others are long term. Short-term clients tend to be rapid responders or early dropouts; long-term clients find progress more difficult to achieve.

Although most of the research is on adults and has significant limitations, there appears to be a subgroup of clients who make progress early in treatment (averaging at the fifth session), which accounts for much of their total improvement. For instance, in a study of a 16-session manualized cognitive-behavioral treatment for depression, 39% of those who completed treatment showed a pattern of early sudden gains, which accounted for half the total improvement they reported at termination (Tang & DeRubeis, 1999). In another study, depending on the criteria used to define "sudden gain," 17% to 56% of the 135 clients who completed treatment in three clinics in England were found to have made early sudden gains that accounted for *all* the improvement they reported at the end of therapy (Stiles et al., 2003).

Some clients respond even more rapidly. A meta-analysis of the effect of adult psychodynamic or interpersonal therapy found 14% of patients showed improvement before the first session, 24% of clients made measurable improvement after one session, 30% showed improvement after two sessions, and 41% showed improvement after four sessions (Howard, Kopta, Krause, & Orlinsky, 1986). These rapid responders supply the ingredients sufficient for improvement. They respond so early that client characteristics, such as readiness to change, hope generated by the idea of working on their problems, and placebo and extratherapeutic forces, rather than the effectiveness of treatment techniques supplied by the therapist probably account for much of their improvement.

The research does not tell us the shelf life or nature of these gains. When measured by client self-reports, these gains can differ from therapist's goals and opinions. For example, Kiley, age 6, was brought to treatment by her mother because of crying, failing academics, and loss of interest in friends. Her mother had been depressed since her abusive boyfriend left her, and Kiley's problems covaried with her mother's depression. While another therapist treated Kiley, I provided child guidance counseling to the mother and initially offered reassurance, support to be angry at the abusive boyfriend, and encouragement to increase activities with Kiley. Kiley and her mother improved rapidly and stopped attending sessions when the mother started seeing a new boyfriend. The mother went from feeling hopeless, overwhelmed, and unlovable to feeling attractive, desirable, and hopeful. However, she left treatment before she could learn about her contribution to her pattern of repeated involvements with abusive men. I had hoped that we could work on improving the mother–child relationship and preventing future chaotic and abusive relationships, but she was busy and felt better. I did not view this case as a success, even though the mother reassured me that this boyfriend "is different from past boyfriends. He's older and a Christian."

Early terminators compose the majority of short-term clients. The research on adult treatment indicates that "the modal length of psychotherapy, as practiced in the United States for the last 40 years, is very low. The national mean length of psychotherapy probably varies each year somewhat between five and six sessions. ... This is true for various types of therapy and for a broad array of presenting symptoms. ... These data suggest that the majority of individuals who come to psychotherapy remain in therapy for only a small number of sessions" (Phillips, 1988, p. 669).

In a study of more than 9,000 adult patients (most receiving insurance-driven brief therapies for less severe problems) in six treatment sites in England, one third of the sample received only one session of treatment (Hansen, Lambert, & Forman, 2002). The authors concluded, "Half of the patients receiving psychotherapy receive only about a quarter of the length of treatment that the literature has noted as necessary to observe a 50% response rate" (p. 337). Remembering that one third of the patients were excluded from the study because they dropped out after the initial interview, the median number of sessions for the remaining 6,072 patients was 3 sessions and the mean was 4 sessions. This dropout rate is fairly typical. Garfield (1994) found that 25% to 50% of clients "refuse psychotherapy" after an initial interview. Nationally, one third of outpatient psychotherapy consumers used only one or two visits of treatment. This estimate is lower than other studies because it came from a national survey of *all* outpatient mental health treatment, of which 65% was provided by physicians in 1997 (Olfson, Marcus, Druss, & Pincus, 2002).

There also is evidence that many youths do not remain in treatment long enough to benefit. In the Fort Bragg Evaluation Project, of the 568 youths (ages 5 to 17 years at the start of the study) who were offered just outpatient psychotherapy, early terminators (254) composed 45% of the sample and received less than eight sessions; of these, 37 had no sessions, and 70 had one session (Andrade, Lambert, & Bickman, 2000). In the Great Smokey Mountains Study, the researchers concluded that because "real improvement was not apparent until an individual received more than eight sessions ... we should concentrate resources on ensuring that the service system is able to deliver episodes of treatment of sufficient length to be efficacious" (Angold, Costello, Burns, Erkanli, & Farmer, 2000).

Long-term clients represent a different challenge than short-term clients. They may have more complex or resistant problems or less therapeutic common factors than the early responders. Yet they are more dedicated and motivated to continue treatment than the nonstarters or early dropouts. We might assume that change for long-term clients is more difficult to accomplish than for the rapid responders. As Kopta (2003) summarized, "The effect of therapy is greater in earlier sessions and increases more slowly at higher dosage levels" (p. 728). This body of research indicating diminishing returns for long-term treatment has been used as a rationale for limiting treatment duration based on cost-effectiveness.

The data support a picture of treatment in general: some clients drop out or benefit early in the process and terminate, leaving cases in which change is harder to accomplish. Thus, in the absence of artificially imposed time restrictions on treatment, we can expect that a typical caseload may be composed of (a) short-term clients who show gains in a few sessions or no longer want to continue and drop out and (b) longer term clients who wish to continue and respond more slowly to treatment. By attrition the typical caseload can carry a majority of longer term clients who change slowly and a minority of dropouts and rapid improvers.[1] Treatment in the community may not be as effective as it could be because so many clients drop out prematurely, and the slow-responding clients do not receive enough treatment.

Without relating treatment length to more specific therapist, client, problem, and treatment characteristics, stating how much treatment is needed to generate meaningful improvement is similar to saying that the average number of sessions needed for a medical treatment is x visits, thereby ignoring whether the patient has cancer or a cold. There is evidence of "differential responsiveness for different diagnostic groups and for different outcome criteria" (Howard et al., 1986, p. 159). Therefore, imbedded in the averages are different rates of improvement for different types of problems. For instance, adults receiving psychodynamic and interpersonal psychotherapy for problems reflecting acute stress required less treatment, whereas patients with problems caused by chronic stress required more sessions, and patients with characterological problems required even longer treatment (Kopta, Howard, Lowry, & Beutler, 1994). These authors found that problems caused by acute stress (anxiety, depression, and somatic problems) showed significant improvement in fewer than 10 sessions, with 5 sessions being the average number of sessions needed for 50% of patients to show clinically significant improvement. Problems related to chronic stress (chronic anxiety and depression, phobias, obsessive thoughts, and interpersonal sensitivities, such as being scared for no reason, feeling worthless, having difficulty making decisions, and being self-conscious) showed significant improvement in 7 to 27 sessions, with an average of 14 sessions needed for 50% of patients to report dramatic improvement. Characterological symptoms responded the most slowly. These symptoms of hostility and paranoid and psychotic thinking, such as never feeling close to others, believing people cannot be trusted, having urges to harm others, having sleep problems, blaming others, having frequent arguments, and feeling something was wrong with their mind, showed significant improvement in 50% of patients after 18 sessions, with many of these symptoms demonstrating less than 50% chance of recovery after 52 sessions.

"Clients likely require different amounts of treatment depending on the nature of their problems, therapeutic techniques, living environment and personal resources" (Salzer, Bickman, & Lambert, 1999, p. 236). Characteristics of the clients, therapists, treatment, and settings; the nature and severity of the problems; and the available resources combine to affect how quickly clients improve and when enough improvement has been reached so treatment can be terminated (Barkham et al., 2006, p. 161). In other words we might expect the rate of improvement and duration of treatment to depend on the common factors. These findings of early improvement for acute problems, the need for more sessions to treat more chronic problems, and the duration of treatment depending on the common factors probably apply to the therapy of youths as well.

Among the few outcome studies on youths treated in community settings, some do not provide support for the effectiveness of treatment in the community (Andrade et al., 2000; Bickman, Andrade, & Lambert, 2002; Hallfors et al., 2006). However, the research focused on evaluating treatments that provided only direct contact with the youths and therefore did not include some of the most effective components of therapy. The interventions evaluated were not the most effective approaches because they did not focus on enhancing the common factors or prioritize altering parenting or family, school, and community interactions to change the youths. Furthermore, in general, the research has other significant limitations.[2] The finding that treatment for youths in the community is ineffective may be a function of the lack of improvement found in the remaining difficult cases after the early responders (the low-hanging fruit) have been treated. These studies suggest that this population of more difficult to treat clients did not show additional improvement when they continued in treatment for 1 year (Tam & Healy, 2007). However, Angold et al.'s (2000) study of 1,422 9- to 16-year-olds who also received community outpatient treatment did show increasing improvement for the subset of longer term clients who continued therapy for more than eight sessions. Therefore, extended treatment may be helpful for longer term youths.

I assume that for youth receiving longer-term therapy, treatment in the community can be beneficial, although more intensive treatment is required than solely providing individual therapy for the youth. When the youth's home and neighborhood continue to be chaotic and frightening, when school programs continue to be insufficient, when the youth is noncompliant with medication or resistant to treatment, when parents are not able to actively contribute to change efforts, and where there are few "village" resources of positive role models and self-esteem-building supervised activities, costly interventions are needed to address these problems. This leads to approaches that include the caretakers and community resources and prevent premature terminations.

Often Clients Drop Out of Therapy Too Early

As discussed previously, research indicates that one third of referred clients do not even make it to the first session (Hampton-Robb, 2003; Issakidis & Andrews, 2004). The longer they have to wait before they can be seen, the more likely they are to avoid the first appointment (Reitzel et al., 2006). About one fifth of clients who start treatment drop out after the first session (O'Sullivan, Peterson, Cox, & Kirkeby, 1989), and 50% leave treatment during the first month (Frayn, 1992). Perhaps one third of these early terminators improved (Kazdin & Wassell, 1998; Scamardo, Bobele, & Biever, 2004), but many left therapy with insufficient treatment. One of the most effective ways to improve outcome involves preventing clients from dropping out and keeping them in treatment long enough to benefit and maintain their change. "Holding patients in treatment until satisfactory gains are achieved is a challenging task at times and should be a focus of clinical practice" (Hansen et al., 2002, p. 339).

Sometimes providing therapy feels like trying to help people I sit next to on the bus. They start telling me about themselves, and I start caring and trying to understand them, but I do not know when they are going to get up and leave. As I become more experienced with the route, I become more aware of the usual stops and can tailor my approach to them. I become sensitized to the clients' preparations to leave and the particular feelings and issues that foster leaving. Then I have more of a chance to keep them for a longer ride.

Some of the typical stops on the therapeutic ride arrive when the parents or youth feel as though I will not or do not understand, care, respect, appreciate, or like them. They may worry that I see them as not trying, at fault, or crazy. They may think that I see them as ugly, stupid, boring, too sick, or not sick enough or that I will trick, abandon, use, abuse, ignore, or reject them. These feelings can be generated by my acts or omissions but are usually expectations derived from transference feelings. Clients may drop out later in treatment because of transference disappointments when they are unable to accept the therapy boundary that they cannot be my friend, lover, child, rescuer, and so on and because of sabotage from family members who do not want the client to change or do not appreciate the client's changes. They may leave therapy when they realize how much time and sacrifice will be required per unit of change and that some things will not change as much as they had hoped. Often the more anxiety producing (as opposed to supportive) the treatment is, the greater the dropout rate is (Piper et al., 1999). Sometimes the client's unrealistic expectations, such as fears of being hospitalized, reported, deported or stirring up trouble with authorities, go undetected and cause premature termination. Even when I make an agreement with clients that they will tell me their gripes and disappointments about their therapy and that they will not just leave without first discussing terminating, sometimes they just leave, and I do not have the relationship with them to allow us to process their reasons for leaving.

It may be fairly typical of clients to keep secret their dissatisfactions with treatment. Hill, Nutt-Williams, Heaton, Thompson, and Rhodes (1996) found that therapists "became aware of their clients' dissatisfaction only after the clients abruptly and unilaterally stated that they were terminating therapy" (p. 216). The authors' review of the literature suggested,

A number of factors have been proposed by clinicians as leading to impasses in psychotherapy: (a) client pathology, which may prevent clients from being able to profit from therapy; (b) mismatches between the therapist and the client because of differences in stage of life, personality type, theoretical orientation, or personal issues or preferences; (c) problems in the therapeutic relationship, such as an inadequate alliance, an inflexible relationship, underemphasizing the relationship, or a breach in the attachment bond; (d) a failure to establish or explain goals, or a disagreement on goals; (e) client transference or inappropriate transference gratification; (f) therapist counter transference or personal issues that interfere with therapists' ability to function adequately in therapy; (g) therapist errors, such as misdiagnosis, sticking rigidly to the contract, misunderstanding the client, problems with judgment or lack of knowledge, inappropriate interventions, pejorative communication, doing the work for the client, acting out, colluding with the client not to discuss difficult issues, or not recognizing that the client has accomplished all he or she can in therapy; (h) client shame associated with cultural prohibitions against discussing certain topics in therapy; (i) irreconcilable conflicts and power struggles; and (j) situational or external reality issues, such as moving or deaths of close relatives. (p. 207)

Knowing where the bus usually stops and guessing and anticipating the client's hidden disappointments, expectations, and agendas come with experience.

In the treatment of youths, clients may leave when the therapist does not adequately focus on helping them engage. The engagement process begins with the first contact usually over the phone and continues throughout therapy. Early therapist support of the parent can predict successful treatment completion for youths (Harwood & Eyberg, 2004). Engaging the parent is crucial to secure ongoing participation, less frequent cancellations, and no-shows and to inoculate against premature termination. Although the alliance with the parent seems more related to treatment attendance, the alliance with the youth appears related to both youth and parent reports of improvement, and both alliances seem highly correlated to satisfaction with services (Hawley & Weisz, 2005).

I try to facilitate engagement by making clients comfortable and aware of what to expect. I respond to them with active listening by which I mirror their feelings and demonstrate my understanding. I think of active listening as a fallback technique that I can rely on whenever I am not sure what to do. To further engagement I might highlight our similarities; instill hope for change; identify and respond to their questions, sacrifices, and doubts about seeking treatment; reflect their healthy ambitions and strengths; and correct their negative feelings and projections about me, while allowing the positive ones to go initially unchallenged. I may have to convey my caring for those clients who need to know that I care about them before they care about what I know.

Stigma, embarrassment, and anxiety can conspire to subvert treatment, especially for adolescents. William is an example of a client who was difficult to engage. He initially appeared calm and collected despite his long history of chaos, abandonment, and abuse due to his parent's drug addictions. I felt our first session went well, even though he came in asking for medication only. So I scheduled two more appointments before his psychiatric evaluation. I was surprised that he refused to come to either of our sessions. When he did attend the meeting with the psychiatrist, I herded him into my office and tried to engage him. I said that I wanted to work with him, but he seemed torn between trying therapy and just using medication. I asked him if it was like when I was on a plane at night looking out of the window and seeing flames coming out of the engine: "You want to tell the stewardess that the engine is on fire, but you decide it's probably normal, and it would be too embarrassing to tell her. But then you are afraid the plane will crash, and you don't want to die, so you think you'd better tell her. But it could be normal, and then it would be embarrassing. So I didn't say anything." He laughed but did not start talking.

I continued. I said that I thought therapy was for the brave, and I could understand how scary it could be, but nothing he could say would surprise me because I had heard just about everything in the past 30 years. Whether or not he told me the worries, the important thing was to get comfortable with people, and if he could get comfortable with me, he would be closer to being comfortable with others. Because he remained silent, I went on. I suggested that I was easier to talk to than other people because what we talk about is confidential, and I could not tell anyone unless he told me that a kid had been abused or neglected, an older person had been abused, or he was a danger to himself or others. That meant that I could not talk to parents or anyone unless I had his permission.

I filled the silence with how I thought it was easier to talk to me because I was like Kleenex. He could use me and then leave me behind without having to worry that I would tell anyone. I paused; he smiled but did not pick up the ball. So I continued.

I said that I felt bad that he had given up on me after just one meeting, and I asked if he would give me another chance to get to know him and help him feel more comfortable. I complained that he did not know me, and it was unfair to give up on me without meeting a few times. His guilt, my humility and caring, or something got to him, and he started to respond. He said he had friends to talk to but had not seen them for 2 years since he started home school. I asked if he talked to people on the Internet, and he told me about MySpace and his cyber habits. We started to connect, and he returned and continued. Knowing his history of previously dropping out of treatment helped me to focus just on engagement, work on the positives, and try to mirror his strengths rather than confront or increase his anxiety by probing too deeply. I also spoke to his father about ways he could support William's initial contacts, and his father was helpful. I do not think that William would have returned if his father had not provided the correct balance of encouragement and consequences.

As therapy and informed consent develop, clients gain an understanding of what to expect and what will be expected of them, including the possible goals, procedures, alternatives, costs, benefits, and duration of therapy. The more I can identify and correct their false expectations, the fewer therapy-ending surprises. For instance before exposing anxious clients to their fears, I try to help them understand why exposure is necessary and ask them to agree to being gradually exposed to their fears as they learn the skills to tolerate the anxiety. Some clients find reassurance in knowing that they have a role in controlling the intensity and duration of their exposure.

The treatment of youths requires a strong alliance and at least monthly contact with their caretaker(s). Sometimes youths are taken out of treatment because the parent cannot handle the stress of the sacrifice of time and money and the hassle that therapy requires and/or does not feel that the youth is benefiting enough (Attride-Stirling, Davis, Farrell, Groark, & Day, 2004). Caretakers may not see the gains that the youth has made and may be frustrated with the child's problems. I recently happened to talk to a parent as her child was leaving the building and serendipitously discovered that the parent was about to take her child out of treatment because he acted out in the car after sessions. I was lucky to have the opportunity to help them establish a reward system to deal with this behavior, reassure her about his progress, and keep him in treatment.

The therapeutic alliance is based on shared goals and expectations about therapy and usually indicates that the client likes and trusts the therapist and wants to have a relationship and make changes. I try to be attuned to any directly or indirectly expressed negative feelings about the treatment or me because they could foreshadow dropping out. Certain client behaviors can precede dropping out, such as missing sessions, arriving late, not calling to cancel or reschedule, answering or making phone calls during sessions, leaving early, and requesting less frequent meetings.

For many clients the more similar they feel to the therapist, the more likely they will remain in treatment. Therapist values that are different from the client's can disrupt treatment (Vervaeke, Vertommen, & Storms, 1997). After a while the differences between client and therapist can become assets, but particularly at the start of therapy, they can interfere with engagement. Later in therapy the differences can be more easily overcome when the client is more secure about the therapist's interest and caring.

When the difference in values is obvious, I usually look for its effect on the therapeutic relationship and for ways to minimize the negative influences. If they seem to disrupt engagement, I may try to elicit the client's thoughts about our differences (age, race, gender, status, ethnic background, etc.). I encourage clients to tell me when these attributes seem to interfere so they think I do not understand something. I might ask what they had expected the therapist or therapy would be like and ask what they thought when they realized it was different.

In my practice, reality issues (e.g., safety, food, clothing, shelter, finances, child care transportation, health problems, moving, not being able to miss work or school, siblings with special needs) play an important role in discouraging participation; therefore, case management is often required because the focus may need to be on resolving reality pressures before dealing with the presenting mental health concerns. Making referrals to other services, advocating for the client, and teaching caretakers about their rights and how to advocate for services are often necessary. Sometimes I help the caretaker obtain help from family or friends (transportation, child care) to overcome barriers to attendance. Giving appointment cards, making telephone reminders, if needed, and follow-up calls about missed appointments, and scheduling appointments on the same day and time can increase attendance. Matching clients with the most convenient, accessible, and suitable treatment, in which interventions are appropriate to the client's level of motivation and capabilities, is helpful in reducing dropouts.

The reasons clients leave prematurely can be related to their core problems, and dealing with their feelings about leaving can be the most productive part of therapy. For example, a parent with an anxiety disorder withdrew her child from treatment because she was afraid of the side effects of the youth's medication and feared that I would be angry because she was noncompliant. It took several phone calls to help her tell me about this problem instead of quit. It is such a loss when I miss opportunities to correct clients' projections, misperceptions, unrealistic expectations, and transference tests that disrupt treatment and sabotage their personal life as well.

Sometimes clients call to say they want to stop. Then I have to decide whether to validate their choice, focus on the gains they have made, put a positive spin on what we have accomplished, and reassure them that they can return or to try to persuade them to come in for an ending session to explore their reasons for terminating. Those who call might come in to please me, but often their decision has been made. Some have been disengaging for some time, and I failed to notice.

Major changes in the client's life, such as embracing a new religion or falling in love, can result in terminating treatment. Aspects of fundamentalist religions, spirituality, and falling in love can provide or support defenses against the uncomfortable feelings that led the client to initially seek treatment. They may offer hope through alternative, sometimes therapy-hostile, belief systems that can emphasize acceptance, denial, predetermination, the belief that therapy is basically a narcissistic enterprise, forgiveness, starting life over again, tunnel vision, and/or dissociation. They may also provide a social network that offers relief that can end the client's motivation and present need for therapy.

A frequent stop where parents consider departing involves making a transition from seeing the child's problem as caused by factors in the child that the therapist will fix to accepting a role in having created the problem, needing to change, and being a part of the solution. Most child and adolescent cases require relationships and interventions with the adults who parent the youth and may require helping caretakers accept that although the youth is the identified patient, the caretakers may need to be part of the solution, which could involve changing their parenting, and the parents may need to make changes in their own lives and relationships.

With caretakers, boundaries can be easily crossed between child guidance counseling (working with the parent(s) to help the child), adult therapy (focusing on the caretakers' problems to help the adult), and marriage or relationship counseling. A conservative child guidance approach involves clarifying with the caretakers (a) that the purpose of meeting with them is to help them with parenting issues, (b) that the youth is the client, and (c) that when adult issues surface, the adult may need to be referred to appropriate resources. When I provide child guidance counseling to caretakers, I have to use caution in deciding how involved I will be in their personal treatment. The continuum runs from ignoring the adult problems, to identifying problems and their effect on the child and parenting, to working on the problems to improve parenting, to looking at the effect of the problems on the parent, to increasing the parent's motivation to seek services for himself or herself and accepting a referral, to crossing the boundary and working on the adult's problems to improve the adult's life and relationships.

Probably one third of parents who bring their children to therapy end treatment because they think that the therapist is not working on or is not in agreement with the parents' goals for their child (Garcia & Weisz, 2002).[3] In working with youths, agreement between the parent, youth, and therapist on which problems are the focus of therapy can facilitate continuing in treatment. The parent and youth typically disagree on the problems that the youth should work on (Yeh & Weisz, 2001),[4] and the therapist disagrees with one or the other (Hawley & Weisz, 2003).[5] The teen might want "Mom to stop bugging me in the morning." The mom might want to know, "How can I get Robert up in the morning to go to school? He's late every day."

If the therapist does not agree with the parents' goals, then engaging parents is difficult, and they are prone to drop out. If the therapist disagrees with the youth, then the youth is hard to engage. When parents and youths disagree, I prefer to have them meet and work toward finding common ground. The best therapy is based on our mutual agreement, but the three parties often cannot have this unity of purpose (Garland, Lewczyk-Boxmeyer, Gabayan, & Hawley, 2004).[6]

Therapists share responsibility for the direction of treatment. Sometimes a clients' initial goals are determined by their needs, defenses, and pathology. A paranoid client might want the therapist to confirm his or her delusional beliefs. Parents of a fearful child might want the therapist to collude with them to protect the child from anxiety, as when one such parent wanted a medical excuse to obtain in-home schooling for her anxious son. A delinquent teen might want the therapist to see him as the victim of home and school authorities rather than be seen as contributing to problems. The client's initial agenda must be treated with respect, but not necessarily adopted, and sometimes adopted temporarily as a bridge to other goals, as happened with the mother who wanted "drop-off" treatment for her violent 5-year-old. She wanted him treated while she ran errands. It took months to gain her involvement in child guidance counseling.

The parent's and the therapist's agendas usually have common elements that can form the basis for agreement on goals. For example, one parent wanted me to discipline her rebelling adolescent and support her overly controlling parenting. We were able to agree that we both wanted her daughter to be able to function independently and not get pregnant or abused by boyfriends as she had been. Eventually the mother, daughter, and I agreed that allowing the daughter to gradually earn freedom by displaying responsibility would help her learn from experience and prepare for emancipation. The mother came to see that her relationship with her daughter was a greater protection than the limits she was unsuccessfully trying to enforce when she recognized that if she had had such a relationship with her parents, she would have been safer as an adolescent. She was able to adopt a different parental role that involved helping her daughter learn from problems rather than protecting her from problems.

Sometimes clients are impossible to engage and keep in treatment. They may be exquisitely sensitive and require perfect mirroring to avoid upsetting them. They may be so hostile, so sexualized, so anxious, so depressed, defended, or pathological, or so needy or demanding; present so many transference tests; be so overwhelmed; live such chaotic lives; be so addicted; or be so controlled by others that it is amazing they attended the sessions that they did.

Some Clients Want to Stay Too Long, and We Have to Help Them Leave

Some clients are afraid to terminate, and for them especially, termination can be the most important part of therapy. Termination can require a great deal of planning and discussion, which can begin early in treatment. Some clients may need to clarify what ending treatment means to them and develop realistic expectations for what can be accomplished and for how long it will take. Clients with unrealistic dependency expectations usually need to learn better skills to face risks and meet their needs in relationships in their daily life rather than to expect the therapist to meet these needs on a long-term basis. If termination is not done carefully, gains that have been made can evaporate, and unhelpful transference feelings can be confirmed. Even after significant improvements and a close relationship, clients could leave therapy concluding that the therapist was just like all people—rejecting, uncaring, and so on.

Sometimes clients stay in treatment too long because the therapist and/or the client have not developed clear goals and their associated ending points. We can always find more problems to work on, so it is difficult to decide when the client has had enough therapy. "We need to decide which goals we are pursuing … 'enough' could mean (a) clinical improvement, (b) no longer meeting criteria for medical necessity or for a psychiatric diagnosis, (c) as much improvement as would be expected for this particular patient, (d) enough improvement to minimize the likelihood of reoccurrence or reentry into treatment, or (e) enough to ensure normal functioning" (Lutz, Martinovich, & Howard, 1999, p. 577).

When clients are resistant to ending, they might be weaned by scheduling less frequent sessions. They may be more accepting if termination can be presented as an experiment in which they take a break from therapy and see how things go without treatment. Particularly anxious and dependent clients may need reassurance that they can return. We might discuss what they think could cause them to return and that it is common to come back when they face new problems and developmental stages. I try to leave the door open and the light on.

CHAPTER 6

Managing Treatment

A Referral! What Should I Do?

Over the years I have found that some stages of the treatment process have become fairly well mapped out so that I have clear agendas and a host of questions I can draw from. This structure reduces anxiety for the client and for me so that I do not have to think about myself and what I will do or say. I can more fully focus on observing the client, understanding his or her feelings and intensions, and fostering engagement. Because I act fairly similarly with each client during these stages, I have a more developed sense of what to expect, so client behavior is easier to interpret.

Starting Treatment: The Initial Phone Contact

Usually I receive a referral form with identifying information and the caretaker's presenting concerns that caused them to seek treatment. I call the caretaker, and this is our first contact. In about 10 minutes I want to do some screening, make a connection, schedule an appointment, and prepare the caretaker. I introduce myself and say that I have a note saying he or she is looking for help with a youth because that youth is having the problems described on the referral form. I mention the problems to indicate I am informed and to save time. I do not want to be drawn into a discussion of the youth's problems at this time. After clarifying that the referred youth is appropriate for outpatient treatment and not in need of a crisis evaluation because of imminent danger, I say that I would like to meet them to do an assessment. I ask about their schedule. I wonder if the parents' availability and attitude toward me is related to their youth's problem. Do they cater to me at their expense? Do they have little time for me, so I must fit into their schedule? I set up a meeting time that is the least disruptive to them and to me, and I explain what to expect at that meeting—many questions about the youth's problems. I discuss when, where, and how long the session will be (usually 90 minutes); give clear directions to my office; explain fees; instruct them about the papers they should bring (especially previous evaluations and the latest court documents confirming custody and authorization to seek treatment); and give them my name, phone number, and policy about cancelling the appointment. I ask if they have any questions. I want them to know what to expect—an assessment, not solutions. Better attendance at the intake appointment has been found in parents who have been helped to have clear expectations about the meeting and positive feelings about the therapist (Bonner & Everett, 1986) and in parents who receive a follow-up telephone reminder or a letter explaining what to expect at the intake meeting. Kourany, Garber, and Tornusciolo (1990) found that such pretreatment contact led to a 12.9% no-show rate compared to the usual 34.6% no-show rate.

I clarify who can authorize treatment. Minors younger than 13 years of age who live with their parents require consent to treat from their custodial parent. In cases where parents are divorced, I clarify if both or either parent can authorize treatment and ask for the most recent court order. In California minors ages 12 to 18 years may obtain outpatient mental health treatment without parental consent if the minor is in danger of serious mental or physical harm to self or from others if they are seeking treatment for rape or abuse, treatment or prevention of pregnancy, a reportable disease, or a substance abuse problem. Unless the parent or guardian is a threat to the youth, I seek the youth's permission to contact the caretakers and try to gain their cooperation and involvement.

For wards or dependents of the juvenile court, a court order is required to clarify who has the power to authorize care. Sometimes the judge orders treatment. Sometimes the probation officer, social worker, parent or guardian, foster parent, or an adult relative has been given permission to authorize treatment for the minor. Court-declared emancipated minors, financially self-sufficient minors older than age 14 years who live apart from parents, minors on active duty in the armed services, and minors who are or have been married do not require parental consent. Contacting their parents may conflict with the clients' privacy rights.

As the initial phone conversation progresses, I try to decide who should attend the first session. Selecting who is invited can be a major intervention. When the client is a child, I prefer to meet first with the important adults in the child's family to obtain the history and then assess the child in later sessions. Having the child attend could be a distraction, and the parent might be reluctant to say things with the child present. If a father figure is involved, or if it appears that his involvement could be beneficial, I make every effort to have him attend. Sometimes scheduling difficulties, the lack of child care, or the parent's preference determines who appears at the intake. Parents without childcare may need to bring the child to the intake, so the session provides an opportunity to observe the parent–child dynamics.

If the client is an adolescent, I discuss with the parent on the phone some of the advantages and disadvantages of inviting the teen to our first meeting. I often rely on the parent's decision. I might ask the parent to consider if the teen would contribute to or inhibit conversation. Would talking about the past with the teen present be helpful or detrimental to the teen? Would it make forming a relationship with the therapist easier or more difficult because of the openness and visibility of the process and the teen's knowledge that the therapist is aware of his or her past and present problems?

The First Meeting With the Caretaker(s)

In the "first session … whether the patient is a child or an adult … ideally, the therapist seeks to establish a beginning therapeutic alliance … ; convey the ground rules and expectations of the therapeutic relationship … ; gain a preliminary understanding of the patient's problem; make some exploratory interventions; and formulate a preliminary treatment plan" (Stern, 1993, p. 165). The therapist's initial interpretations of the client's situation are highly influential and can cement or sabotage the alliance.

For the therapist there is a tension between wanting to hear the client's story to start helping and needing to discuss the rules of engagement. For the parents there is a tension between wanting to tell their story to receive help and having to listen to procedural information. My mistakes have come from erring on the side of dealing with the client's problems at the expense of not taking a detailed history and not covering certain ground rules, such as discussing informed consent, the limits of confidentiality, office and emergency procedures, and the limits of therapist availability.

I deal with the limits of confidentiality early in the intake. I tell adults and teenagers that what we talk about is confidential and that I need their written permission prior to telling anyone what we discuss. However, there are exceptions. If a youth, disabled, or older person is neglected or sexually, physically, financially, or emotionally abused, or if a client is a serious danger to himself or herself or others, then I am mandated to report the danger so they can get help. I might be court ordered to disclose information, and third-party payers might require information to authorize payments. I may explain that the USA PATRIOT Act permits the government to seize records and forbids the therapist from telling his or her clients that records were taken. I explain that except for these exceptions, I need their written permission to tell anything about them to others. I ask them to sign releases of information to allow me to contact and get records from school, the family physician, and others who know the youth and could be helpful in the assessment and treatment, such as teachers, probation officers, child care providers, and previous therapists.

When working with parents of teenagers, I make sure they feel comfortable allowing, or they at least agree to allow, their teen the privilege of confidentiality. If parents insist on being informed about their adolescent's disclosures of petty criminal activities, consensual sexual activities, and/or all substance use, then I inform the adolescent about this reality. I try to lead reluctant parents through the costs and benefits of allowing the adolescent confidentiality. Many adolescents report they would not seek treatment for concerns about sexuality, substance abuse, or emotional upset if their parents had to know about the visit (Saul, 1999). Adolescents vary in their need for privacy just as parents differ in their capacity to therapeutically handle what their youth say. Some parents might punish, restrict, harm, or withdraw their teen from treatment, so it is understandable that teens may fear retribution and withhold their concerns. Negotiating confidentiality boundaries with caretakers and reaching a mutually acceptable arrangement can be a necessary and productive part of treatment.

The youth may say things that the custodian is entitled to know: if the youth is endangering himself or herself or others or perhaps if the youth is about to commit a felony, then parents might need to know. The value that therapists give to the youth's autonomy versus the youth's safety contributes to the therapist's decision. Disclosing typical adolescent experimentation is usually erring on the side of being too safety oriented. Not telling about mandated reporting issues and seriously endangering behaviors is erring on the side of being too autonomy oriented. Wherever the therapist draws the line, the negotiations should begin in the discussions of informed consent that define the limits of the parents' access to the youth's disclosures. These boundaries can then be amended as issues surface. Different states have different laws about the parent's access to the child's records (e.g., New York and Illinois allow youths 12 years and older to control access). The informed consent discussions can help the youth accept the limits of confidentiality and understand that the therapist's intention in making disclosures is in the service of protecting the youth and/or the safety of others.

We have to balance the parents' right to know and their ability to be helpful with the damage to the therapeutic relationship that might be created by informing the parents. Sharing information with a parent can rupture the therapeutic relationship with the youth. Not sharing can rupture the relationship with the parent. If the youth will feel betrayed, the dangers would need to be robust to warrant telling the parent. If disclosures could be relationship breaking and the parent needs to know, then having a conjoint session to probe how much the parent already suspects can be helpful to possibly address the problem without having to break confidentiality. Many times the caretakers already suspect the youth's problem behaviors. Sometimes the youth can be encouraged to tell his or her parent by exploring the costs and benefits of disclosure and the reactions that can be realistically expected from the parents. If I need to deny a parent access to records or treatment information I develop and document in the chart a plan to involve the parent(s) in treatment. Confidentiality and minor consent are too complex to be fully treated here, so the reader who wishes more information is referred to the publications of the Adolescent Health Working Group at http://www.ahwg.net, where links to other resources are available (Simmons, Shalwitz, Pollock, & Young, 2003).

I anticipate that confidentiality can cause problems. Teens may use therapy to manipulate parents. They threaten to tell negative things about the parents to the therapist or may tell the parents that the therapist recommends certain things or thinks certain negative things about the parents. I promise parents that I will not believe everything the adolescent says about them if they promise not to believe everything they hear about me, and they are encouraged to tell me about concerns they may have. Parents have asked if I said they were stupid or crazy and if I said they should let their teen go to a certain party or have a later curfew or bedtime. I usually do not tell parents what the adolescent said in sessions, and I typically tell parents that I will share our conversation with the teen. Even young children tell parents stories that need correction, as I learned when an upset parent of a kindergartener phoned me to ask, "Did you take my daughter swimming last session?"

Clients require additional disclosures about their confidentiality when they are court ordered into therapy. The court may want quarterly reports about the client's progress and the therapist's assessment of the diagnosis and potential to reoffend. Reporting to the court places the therapist in a dual role—therapist–confidant and judge–snitch—and reporting presents the client with a conflict between openly disclosing and needing to manipulate the therapist into providing a positive report. It is difficult and sometimes impossible for treatment to take place under these dual mandates. I clearly define my role with court-ordered clients. If I am their therapist, then I will not report to the court what they say, because reporting might influence what they could discuss and distort the therapeutic alliance. With delinquent youths I explain to the court how reporting could derail treatment, and I usually compromise with the court worker or probation officer by agreeing to tell them whether the client is attending sessions, what our goals are, and whether the client is working in the sessions. I then explain this to the youths and make sure they understand that except for mandated issues, I will not tell the court what we have talked about. I explain confidentiality to children by telling them about the three hurts. I say that if someone hurts them or they hurt someone or they hurt themselves, then I have to tell people so everyone can be safe. I also indicate there will be times when I, or we, might need to talk to parents about what we are doing.

Parents facing divorce and custody conflicts can also place the therapist in a dual role. I initially make it clear that I cannot provide treatment unless they agree that what we discuss in treatment is confidential. Any agreement to discourage using information obtained in sessions in a divorce or custody battle is not legally binding. However, parents usually accept the agreement. If they later seek the therapist's testimony or a report to the court, it places the parents in the situation of being seen as putting their interests ahead of the best interests of the youth. I cannot be their advocate or evaluate the parents for the court, because giving me that power would cause them to distort what they would want me to know and subvert therapy if they did not like what I reported. If they need an evaluation or someone to testify for them, then I help them find a professional to provide the service. When a report to the court is required, I try to meet with the stakeholders and present what I intend to tell the court so I can deal with objections and make adjustments when necessary. I seek their permission to release the information even if I must release the information anyway. Agreements cannot be made that place limits on the client's ability to file a licensing board complaint. I treat with caution clients involved in custody battles because they are the most litigious and physically dangerous.

Once ground rules are covered, the focus of the first meeting turns to taking a history. At the intake some caretakers may initially feel anxious about giving a history and view the history taking as a frustration. However, they almost always find it illuminating and discover new connections as they begin to share the intimate story of their life. This process helps them bond to the therapist, therefore it is preferable that the therapist who will work with the family do the intake. I do not expect to get all the information in the first meeting. My focus is on reducing anxiety and creating engagement so I can work with the family.

Even taking a history before intervening has become somewhat controversial. There are arguments against taking a history. Behavioral therapists, especially, contend that taking a history is a throwback to the days when therapy emphasized insight and catharsis, and because they see therapy as focusing on building skills, then knowing the cause of the deficit is not particularly important. In addition, focusing on what is wrong or on painful past experiences is uncomfortable, causes sadness rather than motivation to change, and can lead the frustrated client to drop out of therapy. However, the argument for taking a history seems valid. Gradually disclosing intimate details usually increases the client's engagement with the therapist and strengthens the therapeutic alliance, which enables the client to tolerate anxiety, invest in treatment, and disclose more. The therapeutic alliance is an understanding between client and therapist that they are going to work together to create changes that will ameliorate problems.

Some clients are reluctant to revisit the past because they anticipate they will reexperience unpleasant feelings and be reminded of the negative conclusions they made about themselves as a child and may still believe. It is the therapeutic relationship that allows clients to explore their past and correct the unexamined misconceptions (especially self-blame) with which they have been living. In fact, one of the conceptual models of therapy postulates that events that happened to a youth were understood in accordance with the youth's immature thinking (often under extraordinary stress) and have remained unexamined until later in life. Therapy then provides the opportunity for clients to overcome their fear of exploring the past and use their adult thinking capacities and knowledge to construct a new understanding of their history. An example of correcting a childhood misconception was generated by a teenager who, at age 7, began blaming himself for his parent's divorce because he was blamed by a parent and because he overheard his parents argue about how to discipline him for his messy room on the night his father walked out of his life. He egocentrically thought that if he had cleaned his room, they would not have argued and subsequently divorced. When he revisited this painful time, he realized that issues that children are not aware of, such as infidelity, substance use, domestic violence, and disagreements over money, actually led to the divorce.

History taking is necessary because the cause of the problem can determine the diagnosis and treatment. For example, failures caused by learning disabilities, attentional problems, retardation, family chaos, abuse, medical problems, anxiety, or depression would each require different treatments. Taking the history can also identify the clients' personal and family resources and liabilities and the clients' theory of the causes of their problem and expectations for treatment, which can strongly influence the treatment plan. Furthermore, failure to take an adequate history is unethical and could lead to civil and licensing actions.

Early in the intake I ask parents and adult clients to describe the problems and concerns that brought them to seek services. This is a good place to start, because most nonchild clients are motivated to discuss what is bothering them. I look at the history of each presenting concern and sometimes am able to guess their causes by identifying what changes were happening when the problem emerged. When interviewing resistant adult clients, Eron and Lund (1996) suggested asking "the mystery question" to obtain historical information and the clients' understanding of the evolution of the presenting problems: "The mystery question assumes a typical form: How did a person with X preferred attributes (competent, independent, in control) wind up in Y position (being investigated by probation or Family Court, being scrutinized by other adults, being pressured to come to therapy)?" (p. 254). The presenting concerns usually lead to identifying the client's goals and theory of how to accomplish them. These goals "may be the most important pieces of information that the therapist can obtain" in the intake (Duncan, Miller, & Sparks, 2004, p. 73).

I take a detailed psychosocial history that includes questions about the client's pregnancy, birth, delivery, developmental milestones, and early environment. I ask about the client's parents and caretakers and the quality of the care and attachment they provided. I ask about siblings, other close family members, and other relatives with problems similar to the client's. I ask about family, cultural, and spiritual affiliations; history of abuse; use and abuse of substances; and exposure to discrimination and real and media violence. I ask about involvement with the legal system, previous medical and psychological problems and treatment, medications and their efficacy, educational and employment history, people in the home and daily life, and suicidality and unusual perceptual experiences. I ask about eating and sleeping habits, chores, friends, routines, habits, current stresses, and finances (including credit card debt). I identify strengths and community and extended family resources as well as potential obstacles to treatment. By the end of the meeting, I want to have a preliminary understanding of the parents' concerns, why they sought treatment at this time, and what they think will be helpful. Often the clients' goals and theory of change are more realistic and informed after the history has been detailed.

I ask if there are other things that would be useful for me to know, and I ask about the clients' reaction to our meeting and answering all these questions. I ask if they have questions for me. I am not overly concerned with trying to ask everything in the first meeting. I usually say that if they have any problems working with me, it is important to tell me as soon as possible, because I want this to be helpful. I mention that it is important that throughout our work together, they tell me when it seems we are not going in the right direction. I might end the session by saying that I am looking forward to working with them.

When the intake is just with parents, I ask what they intend to tell the youth about coming to his or her first session. How the youth is prepared can facilitate or harm the process. Hearing the parents' thoughts about preparing the child also can be diagnostic of their sensitivity to their child and parenting ability. Usually, I cannot learn from children what their parents told them because when I meet children, they typically say that they do not know why they came, what problems they have, or what their parents are concerned about. I anticipate that children might be anxious and that some, upon hearing that they will be seeing a doctor, might even expect to receive a medical examination or a painful shot, and older youths might expect dire consequences, such as being hospitalized, removed from home, or lectured by the parent's ally. I would like the parents to tell their young child, "We went to see a doctor for children who is not like our regular doctor but more like a worry-doctor, or a feeling-doctor, who helps kids with their feelings and problems by talking and playing. We thought you should go because you are upset about things or doing things that are a problem. We told the doctor (who was very nice) about you and all of us, and he wanted to meet you and hear your ideas and get to know you." With adolescents I expect parents to be more direct and mention that they told their view of the problems they and the family are having and that the doctor wanted to hear their side of the story.

As I progress through the intake and early meetings, my focus is also on making a diagnosis to aid in selecting treatments. The diagnosis is generally based on the history from caretakers and observations of the client. Sometimes psychological and/or educational testing is helpful. One of the advantages of treating children and adolescents is that teachers and other professionals who know the youths can inform the initial diagnostic impression. I have rarely been disappointed after talking to a teacher. Teachers have a unique position in that they see 30 to 60 agemates a year under a variety of situations, have access to youths' educational history and testing, can put youths' behavior into perspective, and may offer observations about the parents and the youths' relationships with peers.

I look for opportunities to try to reduce anxiety by identifying and correcting client misconceptions about beginning therapy. For instance, a client who is worried that the therapist will tell everything to his parents might feel more comfortable after a discussion of his or her confidentiality rights. I tell clients that part of therapy involves their telling me any complaints or concerns about treatment they may have and that it is important for us to keep working together until our goals have been met. I might explain to parents how play, art, and activities used with their child are therapeutic so parents value what their child is doing instead of thinking that our sessions are "just play." It is not unusual for parents to anticipate being blamed or to initially wonder whether their youth's problems are caused by a mental health condition or are normal behaviors. Some parents might ambivalently accept counseling "feeling they had no choice" (Lazear, Worthington, & Detres, 2004). These are issues that may need to be identified and discussed early in the process.

The First Meeting With the Young Child

I usually meet individually with the child for the assessment, which can last several sessions and might include psychological and/or educational testing. The assessment session of the child begins with observations in the waiting room. I anticipate that young children will be more anxious at the first session; I know that I am. So my primary focus is to make them feel comfortable and want to return. Some children ignore me when I approach them in the waiting room. They avoid eye contact, cling to their parent, or busy themselves in an activity. If they avoid me, I might talk to the parent in hopes that the child will wander over so the parent or I can introduce us. When children are hesitant to separate from their caretaker, I may try to connect with them in the waiting room by joining in their play until they are more comfortable with me, and I think they will accept my invitation to go to my office, where they can continue with the toys they are playing with or can see the other toys and things that are in my office. If they still will not accompany me, I invite the caretaker to join us. When the child is more comfortable, I wean him or her from the parent. After 10 to 15 minutes, the child typically does not object to the caretaker's leaving the session after being reassured that the caretaker will be in the waiting room nearby, and the child is free to check in with him or her. When the child refuses to separate from his or her parent, it is often because the parent conveys his or her anxiety to the child, so the parent needs to trust the therapist before the child is ready to be more independent. Such parents may be anxious or have worries about men or the system or have had problems with previous therapists. Before feeling comfortable, they may need to see the therapist interact with the child in a way that allays their fears. Children usually accompany me easily or with initial anxiety that fades as we start to interact.

Particularly hyperactive and deprived children are drawn to materials in my office, and we may begin with their selecting an activity that does not require our interaction, such as drawing or playing clay, while I ask rapport-building questions. Although there are some common questions that I ask all young clients, some questions are particularly relevant to exploring the parents' presenting concerns.

I try to ask open-ended questions (that cannot be answered with a "yes" or "no"), elicit further elaboration, and encourage the child to speak spontaneously. I ask young children questions, such as the following:

> What's your name? What do you like to be called? How old are you? What did your mom say about coming here today?
>
> What kinds of things do you like to do? Do you collect anything?
>
> If you could have two wishes, what would you wish? What's another wish?
>
> If you could be any animal, what animal would you like to be? What is special about that animal? What animal would you not want to be? What is bad about that animal?
>
> Who are all the people who live in your home? What's he or she like?
>
> How do you get up in the morning? Who helps you get up? How do you go to bed at night? Do you like someone to help you go to bed at night?
>
> What is dinnertime like at your home? Favorite food? Worst food?
>
> Who is the best person in your home to do stuff with?
>
> What's fun to do at home? What makes people upset at home? How can you tell they are upset? Are there some things that are not fair at your home? What needs to be changed at home to make things better?
>
> Do you go to school? What grade are you in? Who's your teacher? Is she or he a good teacher? What does she or he do well? Does she or he do things you don't like? What's your favorite part of school? Is there a part you don't like? What do kids play at school? What do you play? Whom do you play with? Whom do you sit with at lunch?
>
> Whom do you play with around home?

The assessment sessions are different from therapy visits, especially in the degree to which I direct and ask questions. In therapy I encourage the child to take more control, whereas in an assessment I control the agenda and ask many questions because there are so many areas that I want to explore.

As the child feels more comfortable, I try to establish some structure and purpose for future visits. I might say, "I met with your mom, and she said you were unhappy at school or worried about going to bed at night or getting into fights at home, and so on. Mom wanted us to meet so I can get to know you, and we can figure out how to make things better." I might show them around the center so they can see some of the fun things kids do and find out what they might like to try. I say, "Kids like to come here. Each time you come here, we will spend some time talking and some time doing activities." I want them to feel comfortable with me and know that we will work and have fun. If the parent is in the session, I might ask him or her why he or she wants the child to come to the clinic. This can be the first time that the parent has clearly told the child her or his concerns and the first time they have talked about them. Their interaction can be helpful in deciding if conjoint therapy is appropriate.

I try to avoid asking questions that will harm our relationship. In the first meeting there usually is an opportunity to draw, paint, build with interesting materials, play a game, make a crafts project, and/or have a snack. These activities are potentially diagnostic and therapeutic. They can promote the therapeutic alliance and provide an opportunity to observe the child's ability to tolerate frustration, share, take turns, manage and express feelings, problem solve, learn marketable peer skills, and learn to follow rules and to help clean up after himself or herself.

I might be more problem focused with older youths who have a more developed capacity to talk about their problems. Some early adolescents cannot or will not discuss problems at the start of treatment before a relationship is established. Pushing them can just create resistance. Some feel uncomfortable if problems are not discussed. Some can disclose too much and then not want to come back.

Value and Develop a Case Formulation for Each Client

There are many roads clients can travel to reach the same diagnosis. Therefore, the variability of clients within diagnoses is too great and the power of treatment techniques is too small to automatically apply a "treatment of choice" to all people within a diagnostic category.

The formulation is the therapist's understanding of the unique client's problem(s), the causes, what triggers and maintains the problem(s), and the preliminary treatment plan for the specific client. The formulation is a statement that places the symptoms into a biological, psychological, social, family, cultural, and societal context. The formulation includes the therapist's best guess as to which factors contribute to the problem. Unlike the diagnosis-determines-treatment model, the formulation considers the clients' unique strengths, deficits, and characteristics (capacity to relate, level of motivation, theory of change, self-concept and self-esteem, intelligence, rationality, developmental stage, environmental stability and support, etc.). These assets and liabilities then inform the selection and timing of the treatment plan and how it is implemented (e.g., supportive vs. anxiety producing, directive vs. elicited from the client, problem oriented vs. strength oriented, etc.).

The specific content of the formulation is related to the theoretical orientation of the therapist. A behavioral therapist might explain the client's problems as caused by learning principles, such as rewards, consequences, and modeling. A psychodynamic therapist might emphasize insights that might be therapeutic, conflictual desires, and how to respond to anticipated transference tests.

On the basis of their review of case formulations from several theoretical orientations, Kendjelic and Eells (2007)

> identified four generic case formulation components: (a) symptoms and problems, (b) precipitating stressors, (c) predisposing events and conditions, and (d) an inferred explanatory mechanism accounting for the previous three components. ... The inferred mechanism builds on the preceding components and attempts to explain their relationship. It is the clinician's hypothesis or explanation of the patient's current difficulties and may be expressed as a core or central conflict, set of dysfunctional thoughts or beliefs, biological predispositions, problematic interpersonal relationship patterns, contingencies of reinforcement, or systemic problems among family members. Ideally, identification of the explanatory mechanism helps to organize and guide the choice of treatment interventions. (p. 68)

The formulation organizes and makes sense of a great deal of information. It makes the client's history, problems and treatment manageable so that the therapist can feel less anxious, understand and care about the client, and feel confident in the tentative treatment plan (Eells, 1997).

Based on the initial assessment, a case formulation might read:

> Jeff was a healthy, good-looking, Caucasian sixth grader who lived with his mother and infant sister in a one-bedroom apartment. His mother brought him to the clinic and reported that Jeff has done well socially and academically, but in the past 2 months he received three suspensions for fighting and lost interest in sports, school, and friends. He did not have problems with eating or sleeping. His parents were divorcing after several years of domestic violence for which the mother felt responsible. Recently Jeff pushed his mother and said that he wanted to live with his father as soon as he got out of prison. Jeff blamed his mother, and possibly himself, for the divorce and felt ashamed that he lacked the money, family, and home that his peers had.
>
> The mother presented as depressed and reported a history of being molested as a child. She appeared to be a nurturing parent who had difficulty setting limits and was overwhelmed with parenting and supporting the family. While the father was in the home, he was the disciplinarian. The mother feared the father would get

custody of both children if she spoke disparagingly of him, whereas the father felt free to blame the divorce on her and tell Jeff, "Mom wants a divorce, and I don't want to break up the family. She won't let me back no matter what I say."

Jeff appeared to have a depressive disorder NOS and an adjustment disorder with mixed disturbance of emotion and conduct. Weekly individual psychotherapy might focus on correcting his misconceptions about the cause of his parents' divorce, providing successes and approval, mourning the loss of his idealized view of his father and the marriage, learning self-talk that might help him deal with depressing thoughts, and developing peer activities and support. Jeff might resist hearing about his father's faults because his love of him seems based on an unrealistically positive view of him caused by splitting and his mother's protecting the father. Jeff may fear losing his father's love and experience criticism of his father as an attack on himself.

Weekly child guidance counseling for the mother might emphasize helping her tell Jeff why she is divorcing his father, increasing individual time with Jeff, which dramatically diminished since the birth of his sister and she became employed, and overcoming her reluctance to ask the grandmother for child care, money, and emotional support. Treatment could focus on helping her set limits and give consequences for violent behavior, correcting her self-blaming misconceptions about the divorce, and feeling comfortable with her anger and the anger that can be anticipated from Jeff when she sets limits and mentions his father's contribution to the divorce. She might benefit from learning assertiveness skills, looking at her resistances to attending a battered women's group, learning budgeting skills, and generalizing her sharing her story from therapist to friends without becoming overly involved in helping them with their problems.

The mother might find it difficult to set limits and be more assertive because of a long pattern of feeling badly about herself because of her history of abuse. But she might be motivated to change to prevent her son from growing up to be like his (and her?) father. The mother might have difficulty allowing herself to be angry or assertive because she expects that others will react with anger, harm her, or think ill of her. She seems uncomfortable with receiving support and attention from others and has a pattern of appeasing others. She mistakenly believes that by giving to others, they will eventually care about her.

Providing Feedback to Parents and Identifying Goals

After having a few meetings with the youth and gathering information from the adults in his or her life, I meet with the caretakers and youth to develop the initial treatment plan. This meeting involves the merging of two processes. First, on the basis of the formulation, I share my understanding of the strengths and problems and what I think would be helpful. Second, using the parents' presenting concerns to guide us, we collaboratively identify treatment goals and the stakeholders' specific contributions toward accomplishing them. I try to facilitate reaching a consensus on the problems to be remediated and a treatment plan that is based on the family's and community's strengths. For instance, after evaluating Teddy I thought that his aggressiveness would respond to several environmental changes. His parents and I agreed that his aggressiveness in school was the most serious problem and a reaction to being teased and having learning disabilities. Teddy was motivated to stop getting in trouble. His parents and I thought that tutoring after school, a more structured homework routine at home (both generated little enthusiasm from Teddy), and more social successes through joining a community activity group and increasing success-oriented activities with the father (both highly supported by Teddy) would be helpful. We agreed that increasing consequences and teaching alternative behaviors to tolerate teasing could be done by the parents and teacher rather than in therapy. Therefore, we decided that the mother and I would meet weekly to help her advocate for and implement these changes and assess their impact on Ted's aggressiveness. The father could not commit to attend regularly but was genuinely supportive. We thought that if an appropriate peer group in the community could not be found, we might want to place Teddy in a socialization group at our center. This feedback session involved a discussion of the child's diagnosis and why the parents' expectation was not confirmed that Teddy had ADHD.

Sometimes the feedback process can involve a discussion of the diagnosis, which can be therapeutic. A name, a diagnosis, can make a problem seem manageable by bringing it from the unknown to the known and giving it a specific course, treatment, and prognosis. Without a name, problems can be like a blank screen on to which the client and caretaker(s) project their worst fears. I once told a client that she had an obsessive-compulsive disorder that was inherited. She looked relieved and said, "You mean other people have this? I thought I was the only one. I thought I was crazy." I have heard similar relief expressed by parents who had previously blamed themselves for their child's problems, until they were informed that genetic and other forces outside of their control were the most significant causes. When there is a risk that telling the family the diagnosis might pathologize, lower motivation and self-esteem, and/or upset engagement, rather than tell the family the diagnosis it might be more helpful to discuss traits from the diagnosis that the client can accept and work on remediating. For instance, rather than tell an adult client that she had a borderline personality disorder, we discussed her struggle to modulate her feelings and her tendency to split and use black-and-white thinking. At the time this was more productive and avoided a possible rupture to the relationship that could not have been repaired.

We are legally and ethically mandated to provide informed consent. Informed consent is typically not fully laid out at the start of treatment. It is a series of agreements made as the client's problems and solutions become evident and the client needs to know what might come next. It evolves as therapy progresses. The challenge is to discuss it in a way that enhances rather than interferes with therapy. Informed consent involves explaining alternatives to, and the limitations, risks, and benefits of, treatment, so that clients can make an informed choice. This discussion of the pros and cons of the multiple options available to clients protects the therapist from legal actions and can promote client autonomy, commitment to treatment, and responsibility for treatment outcome. However, discussing the limitations of the treatment or the therapist can undermine the clients' feeling of hope and their belief in the competence of the therapist and the treatment. Focusing on negatives can create negative expectations and doubt that can undermine engagement and create self-fulfilling prophecies. I try to give the clients choices throughout treatment, share my reasoning about how to proceed, and help clients contribute to developing the treatment plan.

Forming a Therapeutic Alliance With Some Adolescents Is Particularly Challenging

Engaging the adolescent can require additional therapist sensitivities. Quoting from Long (1968), John Meeks (1980) described the process of engaging the adolescent:

> The adolescent is alone driving a car down the highway at 50 MPH, but he has never driven before and has only watched others drive. The therapist is in another car trying to shout advice. If the adolescent can make use of the help, he will; but he has to bring the car under control by himself. And the therapist has to convince him that he is not the [police]. (p. 156)

Adolescents present unique obstacles to engagement because of their developmental stage. They may be separating from parents and may resent adults' value systems and advice. Their desire for independence may contribute to unwelcome feelings of dependence if they conform to adults' expectations. They may view adults as annoying background noise as they focus on gaining peer acceptance and struggle with learning to succeed at something. Engagement can be further complicated by the stigma of being in psychotherapy and being made to attend treatment.

Many adolescents are not oppositional, and many admire and have close relationships with parents and adults. But the hostile autonomy-seeking adolescent can be a challenge and requires special handling. When parents are capable, the most productive treatment probably involves working with them to confront the youth's behavior and defenses, provide contingent consequences, and teach skills. However, I do treat these adolescents individually when their parents are not able to contribute and when I anticipate the youths will appear open to adults who appreciate their perforations, strengths, and struggles and can help them prepare for emancipation. Many previously resistant adolescents are particularly open to treatment at emancipation when they realize that soon they will have to support themselves.

To foster engagement I ask about topics and goals that are meaningful to them and seek their personal story, values, and beliefs. I want to convey that I am interested in them apart from their problems, as I seek to unearth and appreciate their strengths. I may need to collude with the adolescents to avoid exposing their felt deficits and uncovering embarrassing historical information. I accept their appearance, present agenda, and level of commitment to change in the same way that I accept their developmental level. Because adolescents may not seek treatment and may not acknowledge problems, I may need to begin without well-defined goals other than my intention to seek engagement. Therefore, I might focus on eliciting their side of the story, use active listening, and accept and validate their feelings. Diamond, Liddle, Hogue, and Dakof (1999) found that the same techniques ("attending to the adolescent's experience, formulating personally meaningful goals, and presenting as the adolescent's ally") promoted the alliance and resolved ruptures with poorly engaged clients.

With most adolescents it is counterproductive to lecture, present a theoretical understanding of their problems (Do you ever think you are blaming the school instead of seeing your part in the problem?), and interpret the transference relationship (Are you expecting that I will get angry just like your Dad does?). Concrete-thinking and impulse-driven clients may be disinterested in, or frustrated with, abstract thought and be more motivated to develop practical solutions to present problems they have identified, such as conflicts with parents over chores, curfew, homework, bedtime, and use of electronics. I might help such clients negotiate a deal with their parents through which the teen gets something he or she wants and the parents get something they want, such as a later curfew if the client completes homework assignments. Such efforts can involve advocating for the youth with parents, school, or other agencies and helping the adolescent learn the skills to advocate for himself or herself. Through this process clients can see therapy as having potential benefits.

I try to empower adolescents by emphasizing their power to make choices in their life and in therapy. I convey my expectation that they have the capacity to succeed and improve their situation. I expect responsible behavior and a commitment to resolving problems through conversation and negotiation, and I try to help clients see that these skills can help them get more of what they want. A frequent theme is "the more responsibility you show, the less they will hassle you, the more they will trust you, and the more freedom you will earn."

I seek a balance between supporting, accepting, and appreciating the clients as they are and focusing on change by confronting their deficits and contributions to problems. I can find things that I genuinely admire in all clients. Sometimes it is their strength in the face of adversity, their hope that triumphs over experience, their willingness to trust me, their efforts to change and tolerate frustrations that seem overwhelming, their sense of humor, their personality, their enthusiasm or energy, and so on. I make efforts to enjoy and mirror these attributes when this process deepens the alliance. Sometimes the beginning of a relationship is not the time to focus on the client's defects. They can be cataloged for later, if needed.

I try to place the teen in the role of expert. This often involves the youth talking about his or her culture (music, prejudices, "gangsta" icons, dress preferences, NBA dreams, crushes, antiauthority and prodrug attitudes, perforations and tats, etc.). My stance involves being appreciative that they are sharing. Particularly for acting-out adolescents, who possess a sense of personal invulnerability that might be accompanied by ADHD and a not fully developed brain (Weinberger, Elvevag, & Giedd, 2005),[1] considering the consequences of their actions can be a challenge. I try to build on their values, egocentric orientation, and hedonism by emphasizing the rewards they might obtain by engaging in certain actions, and I repeatedly focus on the connection between their choices (behaviors) and the consequences they generate. I might ask, "Is there anything you could do that would convince them that you could handle more computer time [a cell phone, a later curfew, etc.]?" In chapters 9 and 10 of this text, I discuss Jordan's treatment, which is an example of my being quick to describe consequences in terms of improving sexual gratification and making money.

Adolescents can be acutely sensitive to criticism, so I avoid criticism, but if I must be critical, I try to sandwich the negative between compliments and hopeful statements. For instance, I told an adolescent who kept approaching girls by teasing them, "You're so funny. And girls love funny. But they don't want to be afraid of being put down. Do they say you're scaring them? Maybe they'd like you more if they knew you better and saw how much fun you are to be with." Because of adolescents' personal sensitivities, I might talk to them about others' problems and move from the distanciated to the personal rather than directly discuss their problems.

I might elicit problem-related themes with value-clarification questions such as the following: If your friend stole something from your teacher, what would you do? If he stole from you, what would you do? If a boyfriend wanted to have sex without protection, what would your friends think? What would being successful be like for a 25-year-old? Whom do you admire? Is Homer Simpson a good father? What is the ideal boyfriend or girlfriend like?

For some adolescents, dealing with the stigma of being in therapy can be an insurmountable obstacle to forming a therapeutic alliance. They may be at a stage when they feel that a minor problem such as a zit or bad hair day legitimizes staying home. They might believe that therapy is for crazy people and worry that if peers knew that they were in treatment, they would be seen as an "emo" or as "mental." Their discomfort could be compounded by being made to attend therapy by others who insist the adolescent has problems. As treatment progresses I try to normalize and depathologize the situation and emphasize my commitment to confidentiality. I might inquire about peers in therapy and how the adolescent and peer group deal with them, comment on how common it is for kids at their school to get counseling, and ask if and what the adolescent would want peers to know about his or her seeing a counselor. When stigma is a barrier, I try to help them answer the question peers might ask: "Where do you go every Tuesday morning?" I suggest that if they do tell others they can trust, then they might want to present counseling in a positive light so others will not smell shame and tease. I convey that therapy is for the bravest families.

When necessary I discuss who and what to tell others about therapy with the parent(s) and adolescent together. Many adolescents ask that parents do not tell other family members or relatives that they see a counselor, and parents usually agree. Sometimes they decide to tell people they can trust that "counseling is like having a referee for family discussions so we can listen to each other and solve family problems. It's interesting, and it helps us get along better." It is all right not to tell others, not because it is a shameful secret but because it is their private family business in the same way that a mother does not need to tell others how much money she has in her purse. It is just not their business. I frequently see the adolescent with other family members and focus on problems between family members, which dilute the feeling that the adolescent is the problem. I also try to schedule appointments after school. On the other hand, adolescents often enjoy therapy, and they bring their friends.

Particularly with adolescent clients, progress can become blocked by fixed beliefs. They may insist they intend to leave home, drop out of school, have a baby who will love them, return to their relationship with a loser, or beat up someone who is flirting with their boyfriend or girlfriend. These beliefs can be resistant to change through rational argument or attempts to derive insight from the exploration of the emotions and needs that generate or support them.

Sometimes a therapist can modify these precontemplation beliefs by accepting them and then trying to ground them in everyday reality by asking the adolescent to describe what it would be like to achieve his or her goal. For instance, "If you left home or school today, what would tomorrow be like? How would the morning, afternoon, evening, breakfast, lunch, and dinner be like? What would the next day and the following days be like?" As the dream becomes grounded in more realistic expectations and its effect on obtaining satisfaction in love, work, and social realms is explored, some clients become more realistic and move on to other concerns. For instance, Reyena, age 13, was headed toward having a baby who would love her. We spent parts of several sessions elaborating on her dream. She eventually began to question her belief and agreed to observe babies and talk to teen mothers at a nearby school. She even took a babysitting job from one of the mothers and was bored because "the baby slept the whole time." Also the mom did not return on time and would not pay her. She became aware of the frustrations and the patience, money, and emotional support needed to raise a child. I did not believe that I could challenge, try to engage her in a cost–benefit analysis, or explore the needs and emotions that spawned her belief, because these approaches would have been resisted and ruptured our alliance. I supported her exploration "to see what it would be like" so she could be a better mother.

Asking adolescents about peer opinions can identify significant motivators for their behavior. Adolescents are often obsessed with conforming to peer opinions and highly sensitive to what peers will think about them. A belief that motivated Reyena to want a child was that peers would admire her maturity and give her attention if she were pregnant. Reyena was surprised that almost all the teen mothers she spoke to reported being rejected by their former friends, having to leave them to go to a different school, and not being able to party because of the baby. As one teen mom told her, "When the baby comes first, you don't come at all." Teens listen to teens.

The adolescent's engagement in therapy should not be based on colluding with the parents or adolescent against the other family members.

"Having the cooperation of parents, either as active participants or in supporting roles, may be a key feature to engaging adolescents in psychotherapy" (Oetzel & Scherer, 2003, p. 218). Treatment functions best when all family members feel their values, opinions, and sensitivities have been respected, and all stakeholders contribute to solutions and progress.

Ending Therapy

Because termination is so well understood and anticipated, it ideally flows seamlessly out of treatment after goals have been met. Client and therapist mutually agree to end, and they devote part of at least the last few sessions to reviewing why the client initially entered therapy, how he or she changed, and what would bring him or her back to treatment. The client and therapist use this time to consolidate gains, clarify medication and aftercare resources, and share their feelings about treatment, its ending, and their mutual appreciation of each other. The client leaves feeling validated about the decision to end treatment and function independently. Clients with a limited number of sessions are prepared for termination from the start of treatment. In subsequent sessions they are asked what they would like to accomplish before ending, and each session contains a countdown of how many sessions remain. Especially for therapy with youths, an ending ceremony, activity (such as making and exchanging cards), or a "graduation" party takes place.

However, ending can be so anxiety provoking for the client and therapist that most or part of this process is avoided. It may be quite common for therapists to avoid talking about termination and properly preparing their clients (Kramer, 1986). It is understandable that so many clients drop out just before termination. Termination might involve talking about such uncomfortable feelings as guilt for not accomplishing more in treatment (Weddington & Cavenar, 1979). Clients and therapists might feel some disappointment about themselves and each other, stripped of the hope that further therapy will provide the opportunity to correct these defects. Accepting that "this is it" is very difficult. Clients can no longer rely on the therapist (except for the parts of the therapist that have been internalized by the client), and the therapist can no longer help his or her client. Thankfully, there is no rule that clients cannot keep changing after treatment stops. Ending can be colored by or evoke past painful losses that may need to be processed, and clients may feel rejected and abandoned. Clients frequently feel emotional pain from the loss of the relationship with the therapist (Roe, Dekel, Harel, Fenning, & Fenning, 2006).[2] Even positive feelings of appreciation, admiration, and caring can be frightening to share. Because these feelings are so emotionally threatening, it is not surprising that clients and therapists dodge parts of the termination process.

Who Are the Clients?

Trauma treatment is a huge part of therapy today (Gold, 2004). In my caseload the most frequent referrals are (a) girls who have been sexually abused and are depressed, anxious, and feel damaged and at fault and who, especially as adolescents, try to find love in all the wrong places; (b) young boys with ADHD and behavior problems; (c) children of domestic violence and/or substance abusing parents who have led and continue to live chaotic lives, and sometimes are being raised by nonbiological parents; (d) older teens who have avoided academics and acted out but are now thinking about emancipation and are motivated to make changes; and (e) vulnerable youths who have been continuously involved in the mental health system because of chronic conditions.

It is typical for clients to have experienced multiple traumas and losses. In some communities 90% of inner-city young adults ages 18 to 45 may meet the definition of trauma victims found in the *DSM-IV* (Breslau et al., 1998). Ninety-four percent of a sample of clients of a community mental health center reported at least one traumatic event in their past, and 42% had PTSD in the past year (Switzer et al., 1999). In another similar sample, 59% of female clients and 24% of male clients reported being sexually abused, and 42% of women and 17% of men said they had been raped (Hutchings & Dutton, 1993).

Sexually abused youths have become a major part of the treatment population because of mandated reporting and the public's sympathy for this population. They are difficult to treat for a variety of reasons. First, they are prone to feel stigmatized and shameful about what happened to them. They often blame themselves for the abuse and sometimes for the subsequent trauma to the abuser and the family. Therefore they are resistant to talk about the abuse, even though the best treatment probably involves talking about it, correcting misconceptions, desensitizing to the trauma, and being met with a supportive, nonblaming, protective, loving response. In addition, being able to talk about being abused is an important part of self-protection, because molest can survive only in secrecy. Sometimes the parent(s) can provide reassurance and encouragement to the child or adolescent to counter his or her reluctance to discuss the molest in therapy. I usually deal with clients who cannot or will not discuss their traumas by focusing treatment on the sequelae of the abuse (shame and self-blame, stigmatization, betrayal and loss, body integrity concerns, powerlessness, revictimization, predatory behaviors, traumatic sexualization, anger, depression, acting out, and dissociation) (Beverly, 1989; Finkelhor, 1986).

I particularly value working conjointly with the youth and parent. Often a significant contributor to the youth's problem is that the parents did not react therapeutically from the time when the sexual events were disclosed. Sometimes the parents also experienced abuse, and they need to deal with their trauma to be fully helpful to their child. A major focus of treatment involves ensuring safety for the child so he or she can feel protected from further abuse. Teaching the child or having the parent teach the child self-protection skills is a basic intervention, especially for very young children. The strategies that have been developed generally contain the three Rs: recognize, resist, and report. For children as young as age 3, there are videos that present characters such as Pooh, who repeatedly sings, "Say no, run away, and find somebody to tell." Parents and children may leave sessions chanting this refrain, and my colleagues may wonder why clients in my office scream, "No, don't touch me! I'm telling!"

Teaching the parents to provide supervision and consequences for sexualized behaviors is needed when there is the potential that abused clients will be sexual with others. These families need a clear safety plan that protects everyone from exploitation and encourages and rewards telling the caretaker(s) if sexualized behaviors are displayed. Grooming and sexual behaviors require securing secrecy, which the perpetrator may try to ensure through threats and bribes. A major deterrent involves eliminating secrecy and opportunity. The safety plan might describe rules, such as no bathing together, no playing behind closed doors or in forts, and so on. Discovering that they are not the only ones who have been abused and that abuse is so ubiquitous is often a surprise to the family, which reduces everyone's isolation. Older boys are prone to protect themselves from feeling victimized by acting powerful and in control through assuming the role of the abuser, whereas girls are prone to revictimization. Teaching skills, such as assertiveness, social skills, and anger management, while correcting misconceptions, providing successes and approval, and building areas of competency and self-esteem may inoculate clients against these outcomes.

As discussed earlier, sex education is a vital component of treatment for many youths. Adolescence is normally a time of obsessing about body image concerns, but having been molested compounds adolescents' worries. Nonmolested boys worry that things are too small, whereas girls worry that things are too big or too small or not curly or straight. Boys normally talk about getting sex and worry about being rejected, whereas girls present themselves as interested in relationships. (Only recently in some subgroups do girls have societal permission to talk about seeking and enjoying sexual acts.) Molested youth are different. The girls often avoid sex or are sexually active in the service of pleasing others by trading sex for affection and attention. They usually find that sex is not enjoyable, and they may not have the skills to enjoy sex. They may talk freely about sex and not have the typical anxiety that nonmolested girls display. Instead they can be anxious about being emotionally intimate. I have a list of behaviors involved in relationships that runs from making eye contact, smiling, talking about common interests, holding hands to having intercourse. I have been surprised that when I ask molested, sexually active adolescent girls to place the items in chronological order according to how these behaviors should happen in a relationship, they put them in an almost opposite order than nonmolested youth. They start with having sex and end with or skip the more typical behaviors, such as going out for pizza. It is not unusual for male victims to worry about their sexual orientation and prefer to die rather than talk about it.

Males with ADHD and behavior problems are another frequent referral. Clients with ADHD and behavior problems generally are not good candidates for individual therapy. They typically lack the ability to use techniques learned in sessions to control emotions and behavior in other settings. Their treatment primarily requires working with the caretakers. When I work directly with these youths, it is usually in family or conjoint sessions, unless the parents are unwilling or unable to participate. When ADHD occurs with behavior disorders, it is not unusual to find a similar pattern in the parents and to find that youth and parent collude to project blame and responsibility for the youth's problems, thus reinforcing the youth's belief that the problems are caused by others and he or she is the victim. Such parents can find it difficult to confront their youth's contribution to his or her problems and then consistently give consequences. I once led a group to teach behavior modification to parents of ADHD clients and did not offer enough structure. Most of the parents had ADHD; I had trouble getting a word in, and it rapidly disintegrated into the parents supporting each other's attacks against the school system. The group could not move on to learning parenting techniques.

The use of stimulant medication with ADHD youths is widespread and effective. Close to 5% of 6- to 12-year-olds took stimulant medication in 2002 (Zuvekas, Vitiello, & Norquist, 2006). Because most were boys, probably 7% to 8% of boys in this age group receive such medication. Resistance to trying medication and to ongoing medication compliance are often a focus of our sessions. Parents resist medication because of a variety of reasons. They may have used drugs and fear that stimulant medications are gateway drugs. They may have experienced previous problems with the medication, such as sleeping, eating, or rebound effects, or they may have heard that the medication can stifle growth. Recent research indicates that long-term use of stimulant medication does not suppress growth (Pliszka, Matthews, Braslow, & Watson, 2006; Spenser et al., 2006). Parents may incorrectly believe they can handle ADHD with dietary restrictions of sugar or food additives. These hopes usually melt away with education about the effectiveness of the standard treatment. The debate about the usefulness of eliminating food additives and colorings has been revived since McCann et al. (2007) found that in some clients hyperactivity might be increased by exposure to addictives and colorings. Most reluctant parents are willing to try the medication when they trust me, realize they can stop using it at any time, and discover that the effectiveness of the medication usually becomes apparent immediately, unlike some medications that take months to build up to effective blood levels.

With youths who have ADHD and/or behavior problems, the major work involves teaching the parents routines and contingency management and supporting their advocating for services for the youth at school. It may be very threatening for such parents to enter a school and talk to authorities because they may have had a troubled history with educators. It also is frustrating for the parents to turn to the school with the expectation that school will facilitate access to resources, only to discover that the gatekeepers are under pressure to deny services because of fiscal considerations. Possibly 25% of students may need special resources, but the school system is not funded to meet this demand. I frequently prepare and accompany these parents to school meetings. Under the Individuals with Disabilities Education Act (Section 504), youths with ADHD qualify for assessments, an individualized instruction plan, and services necessary for them to learn. Just as students who are hearing, speech, or language impaired; learning disabled; brain injured; or intellectually, emotionally, orthopedically, and visually impaired whose disability causes a severe discrepancy between achievement and potential are entitled to adapted curricula, so are students with ADHD. Parents need to request an assessment in writing. The school must, within 60 days, provide an individualized educational program consisting of an assessment and plan describing services that might be needed. These services could include psychotherapy, residential treatment (which can require that the child become a ward of the juvenile court), transportation, medical services, physical and occupational therapy, and other services necessary to counteract what is impeding the student from benefiting from educational services. In California alone there are approximately 680,000 students enrolled in special education (Griffen, 2007).

When the caretakers are unable to provide a significant part of the treatment, the prognosis for behavior problems is limited. Behavior-disordered youth are typically not motivated to change, because they see their problems as caused by others. Thus much of what they say reflects their defenses. Clinicians cannot expect a great deal of "truthiness" from behavior-disordered clients. Their reports of their physical, verbal, initiated, and retaliatory aggression and their malicious and disruptive behaviors seem unrelated to teacher's, peer's, and observer's reports (Henry & Metropolitan Area Child Study Research Group, 2006). For example, Randy had ADHD and behavior problems. He was raised by his diabetic grandmother in a gang-infested neighborhood because his father was murdered and his mother was incarcerated due to drugs. He had multiple disasters and limitations to overcome. His problems compounded and contributed to his missing the academic and socialization experiences, parental soothing, and family routines required to develop the strengths and the coping skills needed to form an identity based on self-esteem. He presented with a carefully maintained impersonation of an adolescent, composed of media, peer, and parental images that he incorporated in an effort to reduce emotional pain. He acted like a gangsta rapper. One day he came into the office wearing gold front teeth like his idol. He had begged for these teeth for more than 6 months, and they cost his grandmother 1 month's income. They were stolen the next week, but nothing bothered him. He denied problems at school, with peers, and at home, and his caretaker lacked the ability to provide supervision or consistent consequences. He even reported being successful at football after school, but in reality he never went to the program. Instead he sought the attention of older boys whom he tried to impress with his daring. It took years to force the school to provide services that were too little and too late when they were offered. He refused to talk about the past, was noncompliant with his stimulant medication, and rejected community activities, even though he was a gifted athlete.

Adolescents seek peer approval and experiences of competency to build their self-esteem. Behavior-disordered youth generally seek excitement and immediate gratification and have difficulty tolerating the pressures of more structured activities, so they seek gratification and social approval through activities that do not require skills, such as doing drugs or daring deeds. Randy resisted supervision and supervised activities, especially in the time between school and dinner (the peak time for having sex, doing drugs, stealing, and fighting). Treatment finally had to focus on trying to convince his grandmother that residential treatment was necessary. She refused until the court stepped in and ordered placement because of his fighting and shoplifting.

Although the amphetamines perscribed for ADHD are not among the most frequently misused prescribed drugs, adolescents and their parents need to be monitored for the sale and/or use of prescriptive medication for recreational purposes. A recent survey of 1,086 teens in an ethnically diverse Michigan school district found that almost half the students reported that they had been prescribed an opiate, stimulant, sedative, or antianxiety medication at some time, and more than a third recently received a prescription. "Up to 60% of all students receiving legitimate prescriptions had been approached to divert their medications. About 1 in 10 traded the medication for others. A smaller proportion sold it, and as many as 25%, depending on the drug, said they gave it or 'lent' it to a friend or family member" (Miller, 2007, p. 8). Twelve percent of the respondents in one study reported that they had engaged in nonmedical use of opioid pain medications in the past year (Boyd, McCabe, Cranford, & Young, 2006), and another survey (National Institute on Drug Abuse, 2007) estimated a 15.4% rate of student-reported nonmedical use of a variety of prescription drugs in 12th graders during the past year. There is a thriving secondary street market for prescribed medication. Adolescents and parents who have a substance abuse history may misuse medication.

Much of my caseload consists of youths who have parents who are not, or for an extended period were not, involved in raising their children because of substance use or domestic violence. Single parents or relatives may raise these youths and need a great deal of support through child guidance counseling and referrals to community services. In 2002 in my county, 25% of households were headed by women.[3] The 2000 census indicated that 2.5 million youths lived in households in which their grandparents were their primary providers.[4] There are almost 300,000 such families in California (U.S. Bureau of the Census, 2002), and most of them are in my caseload. For example, Paul came from domestic violence and hated his father for beating his mother, but he treated her in a similar fashion. His mother could not set limits and tried to appease Paul so he would not get angry. Her behavior changed, not to protect herself but when she realized she was reinforcing him to grow up to be an abuser. Paul became motivated to work on controlling his anger because he was ambivalent about hurting his mother and did not want to be like his father.

I have treated emancipating youths who have been resistant to treatment in the past, acted out, and accumulated deficits and habits that make progress a challenge. Some are self-referred and seeking help because they are facing the realization that soon they will have to support themselves. Emancipation can be anxiety producing for the healthiest youths. It is a time when they run into the military, get married, or go to college to handle the anxiety. It is a time when they are re-forming an identity and making choices that have long-term impacts. Some are foster youths whose family and financial support can abruptly stop at age 18. Only recently have new programs surfaced to help fill the void, because people are more aware that these youths are prone to homelessness, addiction, and further abuse. They need a lot of support and referrals to agencies that provide case-management and peer-group support services. Sometimes these youths are former clients, and they enjoy showing me how much they have matured. Sometimes I have been the most constant adult in their life.

A number of clients have chronic or resistant conditions such as Asperger's syndrome, OCD, schizophrenia, bipolar disorders, depression, anxiety, or personality disorders, which are conditions that can be compounded by low intelligence, learning disabilities, and/or other comorbid diagnoses. They often require additional therapies, such as medication, special education, and peer group therapy. Their problems continue, and they require ongoing services. The parents often benefit from education about the disorder, support groups, and help to weather the stresses of caring for a youth with chronic disabilities. These stresses can destroy or strengthen a marriage, so treatment often includes helping the parents support each other. Siblings of these youth can often be resentful of being ignored, and they may require increased parental attention.

Most cases are fairly easy to understand. The patterns are robust and multigenerational. For instance, it is easy to see how a grandmother's alcoholism and unavailability led a mother to be overprotective and smothering so the youth presents with rebellion at the mother's attempts to be close and different from her mother. It seems evident that the adolescent's learning disabilities led to academic failure and low self-esteem, and now, with the onset of puberty and the favorable attention from boys, she has a one-track mind and has totally given up academics. It is unfortunate that understanding is a small part of the process; knowing how to intervene is much more difficult.

CHAPTER 7

Engage Clients by Helping Them Seek Greater Happiness

Teach Values in Therapy That Are Compatible With the Client's Beliefs

I do not want treatment to end prematurely because of a clash of different morals, politics, or values. I try to present myself as having values that will not offend the client and disrupt the therapeutic alliance. Because clients are motivated to be happier, I often work with them to identify behaviors and beliefs that foster the pursuit of personal happiness and promote the well-being of those they care about.

A Frequent Theme in Treatment Involves Seeking a Happier Life

There have traditionally been two approaches to obtaining happiness: one based on obtaining pleasure and avoiding pain and one based on obtaining meaning in life (Ryan & Deci, 2001). These two aspects of happiness involve different processes. Hedonic happiness is derived from accumulating pleasurable experiences and having the ability to savor them by learning to relax and feel content with what one has obtained. In eudemonic happiness, the more effort expended and the greater the challenges that are overcome in achieving self-realization, a sense of meaning and purpose, and accomplishing one's goals, the greater the happiness. The higher the mountain climbed, the greater the reward at the top. Both types can involve tunnel vision that leads to losing track of time and forgetting one's problems.

It has been argued that the search for happiness dominates our cognitions and motivates our behaviors. Aristotle concluded, "While happiness itself is sought for its own sake, every other goal—health, beauty, money, or power—is valued only because we expect that it will make us happy" (Csikszentmihalyi, 1990, p. 1). The pursuit of personal happiness, which Freud called the Pleasure Principle, and the Declaration of Independence, described as a basic right, may be an innate drive. The great minds of each generation have explored ways to maximize happiness. There seem to be three main paths to happiness: work, love, and play. Happiness can to be experienced as a by-product of progressing toward goals in work, experiencing rewarding relationships, and engaging in play. These paths provide opportunities to experience pleasure through mastery and realizing ones potential, merging with others, contributing to feeling part of something greater than the individual self, feeling selfless and absorbed in a process, and feeling freer of worries and constraints. Therefore, often I support obtaining an appropriate academic placement and vocational training, teach the skills needed to improve family, peer and community involvement, and encourage clients to identify and nurture their passions.

Work includes going to school, parenting, managing a household, volunteering, and being employed.[1] Work provides the opportunity to problem solve, find meaning, perhaps contribute something to others, overcome obstacles, and establish and meet goals. Work provides the possibility of accomplishment, competence, intellectual stimulation, understanding, and money, which has the potential to provide food, clothing, shelter, health care, education, recreation, leisure, opportunities, and the purchase of assistance. The relationship between money and happiness is strong at the bottom and minimal at the top of Maslow's hierarchy of needs. Once the basic needs have been taken care of, money does not seem to help people gratify the higher needs. "A larger income contributes almost nothing to happiness," because the happiness of the economically advantaged is related more to friendships, family relationships (Lane, 2000), and enjoyment of work.

Love is a feeling about others expressed primarily in family and social relationships. Clients often have problems because their family relationships have been and are ungratifying. Some have never experienced a healthy, caring relationship. For clients capable of benefiting from cognitively understanding their situation, therapy often can include identifying and correcting pathological interpersonal expectations and misconceptions about themselves that underlie unrewarding relationships. For youths treatment can emphasize helping them experience more loving relationships in which they experience successes and approval, and facilitating the acquisition of the skills needed to allow and maintain such relationships. The therapeutic relationship may provide an experience of being cared for and a template to follow in future relationships.

To be gratifying, social relationships need to be balanced in loving and being loved. Clients often need to learn how to become more giving or more able to receive. A common dysfunctional belief that motivates anxious, other-directed, overly giving clients is that the more they give and sacrifice, the safer and more loveable a parent, partner, or child they will be. On the other extreme some clients try to obtain happiness at the expense of others. These self-centered, overly demanding clients may have problems because they lack empathy, and their misguided attempts to gratify themselves result in exploiting others, who then reject or harm them.

Social relationships are best when both parties have the skills to be honest, nonviolent, communicative, empathetic, and caring of themselves and others and can resolve disagreements in ways that fairly share burdens and frustrations. To enjoy relationships, clients may need to learn to identify and express their needs, goals, worries, and frustrations and select people who can care about themselves and want to help the clients meet their needs and goals. Some clients need to learn to end relationships that are destructive.

Some relationships involve sex, and therapy may need to focus on developing the skills to navigate sex and intimacy. I try to help clients understand that they are not ready to have sex until they can be assertive enough to protect themselves and their partner from harm, disease, unwanted acts, and pregnancy, and until they have a secure enough relationship so they can safely communicate their concerns and know they will be respected.

Play involves recreation, having mindfulness (the ability to experience the present without escaping when it is painful or trying to sustain the experience when it is pleasurable), following passions, and finding joy. This can be accomplished through having hobbies, playing sports, helping others, appreciating the arts and nature, learning, creating, seeing patterns, reading, playing games, exploring, appreciating humor and entertainment, and so on. Play involves being absorbed in a process rather than being focused on an outcome, as in work. Adults can learn to play from children. Walking with a 2-year-old takes forever. Each step involves a discovery. Adults are constantly generating expectations, whereas children are in the moment. For example, if you are baking a cake and an egg breaks on the counter, an adult might think, "Oh, no, I have to clean it up. That yolk could fall on the floor and spread to the carpet. Dried yolk is impossible to clean up. It's what hardens and makes frescos last for hundreds of years." A young child could become fascinated with the color and feel of the yolk and touch, press, push, and pop it without thinking about all the possible things that could go wrong. Play involves allowing ourselves to fully experience the present without concern for consequences time limitations. It's like dancing as if no one were watching. Opportunities for play can be found at almost any time.

Maslow's writing on peak experiences incorporated the view that happiness is derived from love, work, and play when he concluded that peak experiences come from love and sex, from aesthetic moments, from bursts of creativity, from moments of insight and discovery, and from fusion with nature.

Helping clients develop their previously neglected roads to happiness and their unique balance of work, play, and relationships is often needed to resolve their problems. Getting business done before playing can be a useful value for clients who have not developed their work abilities, whereas scheduling time for love and play is useful for workaholics. As Langston Hughes said, "Do what you have to do so you can do what you want to do."

A questionnaire that might be helpful in monitoring a client's progress in becoming happier is available at http://www.sfbacct.com. The Functioning and Satisfaction Inventory (Davidson, Martinez, & Thomas, 2006) asks clients to rate their functioning and satisfaction and the importance to them of eight life domains (work or school, love relationships, relationships with relatives, friendships, recreation, health, standard of living, and home life). The responses to the functioning and satisfaction scales correlate so highly that clients may not be distinguishing between them (Persons, 2007).

Happiness is related to realistic expectations (Diener & Fujita, 1995) and may exist more in the process of moving toward goals rather than in actually attaining them.[2] It also is related to how and to whom we compare ourselves. H. L. Mencken noted, "A wealthy man earns 100 dollars more than his wife's sister's husband." He was calling attention to happiness being dependent on a person's frame of reference, and there is evidence that happy subjects primarily compare themselves to unhappy people (Lyubomirsky & Ross, 1997). Unhappy clients often compare themselves to unrealistic ideals (often from the media and from other images that were incorporated during childhood that contribute to the persons' ego-ideal) rather than to more typical people and reality-based images. They rarely compare themselves to how they were doing previously, so they do not appreciate their improvements. Challenging destructive comparisons and teaching and modeling self and realistic comparisons can help clients to be happier. As my Boston University professor Dr. Verhage's equation explains, Happiness equals Reality over Expectations ($H = R/E$). Although powerful, this equation is an oversimplification, because we cannot just lower our expectations and be happy. In fact, unhappy people seem to already have low expectations for success (Emmons, 1986). Happiness is more readily achieved when goals are valued and realistic (Csikszentmihalyi & Csikszentmihalyi, 1988).

Another equation has been used to describe happiness: H = S + C + V. Seligman (2002a) contended that enduring happiness, not momentary gratification, is derived from the sum of three factors.

S is the set range that biology and inheritance has prescribed (Tellegen et al., 1988).[3] People are born with different capacities for happiness (Lykken & Tellegen, 1996). From studies of twins it appears that about 50% of the variation in a person's present state of happiness is genetically determined, and about 80% of the variation in long-term happiness is genetically determined rather than environmentally caused. This finding led Diener, Suh, Lucas, and Smith (1999, p. 279) to conclude, "It is as hard to change one's happiness as it is to change one's height." Lyubomirsky, Sheldon, and Schkade (2005) identified two other sources of pessimism for changing a client's level of happiness, in addition to the genetically determined set range. They sited the long-term stability across the life span of the "big five" personality traits that are related to happiness, especially neuroticism and extraversion. They found that people habituated to changes in happiness and returned to their usual state, as shown by Brickman, Coates, and Janoff-Bulman (1978), who found that over time, on average, lottery winners were not happier than controls and that paraplegics adjusted to their paralysis and were not as unhappy as one would expect.

However, change in happiness is possible. People do not just return to their set point or adapt to momentary changes. In a longitudinal study of the lasting effects of positive and negative life events (marriage and widowhood) on self-reported happiness, Lucas, Clark, Georgellis, and Diener (2003) found, "Although adaption does often occur, it can be slow and partial, and there are many people who show no evidence of adaption. ... Thus, habituation does not appear to be an inevitable force that wipes out the effects of all life circumstances" (p. 536).

C is the individual's circumstances. Some examples could be a person's health, involvement in a romance, or community, country, or religious affiliation.

V stands for the variables under the person's control. Thinking styles are examples, such as not dwelling on the past; forgiving and forgetting; having faith, hope, or trust; not overgeneralizing failures and problems (e.g., seeing failures as specific and limited); and disputing pessimistic thoughts. "Circumstances" and "variables under the person's control" include the clients' spiritual and community involvement. When appropriate, a focus of treatment might encourage clients to derive meaning, understanding, and comfort from spiritual and philosophical beliefs while supporting involvement in the community to which these beliefs allow admission.

Happiness involves a complex interaction between biology (endorphins, medication, hormones, and neurotransmitters), genetics (introversion-extroversion, excitement-seeking, neuroticism, energy, optimism–pessimism, and temperament), learning (the patterns we develop to process experiences, and how experiences become associated with pleasurable and traumatic memories), and the environment (opportunities, emotional support). There are many approaches to helping clients seek happier lives. I look for opportunities to encourage a client to notice and appreciate the positive in his or her life. Happy people often anticipate and attend to the positive aspects of their experiences and have the ability to savor them, whereas unhappy people attend to disappointments and rarely appreciate or savor the positive. I look for opportunities to teach clients to notice and savor the pleasant while they identify and disrupt interfering cognitions, such as their tendency to judge, obsess, worry, or think about how to get more. For example, teaching a bingeing eater to mindfully attend to the taste and texture of the food she was scarfing down was one strategy, among others, that she was able to use to gain control of her overeating. She had been so focused on what she would eat next that she did not notice or taste the food she was consuming.

Sometimes I try to affect happiness by focusing on the client's locus of control. Happy people often attribute failures to external causes and successes to internal factors. For example, Jerome, a surprisingly happy 8-year-old, demonstrated this when we played pool, as he congratulated himself for his good shots and excused his errors by blaming them on the cue, ball, and table.

Another approach to promoting happiness emphasizes cultivating certain virtues or character styles (Peterson & Seligman, 2004). Martin Seligman (2002a), similar to the Greek philosophers who believed that you have to be good before you can feel good, suggested that we foster happiness through the cultivation of certain personality traits. These virtues or strengths include creativity, curiosity, open-mindedness, love of learning, honesty, rationality, bravery, persistence, integrity, vitality, love, kindness, social intelligence, citizenship, fairness, leadership, forgiveness, humility, prudence, self-control, appreciation of beauty, gratitude, hope, humor, purpose, future mindedness, and the ability to put problems into perspective. Seligman's positive psychology has spawned several therapeutic approaches, including strength-centered therapy, which emphasizes identifying and naming character strengths and virtues that the client possesses or admires in others and then cultivating their use rather than "simply solving problems or engaging in more positive thoughts or actions" (Wong, 2006, p. 135).

In his recent address to the American Psychological Association's 114th annual convention as recipient of the Distinguished Scientific Contributions Award, Seligman summarized some of the research on the effectiveness of positive psychotherapy techniques (Seligman, Rashid, & Parks, 2006). Preliminary investigations have identified two exercises that contributed to a lasting increase in happiness and decrease in depressive symptoms (Seligman, Steen, Park, & Peterson, 2005). One technique asked clients, for 1 week at the end of the day, to write three things that went well during that day and identify their causes instead of focusing on negative thoughts. The second exercise involved identifying and then using "signature strengths" in a new way. The researchers asked participants to find their top five character strengths by taking an online inventory at http://www.authentichappiness. org and then to use one of these strengths in a new way every day for 1 week. Clients have benefited from doing these exercises online or when working with a therapist. Weekly listing one's blessings has been associated with a more positive appraisal of life, fewer reported physical symptoms, and more time exercising. Daily attention to blessings was also associated with more positive affect and with such prosocial behavior as helping others (Emmons & McCullough, 2003). Sonja Lyubomirsky (2008) has compiled research-based happiness-generating activities that can be incorporated into treatment plans. These findings and the zeitgeist of positive psychology should not lead therapists to indiscriminately encourage clients to focus on the positive in their life, because when this task is difficult for a client, it can result in more feelings of failure. For example when sixth-grade students were asked to recall their successes, high self-esteem students reported improved self-esteem, whereas low self-esteem students actually showed a decrease in self-esteem (Rosenfeld, 1976). It is clear that interventions need to be tailored to the individual and their impact carefully assessed. One size does not fit all, because without preparation, well-intentioned interventions may fuel the family and client systems to continue to go in the direction they have already been going.

We May Not Be Able to Avoid Teaching Values

Psychotherapy has traditionally encouraged therapists to adopt a value-neutral stance; however, postmodern thinking has challenged the belief that facts and theories can be value or culture free. Even if our goal is to be value neutral, therapists cannot always evade taking a moral stance that challenges other value systems. Even when we try to help and understand instead of punish or when we avoid judging or shaming, we are promoting values that are now being challenged by popular media morality therapists such as Dr. Laura and Dr. James Dodson.[4] When we support secular or scientific beliefs, value getting an education, and teach people to question sex-role stereotypes, fear-based discipline, or the belief that a wife, employee, or child should always obey authority, we are offering values embedded in a moral system that could clash with the client's values and beliefs. This led Paul Meehl (1959) to suggest that therapists may be missionaries.

Question: So what values and beliefs might therapists teach? Answer: Values and beliefs that help to resolve the client's problems. Beliefs that lead to changing pain-producing patterns and facilitating productive patterns. Values that protect and do not disrupt the therapeutic relationship. Values and beliefs that are only a little different from what the client and his or her community believe. Values that avoid the religious and political "minefield" that can damage the therapeutic relationship if the therapist and client are not in harmony over beliefs that are central to the client's identity.

In the past therapists believed that client improvement was related to clients adopting their therapist's values. However, research indicates that when clients adopt the personal beliefs and preferences of their therapists, the therapist interprets this convergence in values as improvement, but client reports of symptom amelioration do not necessarily indicate a more positive outcome (Kelly, 1990). There are indications that when clients and therapists have moderately similar values, greater improvement results, and clients' religious values tend to be the most resistant to change (Kelly & Strupp, 1992). There are a number of values and beliefs that I find myself sharing with clients in the hope that if clients incorporate them into their lives, then they will be more successful. However, sharing therapist values and beliefs may be helpful mostly to the extent that they help clients cope with difficulties and do not harm the therapeutic relationship. These statements come up frequently in my sessions:

- Thinking about the costs and benefits before acting can be useful.
- The content of the media that the young and vulnerable are exposed to should be monitored and limited. Typical 8- to 13-year-olds are exposed to 6 hours of media a day (Steyer, 2002). Watching television can be addictive, fattening, teach consumerism and create a fearful and sexualized view of the world. Also, it can create a distorted orientation toward conflict resolution, body image, race, and sex roles. It might make some feel bored when faced with slower, less stimulating fare and make others feel dissatisfied with their body. It creates anxieties, and it promises that buying a product can alleviate them. It can also stimulate and desensitize viewers to violence. There are a few good shows for children to watch. The media should be used as a babysitter only on a limited basis and after other resources have been explored. Exposure to violent video games and probably to violence-praising music can cause increased aggressive behavior, cognitions, and affect while decreasing empathy (Anderson, 2004). No wonder the military uses violent video games to train soldiers.

- People should be nonviolent except as a last resort to protect themselves and others.
- Caring for yourself involves eating healthy food, exercising, and balancing caring for yourself with caring for others. As you value yourself you develop the assertiveness to protect yourself and judge others more realistically. When you become aware of your needs, you can eat when you are hungry, rest when you are tired, appreciate others when they meet your needs, and associate with others who help you progress toward your goals.
- As Art Buchwald said, "The best things in life aren't things."
- It is more effective to argue by trying to come up with the most persuasive reasons rather than by trying to win by name calling and intimidation.
- You can love someone, but that does not mean you can get along with him or her.
- Life is not always fair.
- Share, play fair, don't hit, clean up your own mess, and don't run with scissors (Robert Fulghum).
- Your thoughts and feelings need not be judged. You are not responsible for them. They appear in the same way that pictures appear on television; you observe them and are not responsible for what appears. You are responsible for your choices, behavior, and what you say.
- As Thomas Gordon (2000) described, anger is usually a secondary feeling. First we may feel threatened, judged, rejected, ignored, frustrated, or another unpleasant feeling. Then we feel anger that protects us from the first vulnerable, uncomfortable feeling and usually blocks us from constructively dealing with the situation.
- Having passions is usually a good thing, and they should be cultivated.
- The only way to avoid mistakes is to not try anything new. The trick is to learn from mistakes and not repeat the same ones over again.
- Whether people like you or reject you may have more to do with them than with you.
- Feelings do not continue to grow in intensity. If we allow ourselves to experience them, we see that they are like waves. They increase, plateau, and then fade.
- It is important for parents to mirror, soothe, enjoy, and play with their children.
- Discipline is not synonymous with punishment; it requires teaching, modeling, and supporting healthy development.

- There may be a lesson to learn or an opportunity in every crisis.
- You can accept what happened and how it affected you, but you may choose not to forgive the person who hurt you until he or she has earned it with confession, repentance, and restitution.
- Don't automatically believe your assumptions about another person's behavior or intentions.
- "Something to do, something to love and something to hope for" are essential for happiness. (Allan K. Chalmers)

Therapists need to respect and, if possible, accept client values and beliefs, except when their beliefs and values contribute to presenting problems. Some clients hold beliefs that undermine progress, such as male domination, harsh physical punishment, or laissez-faire parenting. For instance, clients may narcissistically believe their needs are more important than others' or repeatedly subordinate their needs to others'. Clients may have overly strict or lax moral beliefs that obstruct change, such as the parent who insisted that masturbation was a sin and repeatedly shamed his son to teach him to stop, or the wife who instantly wanted to divorce her husband of 17 years because "he committed adultery," or the tormented gay adolescent who believed that he was evil and damned. Parents may overly or inadequately value academic achievement, cleanliness, orderliness, routines, obedience, and so on and create problems for the family. These clients can be expected to initially seek the therapist's support for their values and be threatened when they do not receive confirmation.

When clients' values block progress, an initial approach might involve trying to understand the values, identifying conflicting values, and exploring the antecedents and consequences of the beliefs. If this process does not result in modifying the client's beliefs, then it may be necessary to sensitively challenge these values by offering alternative values, preferably elicited from others or from more questioning parts of the client. When religious values (which are particularly resistant to change) may need to be challenged, the therapist might facilitate the client consulting a moderate religious leader in their faith. Many therapists now adopt this middle-of-the-road approach between therapist neutrality, where client values are accepted and therapist values are hidden, and self-disclosure, where the therapist enthusiastically parades his or her personal values before the client (Williams & Levitt, 2007). In summary, therapists need to approach altering client values with caution, for the purpose of supporting treatment goals, and with care to not jeopardize the therapeutic alliance.

CHAPTER 8

Has Being a Therapist Been a Good Career Choice?

Isn't It Depressing Being a Therapist?

I have had to do difficult and painful things as a therapist. I have told parents their child is retarded or schizophrenic and watched them sob. Then I had to help decide if, how, and what we should tell the child. I have had to say good-bye to so many people whom I came to care about. I have had to make life-changing decisions about removing children from their parents, hospitalizing, and reporting abuse and neglect. I have listened to repeated, inescapable horrors that made me hate humans. I remember the three sessions where an immigrant father told for the first time the story of his 7-year journey from Vietnam to America. He almost drowned, was repeatedly robbed and attacked by pirates, frequently faced death by starvation, was arrested and sent to prison camps, experienced periods of total hopelessness, and watched family members brutally murdered. As he told this story to me and his 14-year-old son, who looked like he just stepped out of the pages of GQ magazine, we felt his pain and strengths and understood his unrealistically high expectations and controlling parenting. I remember the 34-year-old mother of four children ages 4, 5, 11, and 12, who told them she loved them but could not take care of them. She stood and left. I froze in disbelief. The youngest two crawled under separate tables and cried. The oldest just sat as if the air had been let out of him, and the other ran. I had to decide what to do next. I watched a 22-year-old die of kidney failure. His body had rejected two kidneys, and he refused to give up doing drugs, so he could not qualify for another transplant.

So much is written about secondary trauma and burnout that obviously therapy can be a strain. Trying to help clients change can be frustrating. Listening to the horrors people are exposed to and their pain is a taxing routine. However, I find it equally inspirational seeing the courage and strengths people have. Yes, I feel their pain, but I am very busy thinking about doing therapy. I focus on thinking of solutions, trying to identify solvable problems, tuning into process, watching and questioning myself, and observing the client and our relationship. Consulting with other therapists and having a regular consultation group can be helpful in metabolizing the pain.

For me the most depressing thing is when I feel I have made a mistake. I miss opportunities, sometimes because I get distracted or do not notice connections, affects, or intentions. Many omissions can usually be corrected in later sessions. Because most problems are so robust and innervate so many aspects of a client's life, new opportunities to deal with the issue inevitably reappear. That is why they are called core issues.

Sometimes I say the wrong thing. I misunderstand and poorly mirror or make interpretations or suggestions that are not helpful and that puzzle or upset the client. The worst mistakes are the ones I am not aware of making that result in losing the client. Sometimes I can more closely examine, postmortem, what happened and guess what caused the client to leave. Sometimes I cannot figure it out. I try to learn from mistakes and not repeat the same one again. I hate to have clients drop out of treatment because of something I did or did not do. It is a terrible feeling to have worked with someone for a long time and have him or her suddenly stop and refuse to return my calls.

When I have felt burned out I have often doubted my efficacy as a therapist. When I find myself worrying about what I did or should do, and when I continue to worry after a session (that the client might hurt himself or herself; that therapy is not progressing; that I am not sure if I should confront, ignore, or nurture; that I am not sure if something is reportable or if medication might be helpful or if the diagnosis needs to be changed; etc.), I use the anxiety I feel as a signal that I might need to consult with a colleague. Probably the most important skill a therapist needs to develop is the ability to share anxieties with colleagues, ask for their opinion, and share the responsibility for how to proceed. This benefits and protects the therapist and client. I also remind myself that I am not omnipotent and not fully responsible for the client's behavior. I am responsible for mine.

Many times I have been saved from burnout by becoming excited about a new theory or technique, and this has reenergized me. My career as a therapist has involved becoming enthusiastic about a new-to-me therapy, trying to apply parts of it to clients, and then moving on to another technique or viewpoint. This process leaves me with a menu of theories and techniques that I draw on. As I use my judgment to choose and combine theories, I feel like I am inventing a treatment for each client.

There Are So Many Benefits to Being a Therapist

I am paid well for helping people, and I am respected and occasionally appreciated for doing the job. Some people think I have special abilities and can even read their mind. I have the privilege of meeting and learning about interesting people from different cultures and ethnic, religious, and economic backgrounds whom I come to care about and enjoy. They generally trust me and share their intimate thoughts and expose me to intense, dramatic, and emotional stories and situations, through which I am allowed to achieve a high degree of voyeuristic intimacy with minimal personal emotional risk. It feels good to help others grow and change. The job involves an ongoing intellectual challenge, so it rarely feels boring or routine. I get ideas and have experiences that advance my personal understanding and development. I have the opportunity to meet kids who crack up at the riddles, knock-knock, and moron jokes I used to enjoy. At times being a therapist combines love (my caring for my clients and their feelings toward me), work (it is my job, filled with constant challenges), and play (especially when I treat children).

How Does It Feel to Be a Therapist?

I feel challenged and exhilarated every time I meet a new client, and these feelings often persist throughout treatment.

Sometimes I feel as if I am an omniscient, omnipotent guru with powers to understand and help my clients. My words are like pearls to be treasured. My observations and interventions are surgically precise.

At times I am a grand manipulator pretending to clients, and to me, that I understand, can help, agree with, believe everything they say, and really care. I hide my yawns, not knowing the research on their disorder, how much they will have to work and sacrifice to change, my negative feelings and doubts about their potential to change and the effectiveness of the medications they are taking, and being unsure about their diagnosis and what will be helpful for them. Although I can be more enthusiastic about the effectiveness of medication for some target symptoms (anxiety and ADHD), I conceal my concerns about the side effects and benefits of other medications. I deceive clients in the service of building trust and engagement and facilitating their idealizing of me, so they can operate at a productive level of anxiety and be more able to contribute, comply, incorporate my approval and suggestions, and tolerate the frustrations our work will generate. I deceive myself to survive the ordeal.[1]

At times I feel similar to the Empath on *Star Trek* that healed Captain Kirk by absorbing his pain at great personal sacrifice to herself.

Sometimes I feel the way I felt when I was a theatrical lighting designer. I worked tirelessly for months to produce seamless effects, and my greatest compliment was when I asked people what they thought of the lighting, and they responded, "I didn't notice it." I hope clients leave thinking, "I'm not sure exactly what the therapist contributed. I changed pretty much on my own."

Sometimes I am the protagonist in Camus' *The Plague*, who competently observed, documented, and witnessed what was happening with little power to effect or explain the situation.

Sometimes I am the frog in *Frogger* who hops from place to place, avoiding danger.

Sometimes my goal is to avoid getting in the way of the client's efforts to understand and change.

Sometimes I'm a cheerleader.

Sometimes I'm a babysitter who entertains, cares, supervises, and wants to return the children safely and get paid.

Sometimes I am a policeman who must stay attentive through long periods of boredom punctuated by moments of terror.

Sometimes I'm a salesman hawking my wares to disinterested shoppers.

Sometimes I'm the audience watching.

Sometimes I'm waiting for a date who doesn't show up.

Sometimes I'm a repairman who has to tell the person who has been waiting all day for me to arrive that I can't fix it.

Sometimes I'm a traveler visiting strange worlds.

Sometimes I'm a gourmet chef creating new recipes and sometimes a short-order cook providing the usual fare under great time pressure.

Sometimes I'm a gardener watering and fertilizing what I want to grow, weeding, and planting seeds.

Sometimes I'm the guardrail along the highway watching the cars control themselves but being there in case of emergency to limit damage when they are totally off course.

Above all I feel honored to have the privilege of being trusted by so many clients and to have the opportunity to help them improve their lives.

PART 2

Case Studies

CHAPTER 9

A Typical Day

We Are Like Chefs Who Never Eat Out

When I consulted to group homes, I received the most positive feedback for arranging visits for child care workers to observe at another institution. They appreciated the opportunity to see how others performed their duties and returned with new ideas to implement. As a student the most valuable training I received involved doing cotherapy with supervisors and watching tapes of established therapists. As therapists we rarely see how colleagues operate. In the spirit of providing these experiences, I offer "A Typical Day." My expectation is that a few potentially therapeutic events occur during a session, with neutral events filling the majority of the hour; however, I am not always the best judge of what is happening or helpful. The clients depicted are composites of cases I have treated, and the clinical material has been falsified to protect client anonymity.

I arrive at the office at 7:35 a.m.

I am a therapist at a Child-Adolescent Outpatient Treatment Center with 11 other therapists. We receive our referrals from County Mental Health, which authorizes a year of treatment with the opportunity to request further services. Our clients are youths aged 21 years and younger. To best treat their problems, I collaborate with the caretakers, teachers, family members, and professionals involved in their lives. Therefore my day can include working with people of all ages and providing a variety of treatment modalities: group, individual, family, couples, conjoint, child guidance, or school consultation.

I check my e-mail and listen to four phone messages indicating two clients have cancelled. At the center we average a 20% to 25% no-show rate. Because these clients called ahead of time, I am able to schedule someone for one of the unscheduled hours.

Teresa

I make coffee, gather my charts, and review my last session with Teresa and last week's meeting with her parents. I see them on different days. The inconvenience to the parents has been worthwhile, because Teresa and her mom or dad use the time in the car coming and going to her sessions to talk and stop for fast food.

At 8:00 she arrives. Teresa is always on time. The oldest of three children, she is a very pretty 13-year-old with sad large brown eyes and round horn-rimmed glasses that match her hair color and the freckles she hates. Born to a family of accountants, she loves math and is an avid reader. She has been seen weekly for 22 months at our center following a 10-day hospitalization for depression precipitated by her refusal to come out of her closet where she had been found sobbing.

Teresa was referred because of depression, sexualized behavior with peers, verbal hostility toward her gentle caring mother and physical attacks against her father and younger brother. Teresa has been obsessively mean to her brother. Sibling abuse is one of the areas that the field of psycho-therapy has neglected, in the same way that sexual abuse, rape, and domestic violence were once subterranean. Weekly child guidance counseling emphasized helping Teresa's parents give her privileges for using words instead of violence when she was angry, reducing stress in the home by helping a relative and her baby find other housing so they could leave the family home, and realizing that they had been focusing on Teresa's needs at the expense of her siblings. The parents responded by spending more individual time with Teresa's brother and sister.

Teresa has a history of hearing voices when under stress and avoiding peers. Her relationships, especially to girls, are filled with drama and exaggerated feelings of love and hate, which alternate based on the latest incident. Teresa was initially seen at our center by another therapist, who after 4 months asked her to draw a picture of her feelings about her brother. Teresa reacted by withdrawing into a growling ball in the corner of the office. Teresa refused to see him again, saying, "My feelings are none of his business." The therapist transferred her to a girls' peer socialization group, but despite multiple interventions, she was so mean to the other girls that she was asked to leave the group. Knowing about her previous therapy has largely determined my approach. I view her as having a small therapeutic window at this time. Her hospitalization and reaction to previous treatment suggest that we need to keep in the shallow end and focus on managing daily stresses. I am reluctant to pressure her, and I quickly step back when she seems upset and support her when she withdraws. At our first meeting she said she wanted to "return to the hospital and be alone or be with kids that don't know me, because there is always someone that bullies me, like they did in the group." She saw herself as the victim and denied her contribution to peer problems. After a year and a half with me, she is somewhat cooperative and relaxed in sessions, but she is quite controlling. When she is anxious she demands a solitary art, sand-tray, or craft activity; ignores me; and immerses herself in the activity.

For the past year she has been free of hallucinations, nonviolent, and nonsexual since home and school reduced stress. She received As and Bs on her last report card with the help of private tutoring twice a week, which she took seriously. When her parents tried to help her with academics, it was a screaming disaster, and they had to stop. Peers are drawn to her despite her temper, meanness, and projecting blame and responsibility for problems. Once she said, "I'm mean because kids were mean to me, and I'll never forgive them." Her rigid thinking and inability to cope with criticism or correction remain intact. When she was hospitalized she was given the recently very popular diagnosis of bipolar disorder NOS, with borderline features. She was placed on medication, which she refuses to take, saying, "That's for crazies; I'm just evil."

She presents herself as being different from others and slides between punk rocker, gay and evil personas. My guess is that these self-presentations protect her from being acutely aware of feeling different because of having been molested by a motherly female babysitter and the subsequent social ostracizing that occurred following several sexual incidents with peers (some of which she initiated). She was also left feeling lonely and displaced after her only friend moved to Arizona and her parents had two more children. In addition, she reported that she had endured a mean coach who ridiculed her during swim team practice, and was labeled a "biohazard" by a group of girls after she had a nosebleed in class. She is embarrassed by her freckles, glasses and new breasts. As she said about her appearance, "God gave everyone pizza, and I got McVomit."

This morning she runs into my office like a younger child in hopes that I will follow her instead of briefly checking in with her mother. Because I meet with her mother or father weekly, I know how the week went, so our check-in is prearranged to emphasize mentioning successes in front of Teresa. Hearing from Teresa's mother that she had a good week usually starts our session off positively and allows her mother to praise her.

Today there is a white stripe in her hair, and she wears pants and a black shirt, well covered by a baggy Garfield sweatshirt. Teresa usually sits, avoids eye contact, and waits. Today she launches an attack against her mother: "She doesn't drive right, doesn't treat my friends with respect, and is a liar. I'm never going to invite anyone over to the house again. I'd rather bleed to death." Teresa wears her anger as a badge that she is proud of. I ask why she is so mad at her mom today, and she mumbles, "Top secret." I persist, "Sounds like if you told me you'd have to kill me to keep it secret. Did you ever like her?" She responds, "Yes, but I was stupid." I wonder aloud "What could Mom do to make it better?" Teresa chants, "Sand tray, sand tray, sand tray. I won't tell why I don't like her." She ignores my questions and silently sets up a scene in the sand tray. She makes patterns in the sand and carefully buries a few figures. I comment that most of what is happening is going on below the surface, and I don't know what is happening in the story. She smiles and says, "Tuff titties." She becomes annoyed when figures become visible but quickly recovers and finishes with pride. As she cleans up she talks about hating her brother, "I hope his Legos get stolen," and she takes a final swipe at her mother, "I want to go to camp all summer and not have to be around her."

I see a number of molested girls similar to Teresa who refuse to talk about being abused or will talk about it only toward the end of therapy when they are feeling better about themselves. This refusal to deal with molest issues initially pushes me into a psychoeducational direction in which I discuss how common molest is (one third of girls) and how it is not the girl's fault. I told Teresa, "In fact, even if a girl were to beg an adult to molest her, it would still be the adult's fault, similar to a kid begging an adult to run her over with a car, where it would be the adult's responsibility to say, 'No. Adults don't hurt kids that way.' " Then with many youths I might focus on self-protection skills with the emphasis on how molest cannot exist without secrecy, because it is against the law. That is why molesters trick kids with bribes and threats to keep them from telling the secret. I might then work on assertiveness skills to provide protection and empower clients. I want them to know that even though it is scary to tell, and even though molesters may threaten or act nice to trick kids into liking them so they won't tell, they should tell someone they trust, because telling can keep them safe. I have presented these ideas and hoped they would trigger discussions, but they did not.

Rather than try to pressure clients to disclose what happened, I generally focus on correcting the main effects of the molest, which in Teresa's case are probably self-blame, guilt, sexual identity confusion, stigmatization, and identification with the perpetrator, which allows her to feel more powerful and in control. Being molested exposes youths to two roles: the powerless victim, and the perpetrator. Teresa has avoided revictimization and easily victimizes others but no longer in a sexual way. My efforts have been focused on challenging and correcting her misconceptions about her being bad and different that probably lead her to anticipate that others will reject her. I try to show her that it is her meanness to others that causes the rejection and that kids would like her so much more if she would treat them better. When I challenge her cognitive distortions or behaviors, she withdraws into silence or insists she does not want friends. So a lot of her treatment involves weekly child guidance with her parents. This is one of my rare intact families with a helpful father who attends our weekly child guidance meetings. It is also a family in which the pressure of having a child with emotional problems has led the parents to support each other rather than to be driven apart. The parents and I have focused on reducing stress and bombarding Teresa with successes and approval while providing structured (coached and supervised) opportunities for successful initially dyadic peer interactions and now group events. We hope this approach will change the misconceptions she drew from her molest and improve her peer relationships and self-esteem. Then she will not have to protect herself with odd personas and mean attacks. Her teacher has similar socialization goals, and we have all focused on teaching her appropriate ways to verbalize feelings.

The session seemed devoted to enjoying and appreciating her and acknowledging and accepting her anger while wanting to know more about it. As I write progress notes, I feel that I am not doing enough. There are so many topics I wish I could talk with her about, but she can hang up faster than I can call (Jim Croce). Anyway, it is 9:00.

Cassi's Grandmother

I meet with an attractive 55-year-old second-generation Italian grand-mother who is meticulously groomed and dressed. I recently started seeing her for child guidance counseling related to her now 17-year-old grand-daughter, Cassi, who will be ending her year-long individual counseling in 3 months. Child guidance counseling emphasizes seeing the caretaker to change parenting and the youth's environment. The ultimate goal is to help the identified patient rather than the caretaker. Even when we are discussing her grandmother's issues, the goal is to treat Cassi. Grandmother, at Cassi's age, was an excellent student who became pregnant and left school and her religious, controlling parents to work as a clerk in a fabric store, which she now owns. Her innovations of adding sewing and knitting classes and a child care corner have allowed her to be successful despite intense competition from the big chain stores. Cassi came to live with her grandmother when she was a thin, waiflike 14-year-old who refused to talk to or eat with her grandmother. When not in her bedroom instant messaging or talking to out-of-state people in chat rooms, she was hostile, defiant, and argumentative. Cassi's poor grades, discourteous attitude, and black outfits with studs particularly upset her grandmother.

Child Protective Services removed Cassi from her mother because of chronic truancy and repeated physical abuse by Cassi's brother, Don, who dominated the mother's home. Because the mother cannot set limits on Don's continual demands for her money, grandmother pays part of the rent and supplies food at the end of each month. Don ate first, and Cassi and her mom got the leftovers. Although Cassi complained to her grandmother over the years, grandmother did not realize how abusive the home was. When she finally understood, she contacted Child Protective Services and took Cassi, who thought the rescue was "too little, too late."

Cassi received individual therapy while grandmother attended the grandmothers' group that I run. She could not be deterred from minimizing her problems and helping the other grandmothers, so I started to see her individually for child guidance. We have focused on feeling empathy for Cassi regarding her abuse and having a mother who did not protect her. This helped grandmother acknowledge the similarities between how she and Cassie had been raised, which I expected would soften her treatment of Cassie. However, this awareness initially led grandmother to appreciate how her abandonment by her own mother had led to her becoming stronger and more self-sufficient and to seeing Cassi as "needing to toughen up."

A main goal involved helping grandmother protect Cassi from her mother, who periodically contacted her, made promises about the future, and then disappointed her by not following through. Cassi repeatedly went on a roller coaster of emotions with each contact, and the contacts sabotaged her attachment to her grandmother. Once grandmother ended the short visits and insisted that contacts be at least 5 days in duration, the visits became less frequent and detrimental. The mother could seem like Santa for a few hours, but after 5 days her limited capacity to protect and give to Cassi emerged. Cassi's expectations for her mother became more realistic, and she became justifiably depressed instead of angry.

We worked on appreciating, or at least tolerating, Cassi's defiance, which was reframed as her temporary way of protecting herself by being assertive and different from her controlled and abused mother. This helped grandmother appreciate Cassie's defiance as strength and independence and feel less personally rejected by her. I advised grandmother to apologize to Cassi for not realizing that she was being abused and not rescuing her sooner. Grandmother had previously defended herself against Cassi's verbal attacks. Her apology reduced Cassi's hostility, even in the face of grandmother's high expectations for orderliness, politeness, and proper appearance.

Grandmother usually begins with complaints or worries. Today she reports that Cassi has been bugging her to buy her "outrageous" school clothes. Grandmother offered her the opportunity to earn money at the store to buy clothes, but Cassi prefers to guilt, threaten, and manipulate her into giving her money in the same way she has seen her mother influence grandmother, and Don influence her mother. Grandmother says, "If she can't earn it, she can't have it." Personally I disagree, but I say that I concur and am impressed at how she has also begun to set limits on Don and the mother. I check for ambivalence about grandmother telling mother that she will not help her with her latest financial crisis. This week grandmother is comfortable with her decision.

I have an agenda item: I want to revisit a decision grandmother made the previous week. I would like her to allow Cassi to attend a new 10-session Adolescent Art-Therapy Group that will be starting at the center. I explain the advantages, but she is still reluctant for fear Cassi would meet peers who "would be a bad influence." I accept her decision and retreat, not wanting to stress our alliance by examining the appropriateness of controlling Cassi's choices of friends. Two leitmotifs running through all our sessions have been that Cassi's behavior does not reflect on grandmother and that Cassi will soon be on her own and making all her own decisions, so we have to prepare her by allowing her more choices to learn from. I am hoping grandmother can accept a different concept for the role of a parent than the one that several generations of control and shame-based parenting have inculcated. That Cassi should have a voice and a choice is new territory.

They "had a great week," which to grandmother means Cassi was less critical and more helpful around the house. They helped Cassi's mother move, and grandmother saw how abusive Don was by refusing to help, bossing everyone around, and actually threatening to fight Cassi's boyfriend, whom she volunteered to help with the move. Grandmother proudly reported that she was able to validate Cassi's anger and explain again that she had not realized how awful it was all those years. I reacted with praise and appreciation (knowing, but not mentioning, how difficult it must have been for her to acknowledge any flaws). They even had some fun together during the week, which gave me the opportunity to remind her how much better things are in comparison to the beginning of therapy when Cassi refused to acknowledge grandmother's existence and demanded so much from her.

Cassi has progressed from isolating herself with virtual peers to making friends and from refusing to talk to her grandmother to actually being vulnerable and sharing her grief about her recent breakup with her boyfriend. It is difficult for grandmother to appreciate these changes, as she focuses on problems and deficits. Our sessions frequently involve my ignoring grandmother's shortcomings and appreciating her strengths, so she can experience what I want her to do more of with Cassi. We discuss other things they could do for fun, and she agrees to try renting a movie.

It is not unusual to work with caretakers who are angry at their youths. Treatment typically involves a combination of parental contingency management and helping the parent continue to be emotionally present while listening to and helping the youth voice his or her hostility and criticism. Then the youth can feel heard and the parents can consider new ways to respond that might heal the relationship rupture. Grandmother's counseling focused on supporting her use of calming self talk during Cassie's anger, helping her listen to Cassie's blame and complaints without defending herself until later when the relationship was on sounder ground, and acknowledging her contribution to Cassie's pain. At the same time Cassie's therapist helped Cassie attribute her grandmother's reluctance to intervene to her being uninformed and afraid to interfere. As Cassie became less angry, we focused on rebuilding their relationship, which had been strong when Cassie was much younger.

I often try to help caretakers develop enjoyable times with their youths and discover that many parents have no idea how to do this, besides watching television and shopping. It is no wonder that the teens equate love with being given things. I usually start by asking parents what they enjoyed with their parents when they were their youth's age, and I ask teens what their friends do with their parents. When possible I try to build on these activities. The grandmother remembered none. She had few enjoyable experiences as the parentified child in a large family. If we cannot identify mutual interests, I introduce a leisure questionnaire that lists about a hundred activities from acting and archery to zoo trips. I ask the parents to check the ones they would try and to invite the youth to check his or her preferences. Then we see if they agree on any. One of the mutual interests that grandmother and Cassie found was renting and watching movies. I ask about movies that grandmother remembered liking when she was Cassi's age or movies that were important to her that she would like to share with Cassi. None come to mind. She was busy working at the store and raising Cassi's mother. We discuss how they could enjoy the process of reaching a mutual decision at the video store. I try to sensitize grandmother to enjoying the entire process, instead of being frustrated and too goal directed. I want to suggest they watch *Breakfast Club* or *Sixteen Candles* and discuss it, but I refrain.

I write my notes feeling hopeful, seeing the progress, and feeling comfortable ending in 3 months. I admire grandmother's competence in the world and her assertiveness in standing up to her boyfriend, who tells her to send Cassi to a foster home because she is so disrespectful. I wonder if I should invite him to our next session, but grandmother is comfortable standing up to him, and there is no pressing need to change the treatment frame. I am also pleased to see grandmother turn off the money spigot that flowed to her entitled grandson and daughter.

That's two down, and 2 hours until lunch. Because my 10:00 cancelled, I use the next hour to make and return phone calls and review the chart for the very difficult client I called this morning and scheduled for 11:00. I have not seen this mother for 1 month and saw her only twice before that, once while I was taking the initial history to evaluate her 9-year-old son, Barney, who had just been discharged and referred from the psychiatric hospital. It was his second admission in the past 3 years for being a danger to himself and others.

Barn

Barn is a tall, gangly fourth grader with a shaved head, long braided tail, and a history of behavior problems since he had behaviors. By age 5 he had been expelled from several schools and day care arrangements for attacking peers and teachers with anything within arm's reach. He banged his head, refused to comply with requests, and was defiant and retained in first grade. He continued to be shifted from school to school until his present, self-contained, special education placement, where he requires frequent daily trips to the quiet room to regain control.

His 30-something parents are attractive, verbal, bright, and financially successful, but that is where the good news stops. Barn was conceived during what father expected to be a one-night stand. He was surprised and irritated when mother showed up at his house, pregnant. She moved in, and they married. Mother had a healthy pregnancy and delivery, because she "only ate organic food." He was brought home to his parents' volatile relationship. After 2 years of what mother initially described as constant arguing, she left with Barn, whom she described as "a strong-willed toddler who kicked me until he got his way." She worked full time, which required her to be on the road several evenings a month. Barn went into a series of day care arrangements and spent weekends with father. At age 4, after his parents' lengthy and expensive divorce and custody battle, he went to live with father, who said Barn settled down with him but continued to tantrum and threaten mother on weekend visits. The parents went through several cycles of breaking up and reuniting, and Barn started taking medication, beginning with Clonidine and now involving five daily medications.

Barn was 6 years old when his parents moved back in together, and he experienced his first hospitalization because he was hitting himself and others, talking rapidly, threatening others, staying up all night, and reporting that everyone hated him. He told the admissions worker at the hospital, "A voice tells me to cut off my balls and boil them in my blood." Mother believed that his being placed on an antidepressant caused the hospitalization and that his "auditory hallucinations" started because he was taken off Risperdal. His parents separated "for the final time" while he was hospitalized, and he was discharged to live with his father and see his mother on weekends.

For the past year, father has worked from 6 a.m. to 6 p.m., and Barn had been cared for before and after school by father's fiancée at her house. However, she now refuses to watch him, because he recently threatened to push her down the stairs. Sometimes after acting out he feels regret, which he expresses through trying to hurt himself by banging his head and aggressively pulling out his hair. Substance abuse and rage reactions run through both parents' families. From the hospital Barn carries a diagnosis of bipolar disorder NOS and intermittent explosive disorder.

I started with this family 3 months ago by initially meeting with both parents. It was unfortunate that "that woman," as mother refers to father's fiancée, did not attend. Father made it clear he really didn't have problems with Barn: "He behaves at my house." Mother blamed Barn's rebellion on the negligent care father provided. She was particularly critical of his letting Barn constantly play violent video games, watch violent media, and eat canned or junk food. Father denied that any of these things happened at his house. Mother insists on healthy meals and activities rather than electronics. She attributed Barn's obedience to father being a harsh disciplinarian and said Barn is afraid of father and won't talk to him about feelings. She said she cannot control Barn, and when he gets oppositional, she has to call father to come and take him. As I frustrated the parents by obtaining the history, it became obvious that the only thing the parents could agree on was to triangulate Barn in their disagreements by colluding with him against the other parent.

I clarified that the sessions needed to be confidential and documented the parents' agreement that what we talked about could not be used in court. Then, out of desperation, but too early in our relationship, I tried to spin their arguing into a useful reframe. I suggested that they each saw an important part of parenting that their son needed but had become polarized in response to the other parent. It seemed that mother wanted to be more lenient to make up for father's being strict, and father felt he had to be strict because mother did not set limits. I thought that Barn needed them to agree on discipline, so he would have clear limits and not be so confused. I emphasized that Barn probably would continue to hurt himself and others until they agreed with each other on parenting. In a rare moment of unanimity, they disagreed with me. But we worked out a plan for the mother to stick to her rules on weekends and for the father to tell Barn that he had to follow her rules. Father told Barn that he would not pick up him when he calls him until the weekend visit was over. He suggested that if Barn became out of control, mother could call 911.

This had been a difficult intake session, because I did not feel I had established any engagement or therapeutic alliance with these parents, who had been pushed into contacting me by the hospital. In addition, I started to focus on changing parenting methods. This is often a big step. Some parents want their child fixed without their having to change, in the same way that individual clients want their pain removed without having to alter their behaviors or defenses. In this case these parents also wanted to hurt, change, or get rid of the other parent rather than change themselves to be more like the other parent. These parents made me feel similar to Barn. They wanted me to agree with them and blame the other parent. Their battle was so robust, I commented on it, even though it was just the first session.

The next day I saw Barn for the first time. He reported that he liked to be at father's "because he has violent video games, and mother has only little soldiers." He was excited because he had just come from "shooting with Dad, but we only could use cans. I wanted to shoot at rats." He made two art projects while he talked. First he made a gun out of wood scraps with a hot glue gun. Then he drew an alligator-shark with blood-dripping teeth that was about to eat a scuba diver carrying an elaborate knife. He titled his drawing *Mad Alligator-Shark*.

He reported that he had daily problems with cussing and getting angry. He said that he had no friends since Randle moved in first grade, and he didn't want friends: "They'll just tease." If he won the lottery, he would "buy guns." If he could be any animal, he would be "a T-Rex. They eat and kill my enemies. Bite them." When asked about his parents' arguing about him, he stopped talking. Like his parents, he minimized his behavior problems and blamed others. He insisted, "It's their fault. They shouldn't make me so mad."

I saw Barn 5 days later. He was angry at a classmate. "Blaine is retarded. I want to kill everyone, especially the sissies in regular class, first. I want home school. I won't have to talk to anyone who annoys me. I could play with Dad, do what I want and eat what I want. I could play San Andreas and kill people. What's wrong with that? My parents fight. I like violence. I don't like the kids or the teacher. I don't like school, and I don't like to talk." He then drew a bear with bloody teeth. While he drew I brought up the possibility of his joining our peer socialization group, which he rejected, saying, "I don't need friends, and my father won't take me. He works until six."

I called school. The teacher was upset with father. "He sees Barn's violence as 'just boy's stuff' and sabotages the school's behavior modification system by buying Barn what he wants, so classroom prizes are ineffective. He doesn't even look at the daily behavior report we send home."

She saw Barn as obsessed with death and unable to handle frustration. She reported that his violence was shifting from verbal to behavioral. In fact, he punched her, and her chest has been black and blue for the past week. She felt that Barn wants attention from father, who works all day repairing computers, builds computers all evening, or spends time with his girlfriend.

I called mother to see if she could bring him to individual and group therapy. She said she could do this if she didn't have to go to Chicago for business. She then railed against father, stating for the first time that when they lived together he was violent on a monthly basis, had rages, and turned Barn against her, saying, "Your mom doesn't love you because she doesn't let you eat or watch what you want." She said that father's family was violent for generations. His grandfather beat father who beat him, and father fought from the time he could walk and even attacked his mother. The intake appointment had been with both parents. I looked forward to meeting them individually to hear what they could not say in front of the other parent. Domestic violence is typically hidden in conjoint sessions, so I was not surprised to hear about father's behavior, but I could not fully trust the mother as a reporter because of her exaggerations.

Sometimes my job involves searching through the generations, looking for an ego or even a friendly face that I can work with. Because father now refuses to return my calls, I return to the mother for transportation to our sessions. She had said previously she would bring him weekly, but, like the father, she failed to deliver Barn. At this point the case has been open for 3 months, and we have little engagement or therapeutic alliance, and Barn's violence is escalating.

I plan to meet with mother at 11:00. She rushes in 15 minutes late with a dramatic story. She is increasingly hysterical at each contact. She begins. I am the audience, expected to sympathetically take her side. She rapidly reports that they saw the psychiatrist, who wanted to increase Barn's medication, "But I said, 'No. He's taking 10 pills a day.' I take him to appointments. Father never goes. Barn's lippy and rebellious like me. He has to be who he is and learn to control himself without drugs. He's the product of crummy genes and a parent who scares and neglects him. I want him in regular classes. The brilliant minds were nut cases. He has a disease and has to learn to manage it. The teachers can't control their classes, and the kids at that school are violent. That's what he's reacting to."

I mirror her frustration, try to offer reassurance rather than challenge her, and search for common ground. I agree that medication and special education create problems. I agree that we want to get him off as much medication as possible and in control of his behavior so he can be in regular classes with better behaved peers. I commiserate about having to carry the heavy burden. I focus on the need for Barn to have the same rules at home, in day care, and in school with seamless transitions. This triggers her to shift focus. "I'm having a great time with him. Last night at dinner he said he wanted to go back to father's to eat real food. I said, 'No. You can't call him.' And he settled down and ate what I gave him." I comment on how this is different from the past when she would allow him to leave. I suggest that there is a lesson we can learn from this: "Barn needs you to set limits and for both parents to agree and enforce them. Because you and Dad agreed that Dad would not rescue Barn on weekends when he calls, and you insisted on following the rules at your house, he has become more compliant." She responds, "I always wanted to give limits, but I was afraid he'd start banging his head." We then discuss a safety plan for times when she feels Barn might be a danger to himself or her. She seemed calmer when we reviewed ways she has successfully deescalated Barn's behavior in the past and what she could do if these methods do not work.

It is 11:55, and we still have not dealt with scheduling appointments for Barn. She wants to talk about how "school is just blaming home," and I do not have a clue how I can help Barn if or when I see him. I say that I cannot be of help to Barn if I do not see him regularly. I think about how her bringing him to therapy is an admission that he has a problem and how the mother has to provide the transportation and do so much changing while the father avoids the hassle and responsibility. Barn and I are triangulated in their battle, and their failed appointments make me feel angry and not valued. These feelings help me better understand how Barn probably feels. It is really common for parents' problems to affect me in the same way they affect the youth I am treating.

She agrees to bring him next Tuesday, "if I don't have to be in Chicago. I'll call you." I am pessimistic as I write my progress notes and start to think of alternative treatment modalities, because this is not working. Perhaps a program that offers in-home contacts several times a week is needed. Perhaps he can get therapy at school. I plan to talk to the parents about these possibilities. Luckily, it is lunchtime.

I treat myself to a good lunch that I carefully prepare each morning. Today's menu is my favorite sandwich, a ripe nectarine ("half a peach, half a plum, such a fruit"—*Two Thousand Year Old Man*), and a Diet Peach Snapple. A colleague brought in a pie she baked as a bonus dessert. Several staff members eat and discuss our local NBA team, movies, Tom Cruise's outburst against medication and psychiatry and its fallout on our clients, and the nearing retirement of our boss. We try to avoid talking about cases at lunch, but there are often quick consultations and a catharsis or two.

Then it is 1:00 and time for our staff meeting. One of the things I love about my job is I have only one required meeting a week, which alternates between administrative concerns and educational or case presentations. Today it is administrative. Our director requests our input into the annual report he has to write. He asks us to brainstorm about our center's successes and problems over the year. Successes include starting several new groups, replacing a receptionist, and choosing a new director, as our current one plans to retire after 35 years. Problems include needing new trash cans and general agreement that clients are more disturbed. The referrals are more psychotic, are more involved with the juvenile justice system, have more comorbid drug and medical problems, need more in-home services, and present greater scheduling problems because families are more unstable due to of finance, drug, and mental health problems. They seem more difficult to schedule because of unreliable transportation and because more parents are working at minimum wage jobs as the safety net unravels. Many have to spend their money on child care or in some cases have an emotionally disturbed relative care for the child during working hours. This appears to be resulting in a higher dropout rate for new referrals. Our director decides to see if there is, in fact, a higher drop-out or no-show rate and will report back. We discuss possible resources for transportation for our clients, but none seem available. Ding! It is 2:00 and time to see Alexander's dad.

Alex

Alex and his older brother, Kevin, were adopted from a Rumanian orphanage by their divorced 45-year-old father. Alex is a handsome, well-dressed 12-year-old who has lived with his single-parent father for 6 years. At our intake interview, the father brought in past evaluations that diagnosed Alex as having obsessive-compulsive disorder, Asperger's syndrome, attention-deficit/hyperactivity disorder, post-traumatic stress disorder, reactive attachment disorder, oppositional defiant disorder, and learning disabilities. Now that I know him, I can see parts of all of these in him. He takes Concerta, Depakote, and Prozac to be maintained in his self-contained special education classroom. Both boys came to the United States unfamiliar with English. When they first arrived they banded together to scavenge for and hoard food, steal, lie, beat up peers, fail academics, and refuse homework and chores. Six years later Kevin is an A student who was elected to student government and has a girlfriend.

Alex has made significant gains over the past 2 years but lags way behind his brother. He speaks accent-free English. He no longer threatens to kill teachers or gains satisfaction from hurting peers. He is rarely violent, gets some passing grades, cares about his personal hygiene, and earns computer time for completing homework and chores. He used to act on impulse without any reflection but now considers consequences and even shows occasional flashes of empathy for his dad. This progress has been the result of medication combined with the father's learning how to deal with ADHD, developing realistic expectations after mourning the loss of his hope to cure Alex, and implementing and constantly adjusting the home routines and behavior modification program. Alex is left mostly with difficulties related to his attachment problems. He was placed in the orphanage as an infant after his parents abandoned the brothers. He was separated from Kevin, who had only periodic visits, and was raised by a television set. He lacks age-appropriate empathy, is excitement seeking, and worries about monsters, getting his share, and car accidents. He obsesses about watching and playing electronic media but is not interested in peers who play the same games.

I anticipate a session with the father of fine-tuning the behavior modification system, but during the staff meeting, he called to cancel for Alex's peer group and our child guidance session because he has "to take Kevin to the dentist for a chipped tooth. Sorry, see you next week." I check on the pie.

Treatment problems and reality issues contribute to missed appointments in my caseload. I expect weekly clients will miss one of their appointments each month. Sometimes no-shows and cancellations come in waves, and it is frustrating for me. The first of the month and late in the month when funds are low are peak times for missed sessions. Medical appointments, school holidays when clients assume that we are closed, and disruptions to our schedule due to vacations or changes in the frame are all prone to cause failed appointments.

Many of my clients do not call to cancel and reschedule. Some assume I am like a bus driver whom you do not have to call when you miss the bus, because he will not care and just keep doing his job. Some are protecting themselves from anxiety; some have car or medical concerns to deal with. Some are afraid to talk about wanting to stop. Some only want help when they feel there is a crisis or trouble and are not motivated for services at other times. I have clients whose parents live such chaotic lives that they fail appointments because they do not know what day it is.

Just because parents do not keep appointments, their child should not be deprived of treatment. Each client and situation requires a different response from me. I call some clients to confirm appointments. I schedule appointments at the same day and time; work with disorganized caretakers to develop routines, calendars, and to-do lists to bring order to the family; and explore resistances and reality issues that affect attendance. Still, some parents are unable to keep regular appointments. I try not to give up. It is unethical to abandon a client. Our code of ethics says we can stop treatment if clients are not benefiting or are being harmed by treatment. When fewer than half the sessions are being kept, it is difficult to make progress, because when we meet we spend so much time catching up with what has been happening, reestablishing goals, and restarting the stalled relationship. The youth may be harmed by being subjected to another inconsistent, shallow, and disappointing relationship and to treatment that could be ineffective because it is so diluted. Irregular attendance in peer group therapy makes forming relationships much more difficult. Sometimes I have to discuss stopping treatment until caretakers or clients are more able or motivated to participate. I generally tell them we are not meeting frequently enough to make progress and need to meet and decide if we should continue. I leave the door open to their returning, or I try to obtain other services for them, such as in-home therapy or therapy on-site at the child's school. Some of my colleagues travel to see a few clients at their home, but I do not regularly meet in the client's home, because it is so time-consuming and detrimental to my productivity. I do like to have a home visit to see the environment, but sometimes I worry that I am being too intrusive.

I spend the next hour answering phone calls, returning messages, and trying to talk to teachers. One of the advantages of treating youths is the availability of help from teachers in diagnosing and treating. I have rarely been disappointed after contacting a teacher.

Arisa

Arisa, age 13, arrives and is the immediate center of attention in the waiting room. She brought her ferret and everyone wants to see it, but she guards it in her blanket, allowing only brief peeks. I have known her for 5 years now. She first came to the center when she was 8 and had just started living with her active, athletic foster parents after being hospitalized for cutting on herself. With that hospitalization she stopped cutting on her wrists and ankles.

Many of my clients self-mutilate, mostly as a way of avoiding or escaping uncomfortable feelings. Older clients often describe cutting as a way of reintegrating and grounding themselves from a state of dissociation and/or numbed depression. Although it is usually not a suicide-related behavior, cutters do attempt suicide more than noncutters. Therefore cutting requires ongoing monitoring. Cutting may flood clients with endorphins and become addictive. I recently have seen teens receive secondary gain from positive peer attention at school and from the Internet where they can easily meet groups that support and inspire cutting, which can become difficult to control and treat after it has received such strong social reinforcement. Problems are much easier to treat before they become chronic. I am glad her cutting behaviors did not get established.

Arisa was one of two children born to a borderline, drug-addicted mother and frequently incarcerated father, who relinquished their parental rights. Arisa and her brother were removed when she was 6 and placed with her paternal aunt, who neglected them for 2 years. Because of their sexualized behavior with each other, they were sent to separate foster homes. Arisa continued to act sexually and failed two other placements before coming to live with her present foster parents. They will not allow her contact with her brother, fearing they will act out sexually.

When I first worked with her, she refused to do schoolwork and was so controlling with peers that they avoided and made fun of her. I remember our first meeting when I tried to do psychoeducational testing to see if the academics she was refusing to do were too difficult. She squinted and held the paper up to her face and said the writing was blurry, so we could not continue with the tests. Being a keen diagnostician I proudly told her mother that there appeared to be a problem with her vision. The subsequent visit to an eye doctor did not reveal any problems. I quickly realized the depth of Arisa's intelligence and manipulative abilities.

Following 3 years of treatment for sexual abuse at another agency, which described her as "uncooperative," I saw her for 1 year, during which we focused on three areas: trying to motivate her to do academics by instituting a series of behavior modification plans intended to reward schoolwork, stopping her from alienating peers, and promoting her bonding with her foster parents. But her neediness, constant manipulating, and refusal to acknowledge problems and talk about the past or any anxiety-related topics undermined her parents' and my efforts. Each session was a power struggle over eating snacks, refusing to talk, deciding which activities we would choose, ending on time, and not being allowed to take home things from my office. She lied about everything, so before each session I had to talk to a parent on the phone to get a realistic picture of the past week. We stopped counseling, but at Arisa's request, she returned 3 months ago, saying she wanted to talk this time.

At first, weekly child guidance sessions with her foster parents focused on helping them have realistic expectations and goals. Many foster parents, especially those who are financially comfortable, are surprised when the child does not bond and appreciate being rescued. Arisa's feelings of loss and loyalty to her idealized biological parents trumped any feelings of appreciation. They were disappointed that an insatiable sense of entitlement grew where gratitude should have sprouted. She became excited only about shopping, and that was the main thing she wanted to do with her new parents. She did not enjoy the things she begged for, because she instantly focused on the next thing that she had to have. She also rejected their outdoor (camping, biking, hiking) lifestyle, which they assumed she would embrace and share with them. The parents were able to support each other through this difficult adjustment period and try to seek other ways to bond with her, such as over animals. They have a goat, birds, fish, hermit crabs, and the ferret, and the family goes to the zoo almost every weekend, where Arisa volunteers. Her specialty is feeding the bear, which she describes as starving before she gets there.

Arisa enters the office and sits in my chair, hiding the animal. The hour is clearly structured. We talk for half the session and do an activity for the other half. I ask how the week went. She shows me Lovie, and we engage in ferret talk. She relates to animals and cares about them, treating them roughly but with more empathy than she shows to people. She controls them in a narcissistic way, forcing them to kiss her and to accept her affection. I ask about her week, again. She says she already told me. I say, "That's crap!" She offers, "I'm having another birthday party with my boyfriend and two other friends this weekend. It's my third party, and I'm having another next month." Last session she told me about her boyfriend. He is a 16-year-old rock star with his own limo. He is madly in love with Arisa. Because it would interfere with his career, they have to keep the relationship a secret. She cannot even tell me his name. He travels a lot. I do not want to show interest in her real or imagined relationships with boys. I fear they represent an attempt to skip over the developmentally crucial stage of learning about nonsexualized intimacy, trust, and loyalty with girlfriends before relating to boys in sexualized relationships.

She has not mentioned that last week she went to sleepover camp and that two new foster kids (a brother and sister) came to live with them. I bring up the topic of the foster kids. She looks at the clock.

"What's it like having them?" I ask, again.

No answer.

"Does it change things?"

"I get allowance, now."

"Are there any other changes?"

"They [parents] can't blame just me, now."

"Anything else different?"

"I'm the oldest, and I have my own room, and I don't want them in it. I have to go to the bathroom." I ignore the bathroom ploy and ask, "If it works out perfectly, what would happen?"

"They won't be mean to me or my animals."

"How can you get them to be nice to your animals?"

"Treat them with respect." (Mocking my past advice.)

"How?"

"I don't know."

"Is it like when you lived with your younger brother?"

"I don't remember." The session has deteriorated to Q and A—a bad sign.

Knowing that Katrina, the oldest foster girl, is very controlling, like Arisa, I wonder aloud how Katrina feels being in a new home. Arisa says she has no idea. I ask if "Katrina might expect that people will treat her badly, because people usually expect more of the same thing they got before."

Arisa insists she has no idea what I am talking about. I say that maybe she isn't old enough to guess what others are thinking. She responds with, "They expect a loving family that loves them." She focuses on Lovie while I produce a monologue for myself that she outwardly ignores.

"Well, I'll bet she is controlling and won't listen, because she went through some very sad things. She lived on another planet where people didn't take care of her, and she had to look out for herself and protect herself. So, it will take time for her to realize that on this planet she can trust people like Mom and Dad."

Arisa responds, "I don't want to be sad. I don't want to talk about it."

"You have lots to be sad about?" (No answer.) "Thanks for letting me know."

I obey and respect her request, despite wanting to push for a little more exposure to the pain that most of her symptoms seem to be an attempt to avoid. I have not found a way to help her tolerate these sad feelings, so she will not have to devote so much energy to avoiding them. Many clients are resistant to talk about their unpleasant feelings or situations, so we focus on the feelings of others, pets, puppets, and so on. I frequently ask about how others feel, how a 5-year-old in that situation would feel, what kids in the class thought, what teenagers think would be fair, and so on. I want to make it more comfortable to share feelings with me. I have told her about how telling someone you trust can make the sadness less painful. I have said she does not have to carry it all by herself and can leave some here with me. She can draw it, write it, or tell me a drop and see if it feels better. She is getting closer to sharing, because she recently chose an older girl to be friends with who had a similar background and successfully shared some secrets with her.

Rather than push on resistances, which usually creates more resistance, I typically explore the resistances until they evaporate. For instance, were she more able to talk, I expect we would focus on several reasons for not talking about her sad feelings, and in the process of explaining, they would lose their credibility. Were she more motivated, I would focus on ways she could tolerate the feelings. I do not see our being able to do these approaches. I am left with using my relationship to cajole, beg, and plead for a taste of what is presently upsetting her. Desensitizing her to the pain from her past and correcting the misconceptions she drew from her abuse, neglect, and abandonment are possible future goals. Because she idealizes her biological family and denies anger at them, I suspect that she blames herself for the abuse, abandonment, and neglect. Since she fights efforts to correct misconceptions from the past I focus on bombarding her with successes and approval, solving present difficulties, building social skills, and seeing the connection between her behavior and the consequences it generates.

I change the subject and ask about camp.

"Do you know what else I'm wondering about?"
"No."
"Camp."
"It sucked. There were bugs, and the water was too cold. I didn't know anyone."
I move away from feelings to knowledge.
"How many beds in your bunk?"
"Eleven."
"The food …"
"Good."
"The activities …"
"Fun, I guess. I didn't do most of them, because they were on grass, and I'm allergic to it."
"What did you miss most?"
"My boyfriend."
"Did you miss Mom and Dad?"
"No."
"Were you friendly?"
"Yes." (Sarcastically.) "I was nice and not rude. Our time is up." She is a clock-watcher and a master at toying with me.

It is activity time. She usually draws or paints peopleless art with large black circles or idealized homes surrounded in blue. She might say a little about the central object: "That's where Auntie lived." If I try to explore further—"What would this part say to this part?"—she typically says she does not understand. This week it is my turn to pick an activity, and I suggest pool. She agrees. I say, "This time" (and I do not say, "Unlike last time when you cheated, quit when I took the lead, and constantly put me down") "I want you to treat me the way you would like to be treated. I would enjoy it more if you would show good sportsmanship and say stuff like, 'Nice try. Good shot,' and play fair and take turns with no cheating." We play; she complies with my request, at first mockingly but eventually with more sincerity. I model the same behaviors. We both have a good time. When I first met her she refused activities, saying her knees, arms, or somethings hurt too much to play. She once said that she could not play ping-pong because she might sweat, and she was allergic to sweat.

Our sessions have focused on teaching how her behaviors cause the consequences. For instance, if she is mean (does not share or take turns, ignores, cheats, name calls, boasts, lies, does not think about what the other person wants), kids will be mean to her. She knows this and, in part, wants them to stay away if she cannot control the interactions. Therefore, trying to have a fun time in therapy is a priority. I want her to experience the kind of relationship she is missing. I enjoy her, and we have fun in our sessions, sometimes because of our dueling. When I meet with her parents in child guidance sessions, a major focus is on identifying activities through which they can enjoy her. They have found family council meetings to be helpful and have been enjoying her at the zoo and through animal-care adventures. These activities, rather than rewards and punishments, have led Arisa to start to bond with her mother and to do schoolwork. Her grades have improved from Fs, and anticipating retention, to Cs.

As I write my progress note, I think that Arisa will not be able to talk about her present stresses or past family until she is more secure and successful in this family. However, missing her biological family and their unstructured lifestyle (do no homework, stay up at night, sleep in, skip school, eat what you want or can forage) and now sibling rivalry have been interfering with attaching to her foster parents. Today she talked more than ever before. Even though we struggle each week, there is a connection, and she knows I get a kick out of her. We maintain a delicate balance between my pushing for change and talking about feelings and her protecting herself. I must remember to keep feeding the relationship, so she can experience the caring and enjoyment she shows to her ferret.

Jordan

It is 4:00, and my 5:00 cancelled, so I feel comfortable anticipating that the next session could last 90 minutes. I usually see Jordan individually and have monthly contacts with his grandmother. Today I will meet with them together, because she is threatening to kick him out. Jordan is a tall, handsome, muscular, tattooed, gang-identified, African American 18-year-old whom I have been seeing weekly for the past 14 months. He is on probation for assaulting a man who crashed into his truck late one night. While he was in juvenile hall, he reported feeling suicidal and was referred following discharge. He was also court ordered to attend counseling, perform community service, attend drug counseling and AA, stay on probation until he had several clean drug tests, attend school, and comply with his grandmother's directions.

I first met them in a conjoint intake. I wanted to see them together because from the referral sheet I anticipated he would be a conduct disorder, and therefore treatment would not be relationship oriented but dependent on creating clear expectations and contingent consequences. The grandmother was most concerned about his anger. "He has a hair trigger and can go off at any time." They agreed that he was not suicidal anymore. The history revealed that Jordan was raised by streetwise crank addicts who lived violent and chaotic lives. He dropped out of school in eighth grade while getting all As, and at age 14 he left home with his 12-year-old brother, Wayne. He worked construction and sold pot until he was hospitalized for cutting his wrists after he hurt his back framing a house, could not pay the rent, and faced homelessness. He returned from the hospital to sell and abuse crank, pot, and alcohol. He described himself: "I was 'The Drug King of East Oakland.' We had it all before I was arrested. I had a red Ranger and always had a huge roll of cash and lots of bitches. I'd go 'rolling down the street, sippin' on gin and juice.' " With the help of his "homies," he was proud to be able to provide for himself and Wayne. He was angry and fearless and took pride in his violence and ability to humiliate anyone on the basketball court. He was used to having no rules, sleeping all day and running all night, being his own boss, and caring for himself. This made living with his church-going grandmother a bit of a challenge.

I was impressed with the grandmother. I thought she would maintain a good balance between limits, confrontation, and nurturing and would naturally do the same things at home that we would focus on in conjoint sessions. I was impressed with Jordan's caring and respect for his grandmother and concern about his upcoming emancipation. So after two individual assessment sessions with Jordan, I proposed individual therapy with him, monthly child guidance, and conjoint sessions when needed. The grandmother volunteered to provide transportation. It is very difficult to maintain a relationship with a teen client whose caretaker does not supply transportation to meetings.

The decision to see both the adolescent and the parent separately has risks. Adolescents have difficulty believing that you will keep what they say confidential, especially if you meet regularly with their caretaker. They may assume you will tell their parents everything. On the other hand, it is generally impossible to work individually with conduct-disordered youths, because they are so unmotivated to change, dishonest, manipulative, and too egocentric to form relationships. Their major defenses typically involve projecting blame and responsibility, and they describe themselves as victims, because they minimize or ignore their contribution to problems. Therefore, without constant reality rubs from parents and teachers, the therapist risks being manipulated into siding with the youths against the "uncaring adults who misjudge them." This pattern subverts therapy, because the therapist becomes another easily manipulated adult who reinforces the client's defenses and behavior.

Another approach is to have separate therapists see the adolescent and parents. Then the therapists must regularly communicate so they can have a full picture of what is going on. I usually prefer to see the client and parents together in conjoint sessions, because the youth can be confronted directly by the parent, and it is more difficult for the youth to lie and manipulate. It is no wonder that these clients bolt from treatment, because therapy for conduct-disordered youths usually emphasizes confronting behavior and defenses, teaching the connection between the client's behavior and its consequences, and helping the parents supply appropriate consequences. Tactfully confronting and teaching without alienating the easily angered is a skill that is required here.

We initially identified anger management as needed for him to avoid returning to juvenile hall, which was his main goal. The basic cognitive-behavioral techniques of anger management, identifying triggers and developing self-talk and behaviors to calm and avoid the situation, usually can be effective (Sukhodolsky, Kassinove, & Gorman, 2004), but are difficult to install because the anger comes on so suddenly, and many clients (despite efforts to help them recognize the anger) often have difficulty learning to observe themselves. Therefore the techniques to manage anger do not affect their impulsiveness. Jordan surprised me by having the ability to think about and observe himself and the situation, instead of just reacting. He usually experienced people approaching him or looking at him ("mugging him") as a possible threat. As I later came to understand, there was some reality to his concern, because "you never leave your gang." Being seen especially by a male also triggered thoughts of others thinking he was weak, gay, and could not defend himself. Rather than explore these concerns, I labeled his anticipation of danger as needed for living on the street but not adaptive to what we have come to call "civilian life." "Here we try to get along and accomplish our goals. When we don't like someone, we stay away from him." I suggested that perhaps these strangers just looked at him and thought, "I wonder what the tattoos mean. I wonder what he is like. Maybe he can give me a ride or help me with the assignment."

We talked about what triggered his anger and decided that most occasions seemed related to his hostile appearance and presentation. He avoided eye contact with males and greeted them with indifference or hostility. I said they might see him as "shy or stuck up," which surprised him. By negatively labeling his avoidant behavior, he seemed more motivated to change it. We discussed important issues about friends, such as what are they good for and how do people make friends. His orientation was that the male peers with whom he went to school were potential opponents or customers. We looked at alternatives: "They can tell you about jobs, teach you school and workout stuff, play basketball and spot you while working out, agree with your opinion, help you accomplish your goals, and introduce you to their interests and to girls. They could be better than being bored." I particularly emphasized hedonistic advantages that coincided with his developmental and moral level.

I was impressed that he started to think instead of to instantly react with a threatening display to being seen and approached. When he described walking away from a fight with a classmate who kept asking him questions about his gang affiliation, I focused on the nonthreatening reasons why he could have asked these questions and ended finding myself saying, "You keep getting close to fighting because you don't like what they are doing and think violence is the way to change them. What right do you have to try to change others? That's their business. You don't like people in your business. Why get mad because they don't follow your rules? They probably don't even know the street rule is 'Don't disrespect me by looking at me.'" Somehow this intrigued him, and he later gave examples of controlling his anger by saying to himself, "I'll let the fool be like that." Probably the most helpful anger control technique was orienting him to consequences. He eventually described situations where he did not fight because "I could beat him up, but I'd get suspended again. He's not worth it. I don't need more problems with the PO [probation officer]." Before, looking out for himself meant fighting to defend his reputation. On the street, being afraid of him meant respect.

Jordan agreed to attend school, which he saw as a 3-year slog with little benefit. He wanted to work to make money that he said would be used to get a car and apartment and to take care of his brother. His gang affiliation and sensitivity to being challenged and disrespected led to daily struggles to control his anger. Therapy continued to focus on anger management. He fought, got suspended, and avoided academics until his grandmother agreed to a compromise plan of allowing him to work and enter a GED program. After 3 months he scored 98% and passed the GED. He dropped out of Alateen and drug therapy and accepted trying NA for 1 week, which he did, exactly. He got his anger under better control, performed well in several jobs, and continued to avoid hard drugs but did use pot daily and binge drink. Therapy focused on developing the skills to have nongang- and nondrug-related relationships and activities. He started a junior college class and devoted himself to conquering girls, but he lacked the motivation and study skills to succeed academically. Therapy centered on his daily struggle between seeing himself as able to succeed in civilian life or returning to the streets. He identified some skills needed to accomplish work and relationships with employers and fellow employees. He continued to smoke and drink because, he thought, it helped him avoid the pain of all the terrible things that happened to him and to cope with boredom and social anxiety. On a cognitive level he realized that to succeed he needed to get business done before using drugs, control his anger, use condoms, and give up trying to help or change his mother or incarcerated father. On an emotional level I suspected that he would continue to act out until he mourned the losses of his parents, brother, and childhood.

Instead of seeing girls as similar to his mother, he started to treat them with more respect and even began to care about a girl. Jordan's hostile attitude toward women was deeply ingrained and shaped by his mother and the street drug culture. All his relationships with females have been purely sexual except for one girl, whom he rejects as a burden, because she has continued to call and want him to get off drugs and treat her reciprocally. I told him he would probably continue to disrespect women as long as he played it safe and chose women who lacked self-esteem. I presented college girls as different from his past street girls. In therapy we talked about how college girls might be looking for a relationship, and he described his technique for getting girls. He basically gets loaded and asks them if they want to party. He makes it clear that he wants just sex and does not want a relationship. He has never dealt with them sober or without conquest in mind.

I commended him on his honesty and said he was missing out. I continued to appeal to his hedonism by saying, "If you think sex is good with someone you don't care about, you should try it with someone you care about. It's even better." He ended the conversations with statements similar to "I don't want a relationship. I'm too young to be with one girl now." I was surprised that he has been so monogamous with his present girlfriend of 3 months. Although he describes how he could use her and how difficult it is to have to consider her feelings, he is still with her and learning what a relationship is from her, his grandma, and me. This is so different from his street life, where nongang relationships were disposable, and he could just move to another one without consequences or even feedback.

He became less expecting of violence and started generating plans for a future in society rather than returning to street life. He talked about things besides drugs and violence, enjoyed leisure activities (basketball and working out at the gym), and kept distanced from his painful past and dysfunctional family. He experienced how it felt to be given to and the burden of having to think about the needs and feelings of another person. He had longer periods of sobriety and explored its costs and benefits. A lot of therapy time was devoted to trying to develop ways to cope with boredom, social anxiety, and painful feelings to reduce the need for drugs while emphasizing the negative consequences of pot use (probation; loss of money, car, girls who are not druggies, education, job, and family).

Today we are having one of our conjoint sessions, because after 14 months of consistently attending weekly individual sessions, Jordan failed three of our last four meetings and I called his P. O. Two weeks ago he said, "It's all bad, and it's all my fault. I'm fired, and I'm broke." He described gripes about his boss and job as justification for not showing up at work for the second time in 2 weeks. His grandmother was in the hospital, so he spent the weekend "loaded at the bitch's [girlfriend's] house." He has been an excellent worker at three jobs over the past year, earning close to $8,000, but he left each job feeling angry and taken advantage of. Despite his often-stated goal of working to earn money to buy a car, move out, and care for his brother, he spent his earnings on pot. As he ended the last session depressed and failed the next one, I wanted to meet with him and his grandmother to assess the situation.

> They enter the office without looking at each other.
>
> Jordan begins, "Things aren't good, feel me? My brother, girlfriend, P. O. and job. Everyone's pissed at me."
>
> The grandma adds, "I'm pissed too."
>
> "I don't do nothing to you."
>
> "You won't talk to me. You avoid relating to my feelings."
>
> "I can't." ("You won't," I think, "because you speak about your feelings in therapy with sensitivity.")
>
> "You disappeared for 2 days without a word."
>
> "My life has always sucked. It's been one long, bad life. I never want to trust anyone. I want to take care of my problems, myself. I don't want your help. I don't want anyone upset about my behavior."
>
> "Well, we can't continue as a family living in the same house when you lie and go gone. It's a problem."
>
> "I need to do what I need to do to be successful, and I need my own space. Feel me?"
>
> "If you want to be successful living with me and get my help, you have to change. I want to help you if your goal is college and work, but if your goal is job and drugs, count me out."
>
> "You're too close to my business. I have to learn it on my own. You criticize me all the time. You want me to do what you want."
>
> I intervene, "I thought you both wanted the same things: college, job, and emancipation." They agree, but Jordan returns to being uncomfortable with the burden of a relationship. "She wants to go through my finances. That's my business."
>
> "No. That's my business. You wrote me a check that bounced. To stay with me you have to show me you are saving money."
>
> "I don't need that."
>
> "I can't trust you are saving it. Your check bounced. You deceived me. I feel used."

"I never had parents. I'm supposed to have them now?"

"You have to show me you are saving. I have a problem with that. The PO said to kick you out. 'He's 18.' But I want to help."

"My parents weren't responsible for me. I never had it before."

"I'm not going to give up."

"I didn't ask for your help. *You* wanted me to live with you."

"With conditions. We always had conditions. I told you, if you steal from me or use drugs in the house, you can't stay. There are rules. You don't want to be sensitive to my feelings."

"I am sensitive to your feelings."

"I need proof of savings."

He fell silent. I do not press for closure. I think he needs time to think about it. Grandmother knows that Jordan's behavior will speak for him and will be judged, so it is not worth reacting to what he says, now. I summarize the session saying that the grandmother laid out her conditions for Jordan to stay, and he needed to think about the costs and benefits. I was impressed at his rationalizations to avoid admitting that all the money went to pot. When I see him and we review the consequences of smoking pot, I will add, "It could cost you your home and relationship with your grandma."

I thought they would continue this discussion on their own. I was very impressed with grandmother's confronting his behavior while reaching out for more connection and being sensitive to the costs and benefits of a relationship, especially for Jordan who has not experienced a trusting one. I am anxious about how Jordan will respond. I want closure, but I have to wait. So much potential, but so much to overcome. I hope he comes next week. I would like to help him tolerate the costs of trusting and engaging with his grandma. I hope he will come regularly. I want to keep working with him. I also worry that despite the grandmother's assurance that she can straighten it out, he has been dropped from Medi-Cal for the past month since he became 18. Without Medi-Cal he will not qualify for another 6 months of treatment that I need to request soon. I think I will call her tomorrow and see what happened after the session and tell her I appreciate the sensitivity, caring, support, and limits she offered. She was a great therapist.

This was a fairly typical day.

CHAPTER **10**

Three Month Follow-Up

Teresa

I saw Teresa five times in the next 7 weeks.

Session 1: Teresa continues to avoid eye contact. I focus on what she has been doing this summer with the hope of increasing socialization opportunities and replacing mean attacks with social skills. I hope that her boredom at home and anxiety about going to sleepover camp for a week will motivate her to focus on these areas. But she responds, "I watch cartoons, ride my bike, and do sudoku. I like being at home alone." She says she is not bored and does not want to see anyone. I ask about the math camp she will be going to next week. She reports she won't know anyone but wants to get away from her mother and will not say why. I ask if she wants to make friends and she says, "Depends," but will not say on what. I talk about how I made friends when I went to camp. With nothing to lose I tell her everything I know: "I was friendly and smiled at people, asked them questions about where they were from and if they had been to camp before. I asked where things were and what came next and asked questions about what they told me. … I learned to make friends in kindergarten where they taught me to share, take turns, give compliments, and not run with scissors. You don't ask me questions." She responds, "Next time. I want to draw, now."

I give her a beautiful butterfly, basket of wood pieces, colored foam shapes, and a hot-glue gun and ask her to "make a comfy world for this butterfly." She makes a tiny bed and computer for it. She does not like what she made but can't or won't say why and loses interest. Then she becomes engrossed in painting and produces a green world with a brown tree. She colors the bottom half of the paper white and puts red leaves on the tree that look like blood. I ask if she were a butterfly where would she belong in the picture and what would she need to be comfortable. Teresa says, "It isn't a her; it's a he." And she continues to work on the red leaves without answering questions or placing the butterfly in the picture.

I was being excluded and just watch, wondering what her art means to her. Is she the tree? Why white? He not she? Blood equals shame? Again I feel inadequate to the task of making more (or any) use of her art. Maybe an art therapist could ask the perfect question. In the past when I asked questions, such as, "What would happen to this part if this part went away?" she put less effort into the project and seemed resentful of my intrusions.

I end by wishing her a good time at camp and say I am looking forward to hearing about it.

Session 2: Two weeks later she returns. She liked camp. "I played with Daniel. I made friends with everyone, but Liz didn't like me. She was evil. I was evil and scared her by talking in my sleep." She will not elaborate because she is excited about the movie they made and silly dress night where she regrets not wearing all black. She seems pleased about how well she got along. She speaks a lot about whom she thinks is evil and not evil. She has the ability to find an evil scapegoat in any group. Rather than point out how rotten the scapegoat feels and how she knows because she was one once, I ignore the ubiquitous evil references and mirror the approval she got from others and the fun she had.

She paints a blood-red sky with evil angels and refuses comment. I am pleased she had some successful social interactions despite her focus on enjoying finding an evil person to scapegoat. I wonder if she is testing me to see if I will still like her, even though she is so mean to me. I do like her very much.

Session 3: The next week she continues to rail against her mom and brother and the weekend houseboat trip they just had with another family. My requests for elaboration or more specifics go nowhere, and I focus on her second week at sleepover camp that is coming up. I say, "If you want friends you have to be friendly. The kids will like you if you let them. They don't know anything about you except how you treat them." She refuses to describe any hopes or desire to make friends or to commit to being friendly. She is excited to be going to this camp session with a classmate and maintains she does not care about meeting new friends. She continues to hate and criticize her mom and refuses to give particulars or to look at how to improve their relationship. She spent the past week isolated with the latest *Harry Potter,* for which she and her mother lined up at 4:00 in the morning to get. She was 13th in line. I wonder out loud if the kids at camp have read the book and what they thought about it. We talk about the book, and I hope she will do the same with peers at camp. I ask whom she would be friends with at Hogwarts, and she smiles and says, "Harry, of course."

Session 4: She returns from camp and starts the session saying, "I made friends with two people, a boy and a girl. There was a boy who liked me, but I dropped him and Samantha dropped her boyfriend, too." We talk about Samantha and her boyfriend, and I try to help her learn lessons from their relationship. This session she paints a love picture for her mother depicting her mother and her bike riding with smiling stars in the black background. She talks about how much she loves her mother and how strong her love is. I cannot get any sense of what led to this change.

I ask about school starting, and she says she had "a bad dream" about the first day. She couldn't find her locker and then couldn't remember the combination. I say, "I used to have dreams like that, too. And lots of kids are telling me stuff just like that. I just heard two scary dreams about starting school. Did you ever have the one about being called on and you can't remember the answer, or the one where you go to school and forgot to wear clothes?" She smiles and looks less upset. I remind her about her good grades last year and ask what her thoughts are about being in an advanced math class.

Before we can talk more, she blocks further discussion by saying she knows it will be easy, and she has enough friends. So I hope that her summer successes will make her feel more competent and allow her to be more open to peers and use fewer preemptive strikes. I continue to monologue about being friendly and giving compliments and the positive consequences they elicit. I wonder aloud about how her mother will feel and react to Teresa's present of the art she made.

Session 5: This is our last session before school starts, and we are preparing in session, and she and her mother are preparing at home. She reports, "Ann and Tracy are evil. They put people down, and that's my job." I laugh. "I'm having friends over tomorrow for swimming. They think they are popular, but they aren't." We talk about being popular, and I take the Detective Colombo–like stance that I do not understand what being popular means to kids today, because adults do not think that way, only kids do. But she will not elaborate about the popular kids. I tell her that I think being liked has to do with being friendly because we pick people to be our friends who like us and that being cool is being yourself and liking yourself. This captures her interest, and she tells me what kids today are like, describing mean girls and how she is drawn and repelled. We both laugh about how much we liked the movie *Heathers* and how mean they were.

I ask how her mom reacted to the present she made for her last session. She says her mom liked it, and then she paints a love picture and writes a poem for her dad. She fills the page with a heart with a light in it. The heart is floating in black, accompanied by a poem carefully etched with the calligraphy pens she allowed me to teach her to use:

> I live in the night,
> But there is a light that shines bright.
> Drenched in blood
> I keep up the fight.
> I know you know
> I love you so.
> I'd feel dead inside and have to cry,
> if you don't see through the lie.
> I won't be mean to you.
> Don't be sad.
> I love you, Dad.
> I say, "He loves you, too."

I take this and last week's art to be an expression of her realization that despite her faults and meanness, her parents love her, and she loves them. This dramatic shift from making isolated, black, and bloody art that allows her to avoid contact with me to making loving gifts and being more open with me should not be viewed as reflecting a core change. Teresa's orientation to her parents and peers remains self-protective. However, she is allowing herself to publicly express and at least temporarily explore these loving emotions and risk being more vulnerable. I am not sure what this will lead to next, but as she develops a balance between intimacy and isolation, an angry retreat would not surprise or disappoint me. I end with a porcupine story where the porcupine's quills keep a bird away until he learns to control his quills and the bird can get close without being afraid. I pick birds because I know she loves her bird, "because the bird doesn't make humungous dumps in the backyard" (like the dog does).

Next week she will have started school. I did not review social skills, because I expect problems and do not want her to withdraw, thinking she disappointed me by not using them. As the pressure of anticipating school increases, she is bringing compliments and art projects to her parents and gaining reassurance from feeling close to them. They are providing supervised social opportunities with school peers. I hope she can allow some of them to get closer too, as she did this summer.

One month later: Teresa started school, got teased, and felt embarrassed. She took out her frustrations on her mother, who sensitively taught her the comebacks she used when she got teased as a child. In sessions Teresa complained about her mother, and I kept asking her what her mother did to deserve all this anger. All I got back was that she demanded a hug a day, and not only was that bad but while Teresa had a friend sleep over, she asked for a goodnight kiss in front of the friend. Teresa indignantly reminded me, "I'm a teen." She then gave another reason for hating her mother: "She took Robert [her brother] to the movies and wouldn't take me, because she says I treat her so mean." I said I understood how Teresa and her mother could feel hurt by each other and continued to say that I did not understand why Teresa was so mad at her mother.

While her mother drove her home from that therapy session, Teresa asked her, "What's the Guinness record for hating your mom? I've been mad at you for 7 years." It appears that in first grade after reading a book about very tiny people and their pets that live undiscovered among humans, Teresa obsessed about wanting to meet them. She was sure they lived in her house, and she left food out for them. Her mother played along, took the food, and left a thank-you note in very small letters saying, "We liked the fud." Teresa told her mom that when she found out that the note came from her, she started hating her because "You tricked me."

Her parents and I do not know how significant this disclosure will be. I hope it will allow us to work on forgiveness and improve their relationship. I hope Teresa will continue to talk more to her parents and me. She has been less hostile at home and at school since disclosing this possible source of her anger. However, I suspect there are other gripes about her mother that are probably related to the molest concerns, because being tricked about the "little people" does not seem sufficient to generate such a strong response. In addition, perhaps being pressured to be closer, dealing with sibling rivalry, or wanting her father all to herself play a role in fomenting her anger. She is doing better with peers but is having some problems with homework completion. I am not concerned that she is devoted to first being comfortable socially. Her priorities make sense to her parents and me. It is just the beginning of the school year, and she is off to a good start "with a girl that has freckles, too."

Cassi's Grandmother

We had four meetings over the next 7 weeks.

Session 1: I meet with grandmother, who is pleased. "We left last week and kept talking and had some great days. Then her boyfriend, Craig, called to say he had a new girlfriend." Many teen clients are referred because they are a danger to themselves. The girls have often just broken up with a boyfriend, and with the loss they feel they are worthless and will never have another boyfriend, ever. As Craig was her first love, I worry she could hurt herself. The relationship had been intense with constant phone calls and inflamed by the grandmother's efforts to prevent contact. Cassi was controlling and smothering with her boyfriend, but he seemed to comply with her demands.

Once reassured that Cassi is not suicidal and that her eating and sleeping are returning to usual, I focus on the opportunity this loss offers for Cassi and her grandmother to get closer. Grandmother reports that they had seen a movie and laughed and laughed. Cassi even asked her if she could stay after she was 18, but grandmother did not answer. When I ask if she could stay, grandmother discusses her ambivalence and her boyfriend's desire to have a calmer and quieter house like they used to have. I accept her position, despite my wish that she would grant Cassi's request. A positive change this week is that Cassi, who previously refused to work, is now working at the store a few days a week and "is good with the customers; I thought she would be rude." She is even helping in the child care part of the store and enjoys watching the children while the mothers shop. We end the session sharing thoughts about how much better their relationship seems.

Session 2: Grandmother begins by saying that Cassi complains that she is so depressed. When I question further, she reports several incidents of Cassi laughing happily and playfully teasing her. I do not think she is all that depressed. I talk about how depressed people often emerge from their depression with anger and that she might expect anger and view it as an indication that Cassi is feeling better and not blaming herself as much. I think that Cassi is also getting a lot of secondary gain from this breakup, because she is now staying in bed, playing video games, watching TV, and calling friends about Craig. I am pleased she is getting peer support. She is also talking to three guys about it, so I am not that worried. I am concerned that she is avoiding food and liquid, has lost five pounds, and is throwing up. I wonder if she is dehydrated, and the grandmother wants to take her to her primary care physician tomorrow, especially because Cassi, her grandmother, and the grandmother's boyfriend are going to visit family on the East Coast and "the tickets are paid for." We end the session focusing on how they can enjoy each other on their trip.

Session 3: They're back, and we start with a brief check-in with Cassi, grandmother, and both therapists. We meet once a month for about half an hour. Grandmother begins, "Things aren't good." (Cassi smiles.) "I heard her tell Macey that she is 4 weeks pregnant." Cassi puts her fingers in her 17-year-old ears.

"I took a pregnancy test. I don't want to talk. Shut up." Fingers go back in ears. I ask her why she is so mad at her grandma.

She says, "I just am. She's too much. It's my life. It's not you. It's my problem."

"No, it's mine. I live with you. She has to go to Planned Parenthood and decide what to do. I told her the consequences, but she says I'm old and don't know anything. I slapped her." (I do not make a suspected child abuse report.)

"I shouldn't be hit. She's lucky I didn't sock her back."

I ask her what she would like her grandma to do.

"She should leave me alone. I'll take care of it. And she better not tell everyone. She'll tell everyone. Macey is going to take me [to Planned Parenthood]."

I say, "Your grandmother is worried about you."

Grandmother adds, "This is her attempt to get Craig back. His mother is calling me because she read the e-mail Cassi sent to Craig."

Cassi's therapist summarizes and ends the meeting. The grandmother and I go to my office to finish the hour while Cassi meets with her therapist.

The grandmother says, "Not a week goes by without a problem. I just found out an hour ago. I don't know if she is telling the truth." I ask her how a pregnancy would make her feel, and she opens up to talk about the shame she felt when she had Cassi's mother "out of wedlock." She says she feels responsible for Cassi's getting pregnant. I reassure her that she did make sure Cassi had birth control (an issue on which I had taken a strong stand).

I focus on how this is a very different situation, because she has been very supportive and helpful to Cassie. But we are at the end of the hour.

"Why me?"

I end with, "It's not you. You insisted she get birth control."

As I write my notes, I realize we have plans to end in about 6 weeks, and we haven't talked enough about stopping. I wonder what a good ending for us should be. I wonder if we should end.

Session 4: Grandmother begins, "She won't take a test. She won't go to Planned Parenthood. But I think she is lying. She said she took a test already. I asked her how much it cost, and she said, 'Five dollars.' She insisted she took it. She had a mild period. I checked the trash." I said, "Maybe she is trying to get Craig back or get back at Craig."

She continues, "She is so mad at me. I told her not to see Reanna, whom she was caught shoplifting with, but Reanna meets her at the Teen Center. Now she wants to go over to Kelly's house, and she was so cruel to Kelly last month that Kelly's mother called me. I was so embarrassed. Cassi says they are getting along again now. I don't think I can stop her. She shouldn't go over there. She's not wanted."

"Maybe she is reaching out to girlfriends so she can feel more secure about starting school."

"She won't do any chores, and she wants me to buy her all these inappropriate clothes. She hasn't done a chore since we got back from New York. She insists she washed the car, but I know she didn't. She lies. I'm not going to buy her all that, and I don't want her seeing Kelly or Reanna."

"What else is she doing?"

"Her drawers are so full of papers she can't close them. Her clean and dirty clothes are mixed up on the floor. I told her she had to clean them up before school, and now the papers are all over the floor too. Her friends will think she's a slob. I don't want them in the house until her room is clean."

"You have so many things you want for her. If you could have just three wishes, what would the most important things be? Maybe if you try to get everything she'll just get angrier." She cannot prioritize the things she wants to control in this emancipating adolescent who hates being controlled, probably in reaction to how her brother, Don, treated her and because she does not want to be controlled like her mother. I listen to the many expectations and say, "If you could start with the three most important things for now, wouldn't they be: One, schoolwork, Cs or better. Two, a chore a day. And three, have dinner with you at least three nights a week?"

We discuss these, as well as Cassi's need to get to bed on time so that she can get on a schedule to handle school when it starts. Grandmother talks about how Cassie stays up late and talks to Craig on the phone instead of organizing her room. This leads grandmother to nag her to get off the phone and get to bed. We discuss how there are so many things that worry the grandmother and that the more she bugs Cassi, the more secretive and oppositional Cassi gets. However, during the year the more grandmother insisted on rules, such as no phone after 10:00 p.m., or demanded weekly reports from teachers, the more work Cassi did to have phone privileges and freedom on the weekends.

I ask for three rules.

She offers, "One, Craig out of her life. Two, responsibility for her room and chores. And not have sex, get along at school, get to bed early, not be in everyone's business, make new friends, and stay away from Kelly and Reanna."

I start to feel the way grandmother does, that there are so many things that need to be controlled. I am confused about the costs and benefits of limits. I feel nothing will work. I do not know what to suggest. I do think she should have three requests and focus on them instead of demand everything at once. I do think she should let go of the small stuff, like her room, the laundry, what she wears, and whom she chooses for friends.

Then I realize I am talking about a kid who was telling her grandma a lot (up from zero), had passed her classes, moved from having Internet relationships to going to the Teen Center, got a boyfriend, has girlfriends, was using birth control, had been doing one chore a day (up from below zero), has been working successfully at the store, and was getting along much better with her grandmother until 1 week and 2 hours ago when she "got pregnant," which we really do not think she is. So maybe the pregnancy got us both scared. Maybe we are overreacting, and she is not all that bad and does not need more limits now. I share this with grandmother, and we both smile. Then she lays out three rules: One, when school starts show me evidence you are completing assignments and homework, or we go back to weekly teacher reports to earn phone and weekend privileges. Two, clean up after yourself and do a chore a day. And three, have dinner together three nights a week with the TV off.

As I write my progress note, I think about how the grandma's shame about Cassie's possible pregnancy affected her (our) panic, which led to wanting to control Cassi so they would not be shamed. I see them having to work on negotiating rules, verifications, and expectations. In the process I hope they will continue to accept and even appreciate parts of the other person.

One month later: Cassi and her grandmother will stop next week. They continue to get along better, and grandmother is considering allowing her to stay. Cassi is still working at the store, doing a chore a day at home, and is passing all her classes at school. They are eating together several times a week, and the grandmother is more approving of herself and Cassi. As we discussed terminating and accepting the growth Cassi made as well as the changes she did not make, I asked grandmother what her biggest change was. She instantly responded, "You helped me let go of trying to protect my daughter. I've stopped giving her money that went only to Don. I can't help her until she can say 'no' to Don. It's such a relief."

Barn

Mother failed to bring Barn back. We had an individualized educational program meeting with the parents, teachers, a resource specialist, a school nurse, a psychologist, and the principal. The school reported that Barn was increasingly socially isolated and violent. He had stopped doing the minimal work he had been doing. I said that therapy was not being helpful and asked again if the school could supply either transportation or on-site therapy. They said they could not. We discussed alternative plans. The parents complained that my office was just too far away. We came up with a plan. Barn's therapy would be transferred to a facility closer to father's home, mother would transport him, and father would pick him up when appointments were after work. I had already discussed in-home treatment with the county manager of this case, who said that there would be a 7-week wait for an opening, and in the meantime the family could work with the more convenient therapist. I felt relief to be off the case and pessimistic about Barn's prognosis.

One month later: Barn was transferred to a closer counseling center. His parents continued to avoid contact there. I hope the referral to the in-home program works out.

Alex

I met with Alex's father, who reported that school has started, and Alex is "doing great." We agreed that he has grown more than we expected over the years. He went from needing three restraints a day in school to being mainstreamed in regular classes for some of the day. The father reported that Alex came home excited about his week at computer camp, where he did not have behavior problems. The father indicated that he works "with him on homework, and it's a challenge for both of us. I have to be patient while he matures. You helped me stay the course. It just takes time." He has become skillful at behavior modification and has realistic expectations about how much empathy and caring Alex will develop. We do not know how far Alex can go in forming relationships. We decided to stop group therapy and child guidance counseling for now. But they can return if problems develop. I called Alex's teacher, who confirmed the progress and added that he is having lunch with three boys and talks about video games with them during breaks.

One month later: Alex has controlled his anger and adjusted to the school routine. He and his father are both struggling with math. He still talks about video games to one of the peers. The other two moved on.

Arisa

We had two meetings during the next 7 weeks.

There is a message on my voice mail placed at 7 p.m. on Friday. "Hi, George. It's me. I want Katrina [the oldest foster child] gone. I want her to go to hell. I want their license taken away for foster childing. I want you to call the foster agency and get me out of here, because I don't want to be here, anymore. Call me."

On Monday I call the home, and the father says, "Arisa is struggling for our attention. Today she is getting along with Katrina. The problem is Arisa can't be one of the group. She wants to be first. The special one."

She says, 'You don't love me anymore,' when I give attention to Katrina or Joseph, who is starting to have temper tantrums." We talk about referrals for the foster kids, but they are receiving treatment through their placement agency. I ask if Arisa has any good times with the kids. He says they do play well together, and Arisa says she wants to keep Joseph because, "He's like my son." I tell the father, "It sounds difficult to care for such needy kids now that their honeymoon is over. However, there is an opportunity in all of this. Probably Arisa is so needy and controlling to avoid rejection and abandonment. This is a core problem, and if she can deal with this situation at home, she can learn some important lessons that will affect all her relationships."

The dad requests that we switch to family therapy to reduce the drama. I say, "No, Arisa's anger is more related to her personal problems from being abandoned and rejected in the past, and that is more of an issue for individual therapy. It's not related to how the kids treat her." I also worry that seeing me relate to the foster kids would make Arisa jealous. Jealousy/ rejection would be a helpful focus for therapy with a youth with whom I had a good working relationship, so we could talk about it and resolve the rupture based on her core fears of being unlovable and abandoned. But because she is just starting to talk to me about feelings, we are not at a time in therapy when she could process and benefit from problems in our relationship. The dad agrees to wait on family therapy, and we discuss how parents might use family council meetings and how they can have more individual time with each child. I worry that without being able to enjoy each child individually (without the sibling rivalry), the mom and dad may burn out, the new kids will not attach, and Arisa will feel more displaced. I say that I hope this situation will increase Arisa's talking in therapy. Her phone message actually made me hopeful.

Session 1: Arisa comes in talking and sits in my chair. "Katrina is a liar and is rude." I say that I got her message and ask how Katrina makes her feel now.

"I feel like an outcast. It's like an atomic bomb. They don't care."

"What does it feel like to be an outcast?"

"Unloved, I don't belong. Katrina bosses me around. She lies to Mom."

"Did you used to feel like you belonged before they came?"

"I don't know how I felt."

"I think you felt a little 'outcastie' before they came. Is there a part of you that wants to leave and a part that wants to stay? Are they arguing with each other?"

"A little."

"What does the part that wants to go say?"

"They don't care about me."

"And the I-want-to-stay part?"

"I'd take Lovie."

"What would you miss?"

"My boyfriend."

"What do you want Mom and Dad to do?"

"Mom pays attention to them. Buys them stuff. She doesn't care about me. She likes them better. Katrina is so sneaky. She plants stuff in my room and tells Mom I stole it. They believe her, not me. Mom doesn't believe I don't steal stuff. That hurts my feelings. I'm just another person to them. Then Kat says her real mom loves her and my real mom didn't love me."

I say, "She couldn't love anyone; her brain was taken over by drugs. All she could think about was how to get more drugs."

"I know it's not my fault."

"It was all your biological mom's fault. Your mom now is different from your biomom. She can care for three kids. She can love them, and it doesn't mean she feels less love for you. In fact it means she is the kind of person who has a lot of love to give. It's hard to believe she and Dad have enough to go around, but I think they do. It's hard to feel sure someone cares about you. They sure put up with a lot of your bad behavior and still love you. You said you could feel it when you were in the hospital, and they kept coming to see you. Isn't that proof she loves you? A lot of the time you treat her badly, and she still cares and keeps trying to help you." Arisa looks calm.

I smile. "This is the best session we ever had. You talked to me."

"The third best. I talked the first two times."

"You're getting good at talking about your feelings. The kids are new. She has to make them comfortable."

Arisa responds with a story about a peer at school who was placed in a foster home.

I say, "They won't place you. You are stuck with each other. There is no escape. Resistance is futile." She smiles.

We have gone over the halfway point, and I ask if she wants to play ping-pong. She says we can talk more and goes on about scary movies that don't scare her any more. I talk about my favorite scary movie, and we have a good time. The conversation returns to her mom, and Arisa says, "I know she loves me because she buys me stuff." I talk about other ways to know if someone loves you and how people show love by listening, trying to understand, and doing things to help. We talk about what her mother does for her, and Arisa makes up things she does for her mother and father. I ask if her mom says she loves her. She says she does. I ask, "Do you tell mom you love her?" She says, "Sometimes." But I think she doesn't. I say, "Maybe you both need to tell each other more often, especially now that home is changing so much." She leaves in a good mood.

Session 2: Arisa pronounces, "I have a boyfriend [Dennis], and he's a foster kid, too." She brought him and her ferret to the appointment. They are in the waiting room. I go to meet and greet them. Arisa introduces us and says they are going to the mall after this. She asks if he can join us, and I say, "No, this is my time to be with you. Maybe he can come in for some time at the end." I would like to see them together, but I want to keep our time focused on our struggle to trust and relate. In addition, there is a legal issue that inviting Dennis into the session could trigger. I could be accused of treating Dennis without his parents' permission. Dennis appears to be a cute, frail, happy preppie, who looks younger than Arisa. We enter the office again, and she is excited. "He's 16 [Arisa just turned 14] and a gangster. We are both Crips. We like blue. We were at the mall, and the girls I knew in fifth grade saw us and said he was 'a bad ass.' That's what I wanted."

"What's he like?"

"Sweet, loving, nice to my brother and sister."

"Yeah."

"We agree what we will name our children [Dennis Jr., Jake, Nicki, Scott, and Rebeka with a 'k'], and we'll live on a farm with all kinds of animals."

I switch to school, which starts next week. "Are you ready for school?"

"We went shopping ... lots of stuff. ... Mom loves me."

"Do you have any goals for school this year?"

"Not go. I'd rather watch paint peel off the wall than go."

"Well, I have some goals that you can borrow. How can you make this year great?"

"Go to home school. Dad said I can."

"You wish. Listen, did you learn anything last year from doing the work? You started doing the work and even passed everything. That was a new and amazing Arisa. Can she go to school this year?"

"Maybe."

"And can she be friendly?"

"Maybe."

"I'm worried you are going to go in there and not try to get to know the other kids. How can you show an interest in them?"

"They won't talk to me."

"That was last year when you used to show off and be bossy, and they didn't like that. You don't like Katrina when she tries to control you. They will like you if you just be nice and are interested in them."

"No, they won't."

"Yes, they will. You are very likeable."

"No."

"Yes."

"No."

"Yes, yes, yes. Ask them what they did this summer."

"No, no, no."

"Before we go, how are things going with the kids at your house?"

"Katrina still takes my stuff and says she'll hurt Lovie if I tell. But they let Dennis in the house. He's part of the family."

I wonder if Arisa would like to come up with some things she and Dennis can do together, and I get the leisure questionnaire. We go outside with Dennis and the ferret, and they fill it out when I leave. It's fun to see them get to know each other and talk about their interests.

One month later: Arisa has continued to talk the entire session, do schoolwork and homework, and have lunch with two other girls in her class (something she has never done before, as she felt rejected and chose isolation or older students). In our sessions she stopped watching the clock and demanding things. She seemed so comfortable allowing me to confront her and talking about her anger at the new kids in the home and her love of her boyfriend that I thought I could ask for more feelings. I said that she had made such big changes this year trusting and wanting to get closer to friends and parents and being so brave with me that I wondered if she could trust me with some of the things that happened way back when that made her think people would hurt her. I had asked similar questions over the years and got to see her defenses in action. This time she disclosed being molested and neglected, and we filed a suspected abuse report. I do not know if she will allow us to pursue these topics. But I am hopeful. I am not going to focus on pushing her to tell what happened. I want her to realize that it was not her fault, so she can feel less blame and shame for the abuse and neglect. I will expect her to be upset at her biomother and aunt for not protecting her and to understand the role of substance abuse in their neglect of her rather than think she was the cause. Anger at them would be an indicator that she is not blaming herself. I think this shift will manifest in contemporary relationships by a further decrease in compensatory self-aggrandizement, control, and neediness. This shift might be fueled by her parents' and my appreciating and enjoying her rather than the blaming and criticizing that she expects. Her parents and I will emphasize how unfair it is that she was not protected then, but she is safe now.

Her idealization of her bioparents and aunt is common in abused and neglected youths who use splitting as a defense against being rejected and feeling abandoned. They divide the parent into good and bad and attach to the good parent while repressing the bad one. This allows them to still have a loving parent but at the cost of having to blame themselves for the abuse and neglect, because if they believe the parent is all good, then the egocentric youth must be responsible for the problems. We have come a long way.

Jordan

We had one meeting in the following 7 weeks.

I have been emphasizing a harm-reduction (Tatarsky, 2003) rather than a total-abstinence approach to Jordan's drug and alcohol dependence. Harm reduction is a model of treatment that is presently out of favor, largely because it is misunderstood as supporting the client's rationalizations for continuing to use and is perceived as doomed to failure. He dropped out of several abstinence-based programs (AA and NA), in part because they did not take into consideration his developmental level and level of motivation to change. Developmentally he is a pleasure-seeking adolescent with the typical sense of personal invulnerability and orientation toward individuation, autonomy, and risk taking. This level of maturity leads to his developing a personal identity based on separating from adult influence and making his own decisions. He was initially unmotivated to change his drug use pattern and lacked the skills to support and maintain change.

Prior to encouraging abstinence or even less drug use, therapy focused on developing the skills to support change, on increasing his motivation to change by helping him accept his failure to control his use, and on increasing his awareness of the negative consequences of his dependence. He was already quite aware of the benefits of using. Therapy initially focused on connecting substance use to consequences that are important to him. Because streetwise youths often consider prison a good career move, and because some inner-city Blacks think doing well in school is for White kids, going to juvenile hall and failing academically were not deterrents to using. However, the loss of money needed for a car and apartment, loss of girls with higher self-esteem, and possibly loss of placement with his grandmother were consequences that bothered him.

He moved from denying that his drug use was a problem and seeing it as an asset that he could stop at any time to trying to work out a pattern of controlled use. Controlled use involved continuing his relationship with substances while avoiding unfavorable consequences by using condoms and employing strategies to control his use of substances. These strategies included using drugs and alcohol only after business was done, switching to softer drugs, using at a slower rate, and avoiding peers who were heavy users. These harm-reduction strategies can often either work, lead to new strategies, or lead to realizing that abstinence is needed. Harm-reduction approaches assume that clients turn to substance use as a coping mechanism to handle stresses (boredom, anger, feelings of inadequacy, social anxiety, etc.) and emphasize developing healthy ways to deal with these stresses (Marlatt, 1998).

Jordan is now attempting controlled abstinence. He proclaims periods of abstinence until "I pass my drug test … until the weekend … until schoolwork is done," and so on. Therapy at this stage has focused on how to reduce triggers to use drugs and to identify skills he can use to maintain his resolve to abstain, such as talking to peers about things besides drugs, tolerating feelings and relationships, coping with cravings, learning study skills to handle school demands, and developing nondrug-related pleasurable activities. Unsuccessful attempts at controlled use and controlled abstinence often generate motivation and a persuasive argument for abstinence. In fact long-term studies with clients treated with harm reduction have found that more clients ended up abstaining than moderating.

Jordan clearly needs, but refuses, more intensive drug treatment. His depression, anxiety, and memory difficulties may well be partially caused by ongoing pot use and by emotional- and drug-induced damage to his limbic system. He may have a limited ability to experience enjoyment because of a loss of dopamine receptors from his methamphetamine use.

In the past 7 weeks, we have met only once. I was out of town for a week. Jordan called to cancel two sessions, and then his grandmother went out of town and Jordan made an appointment or two which he did not keep or call to cancel. I kept pursuing, and he finally arrived. He has to travel 45 minutes by bus to reach my office, so we scheduled our meeting right after he had a job interview nearby. I ignore his irresponsibility and play the relationship card. "I've been worrying about you. I've been wondering what happened after our last meeting. We ended with Grandma wanting to see your finances."

"I stopped having finances after that."

"What did you two decide?"

"Nothing yet. She went to Missouri. I don't need her coming at me."

"Did you sign up for classes?"

"I'm taking a business class. I want to be a manager. Why should I take English?"

"Yeah, you'll probably never go to England."

"She pisses me off. That's enough for her. Introduction to Business Functions. Four units. I need six to get a student loan." His cell phone rings. He checks it. Girlfriend. He frowns at her wanting contact that does not lead to sex.

"The more I think, the more I want to go back [to the street life]. Am I supposed to just give it up? It's overwhelming what she makes me do. Go from zero to everything or I can't live there [with his grandma]. She's not gonna run my life. No one is."

"I thought you both wanted the same things, and you both know it's very difficult to make big changes."

"I'm not gonna follow her rules. Too many. I don't need it. 24/7/365 she tells me what to do. I have two options. To let her run my life or go back to Oakland. I don't want her to get stressed out when I do fuck up."

"You don't want to disappoint her."

"I don't want her running everything."

"She just wants college, money, and a job."

"I could sell drugs. I can't do construction."

"Because of your back?"

"And making sandwiches [his last job] won't make me rich. Her feelings are the problem. She stresses me."

"You know you have to deal with other people's feelings, and they have to deal with yours when you have a relationship."

"If she wanted to give to me, she wouldn't ask for stuff in return. I don't need parents. Feel me?"

"Every relationship is like that. There is a giving and receiving that has to balance out. But she's not asking for herself. She's asking you to do stuff for you."

"Why's it her business what I do? She tries to control me."

"Is this all about pot? I think you're fighting to keep smoking."

"I didn't smoke all last week."

"Why?"

"It clouds my mind. I couldn't even sign up for classes until the 11th, and they started on the 16th – yesterday. I barely got into class. I'm mean and irritable when I don't smoke."

"Is she pushing you in a different direction than you want to go?"

"I need to get the fuck out."

"She wants you to get a job, go to college, and not spend all your money on drugs. Is that what you want? I think she would agree that everything else is your business."

"You don't know. She says she wants to help, but there is a big price. She holds all this shit over my head."

"What?"

"Probation, and I owe her money. She wants me to pay rent now that the SSI stopped. If she had given me my social security money, I could be on my own now. She wants me to contribute. I appreciate why, but I didn't ask to be taken in. The rent – OK. That's reasonable."

"She was going to rent out the room before you came. She needed the money."

"She wants to know everything."

"Just drugs, job, and college. Isn't this really about pot?"

"No. I want to be rich by the only means I know how. It's her acting like I wanted to be with her and begged her to stay. She acts like my savior."

"And that's what feels like a burden in the relationship?"

"You saved me from so many fights. I come here and can get all my feelings out. It helps."

"Thanks. That feels good."

"My family is distancing from me. Oakland won't talk to me. My mom, brother, all of them."

"Why?"

"I don't know."

"Maybe because you're getting shit done, and that's a threat to them."

"No."

"You are getting business done: 98%, college, stopped crank and fighting, girlfriend, job interviewing, and jobs. They may want to deal only with people who are like them."

"Yeah, they are afraid I'll call the police on them. I haven't talked to Wayne [his brother] for a month."

"Maybe they are afraid you'll be critical."

"No. I told him to go out big before he gets caught. He knows me. Ya feel me? We were on the run together. Just us two. We went to foster homes together. We shared our bitches."

"Aren't you upset about how he is living his life? Like Dad. I thought Grandma would take him in, if he stayed clean."

"He's not going to go right. He knows only this way. He doesn't want to change. There are consequences. I know she [Mom] loves me."

"Her body was taken over by drugs. She can love only drugs."

"She never was a mom. You don't last long on the street. I have to protect her."

"It's so sad. Such a waste and a pain to people who care about her." I change the subject back to pot. "So you haven't done pot all week? Did you have sex without pot?"

"Two or three times."

"When was the last time before this week that you had sex without pot?"

"Never. Maybe when I was 13."

I think about when I was 13 and watching cartoons.

"What's it like without pot?"

"Pot makes you last longer, and you go higher."

"You say pot clouds your mind, screws up your motivation, uses up all your money, and may cost you everything here [Grandma, college, girlfriends, car, apartment]. Why not just use it for sex?"

"Because I'm so mean. I had only one fight when I did pot every day."

"How about the Seroquel and Lexapro?"

"I stopped it."

"Do you still have some?" Wondering if he sold them.

"Lots."

"They're supposed to reduce irritability. Were you having any problems with them?"

"I'm addicted to the high of not giving a fuck. It's me. I got to make things happen. It's my choice. It's my fault. I ain't gonna be an idiot. I got to grow up. I can't party so."

"You wanna check yourself before you wreck yourself." (Ice Cube.)

"Yeah."

"You don't have to do it by yourself. The meds and NA could help. We gotta stop for now."

We agree to meet same time next week.

As I write my progress note, I can see him returning to the street life. He could go back to Oakland, drugs, easy money, and bitches and be included in his family, or he could stay here and struggle with sobriety, relationships, work, and college. He struggles with this on a daily basis. Id versus Superego. The devil he knows versus the devil he does not know. I would like him to understand that he can succeed here and that the only way he can help his brother and mom is to stay here and be a successful model in the same way that his grandmother is a model for him. I am also worried that his funding for therapy may be precarious. I have to call his grandmother to see if she can have his Medi-Cal funding reinstated and see if she will drive him to sessions.

One month later: Jordan and his grandmother are fighting the system to get his Medi-Cal reinstated. Although we continued to make appointments while his funding was in doubt, he did not keep them until this past month. His return seems related to wanting support to stay, feeling my caring, and his grandmother's efforts to bring him. He continues to struggle with returning to drugs and the streets. He could go either way. He has had increasing periods of abstinence punctuated with substance abuse and violence when drunk. His deadline for getting a job to be able to stay with his grandmother is approaching. He has a clear understanding of the costs and benefits of staying and leaving. I hope he stays.

Jordan has returned to taking his medication and keeping his last two therapy appointments. He has been talking more about being tempted to sell pot, missing his father, feeling responsible for not preventing his imprisonment, worrying about being killed by his gang for leaving them, and feeling frustrated by staying with his girlfriend, who bugs him to stop drinking and fighting. He says that the alcohol and pot stop him from thinking about these painful things. I think that his grandmother is pushing too hard on college. He would do better in a 1-year training program where he could graduate with a skill that employers want. I need to meet with her. He realizes that pot calms him, but alcohol makes him reckless and violent. He agrees that he should not drink, but when he smokes, his judgment goes up in smoke, and then he starts to drink.

CHAPTER **11**
Conclusion

These Cases Involved a Delicate Balance Between Improving Skills and Providing a Therapeutic Relationship

These clients appeared to cling to behaviors, defenses, and cognitive distortions that were useful in their past but were not adaptive to their present situation. They had poor skills for managing affects and behaviors and had deficits in self-concept, empathy, trust, communication, and academic performance. These were unhappy clients creating further unhappiness for themselves and others. They had problems that manifested in their relationships and initially in the therapeutic relationship as a transference test. Rather than provide healing, their daily relationships reinforced their defenses and negative expectations. Their pathological approach to others was a major focus in their treatment, especially when it interfered with forming and maintaining the therapeutic relationship and surfaced in peer and family interactions.

Teresa and Arisa approached others with the expectation that if people really got to know them, others would not like them. I tried to persuade them to use friendly behaviors to protect themselves while helping them experience a corrective emotional relationship with their parents and me that would give them a taste of something they would seek in others. This was difficult to accomplish, because they were so self-absorbed for most of their early treatment that I did not appear to be a real person to them. They were not interested in relating to me and could not view me as separate from their expectations and needs. I felt as if my comments were unwanted and experienced as distractions from their focus on themselves and their needs.

Although phenotypically similar they arrived at these deficits through different paths. Teresa seemed genotypically predisposed to social difficulties. She experienced some traumas, but her reaction to them was influenced by cognitive distortions and seemingly innate difficulties managing anxieties. Her molest was met with supportive responses from her parents and teachers. This would have provided damage control for someone more intact and prevented further explorations, confusion, derogatory self-thoughts, and self-harm. Were she more resilient she would not have adopted a pattern of dealing with others by withdrawing and launching preemptive attacks when she anticipated rejection and condemnation. My attempts to teach her to question her negative thoughts about herself and to use grounding, affect management, and techniques to bind her anxiety were met with a defiant look of enthusiasm. Therefore, skills could not be taught directly. Indeed, they were presented in the context of therapist self-disclosures, discussions of others, and the identification of times in the therapeutic relationship and in Teresa's past and present interactions when she successfully used, or could have used, more adaptive skills.

By necessity my primary focus was on engagement rather than skill acquisition. Much of her therapy involved trying to maintain engagement and helping her experience a supportive relationship that mirrored her strengths so that she could be more engaged with her parents, teachers, and peers. As her problems manifested in these relationships and in therapy, I tried to create teaching opportunities, but this approach usually triggered withdrawal and threatened our relationship. Because I did not want to experience the same fate as her mother and previous therapist, the stage of treatment presented here focused on providing successes, respecting her defenses, and offering approval, which was easy because I enjoyed her so much.

Similar to my work with Teresa, my work with Arisa was more of a relationship than a therapeutic alliance at this stage of treatment. She could tolerate more confrontation of her rejection-causing behaviors, and she was more able to directly deal with past traumas when she began to trust that I was not like her previous caretakers. In fact, similar to working with other clients raised by parents whom they fought with, mildly challenging her seemed to be experienced as closeness, in the same way that calling each other derogatory names and "doing the dozens" is experienced as closeness in some teen groups. Both clients reacted negatively to insight and interpretation, so these techniques were not an important component of treatment at this stage of therapy. Insight is often more helpful and accepted after behavioral change rather than as the motivator of change. Her level of moral development dictated the use of consequences to affect her behavior.

Even after 5 years of intermittent contact with me, her foster parents and I still struggled with helping her engage in a relationship with peers and us. Arisa pulled away when people attended to others or did not comply with her control. We worked on doable behavioral issues (schoolwork, truth telling, hygiene, chores), but the main focus was on building trust and engagement in this egocentric youth. Her parents and I showered her with successes and approval, provided opportunities for supervised socialization, and tried to instill behaviors that would lead to successful academics and peer contacts while confronting and providing consequences for her behaviors that sabotaged her academic and social progress. It was possibly through relationships with animals that she began to learn empathy and feel better about herself. As our relationship deepened I was more able to enjoy her, and she was more able to tolerate my approval. I expect to see her increasingly abandon her defenses and further risk relating to her parents and me.

Cassi initially avoided peers and her grandmother, possibly because she expected control and abuse. She controlled others and displayed anger to feel safe and keep others at a comfortable distance. Much of her therapy involved helping her experience relationships with her therapist and grandmother that did not confirm her expectations. Then she could lower her defenses and further experience corrective emotional relationships. My work with grandmother often involved trying to help her relate to and enjoy Cassi without triggering Cassi's defenses. This was complicated by grandmother's shame-based expectations for Cassie. My appreciating grandmother and mirroring her struggles with her daughter and grandchildren allowed her to be more accepting and less blaming and controlling of Cassi, to have more realistic expectations for Cassi and herself, to develop a strong therapeutic alliance, and to tolerate some confrontation of her parenting.

Barn had never experienced a healthy relationship. I hoped to help him have one with me and to teach his parents to agree on their parenting so he could have consistent rules and expectations at their homes and at school. I thought that the work would first involve getting the parents to agree on discipline. I did not want to work with Barn without their support. I could not engage these parents, who, like Barn, were in the precontemplation stage of motivation to change. I became triangulated in their relationship and pathology, and therapy was ended before it began.

Alex had attention-deficit/hyperactivity disorder (ADHD), and he also carried a reactive attachment disorder diagnosis. He came to therapy with a caring parent, who rapidly formed a therapeutic relationship. Goals centered on helping the father adjust to Alex's limitations in forming relationships and learn to manage a child with ADHD. In combination with an exceptional behavior-modification-based special education program, Alex was able to control his behavior to gain nonrelational rewards. I fear his ability to form caring relationships will remain limited.

Jordan's relationships have been egocentric and exploitative. He expected others to harm him or to think negative things about him. He tended to view others as dupes to manipulate. He showed the ability to relate with caring to gang and family members but viewed all others with suspicion. His addictions interfered with maintaining relationships and learning new patterns. I do not see him progressing further without residential substance abuse treatment. Despite his grandmother's and my efforts to use our relationships and consequences to help him seek further treatment, he presently refuses.

Sometimes We Have to Treat Without First Having a Diagnosis to Guide Us

I was trained to base treatment on diagnosis and that diagnosis informs prognosis. When a client has several diagnoses or the diagnosis is tentative, it complicates developing realistic treatment expectations. We do not always have the luxury of knowing a diagnosis before we treat particular problems, even though treatment selection may hinge on diagnosis. For instance, before treating a client with hyperactivity, suspected ADHD has to be distinguished from age-appropriate behavior, post-traumatic stress disorder, bipolar disorder, agitated depression, anxiety, learning disabilities, low IQ, medical and neurological disorders, environmental causes, and other factors that contribute to inattention, hyperactivity, and impulsivity.

Teresa, Alex, and Barn arrived on medication that increased the complexity of an already difficult diagnostic task. Alex presented on medication that masked many of his ADHD symptoms and made his reactive attachment disorder seem prominent. Barn and Teresa were on so much medication that their diagnoses are still unclear. This masking of symptoms is particularly seen in previously hospitalized clients. They are medicated during a crisis that is compounded by hospitalization and removal from their family. They are assessed by psychiatrists whose mandate is to return clients to their precrisis state of functioning. Because the role of hospitalization has changed from treatment to stabilization, clients are discharged as soon as possible. When these clients later appear for outpatient treatment, they carry a diagnosis that legitimizes the medication that they are taking. But they often do not display the behaviors characteristic of the diagnosis, because the medication is effective, or they were misdiagnosed. Despite the questionable efficacy and safety of medication, probably half of my clients receive psychotropic medication for problems such as ADHD, depression, anxiety, insomnia, aggressive behavior, and thought disorders. Working with a psychiatrist and dealing with side effects and compliance problems have become more a part of my practice each year.

Teresa and Arisa seemed phenotypically similar in their tentative therapeutic relationship, problems making friends, and refusal to acknowledge and work on goals. But they carried different diagnoses, which led to differences in treatment. Teresa's biology predisposed her to be unable to resiliently cope with stresses. Her parents were fundamentally loving, but they could not adequately comfort her. Reparenting was not an issue in her treatment. I never felt that the *DSM* provided much help in understanding Teresa. Arisa's early and continued abuse and neglect taught her the dangers in attaching, trusting and depending on others. She learned to feel safe in relationships only by controlling them and by trying to meet her own needs. Arisa never experienced an early nurturing relationship, so major reparenting seemed required. Jordan's diagnosis suggested that he could tolerate and benefit from confrontation of behaviors and defenses in his treatment. All these clients carried multiple diagnoses. As with many clients, the primary and secondary diagnoses shifted in importance as treatment continued. They were complex cases.

I Had My Goals, and They Had Their Goals

Mutually agreed-on goals allow us to focus therapist–client energy, mutually define the purpose of treatment, and assess its effectiveness. However, overfocusing on goals, especially when clients are not committed to them, can be perceived as rejecting and controlling and can interfere with engagement. It is especially difficult to mutually agree on goals when working with youths. All of the clients discussed here were resistant to establishing goals. I expect this lack of commitment to treatment goals, especially at the start of therapy.

Teresa passively accepted her parents' goals for her, but she became silent and withdrew when asked what she wished to accomplish or how she would like things to be at school or with friends and family.

Cassi's grandmother was able to identify goals at the beginning of therapy, but they were unrealistic. As she learned about Cassi's strengths, accepted her limitations, and accepted that Cassi's behavior did not reflect on her, she was able to acknowledge goals of enjoying and helping Cassi rather than demanding compliance and token behaviors that would make her feel she was a good parent.

Barn's and Alex's goals were a reflection of their problems. Barn was seen only twice and verbalized wanting violence and violent toys. His parents stated opposing goals. Alex wanted electronic things, whereas his father initially wanted Alex to be more than he was capable of being. Therapy for Alex involved a process of his father and therapist mutually agreeing on accomplishable goals.

Arisa refused to talk about goals. This limited her progress. Her parents and I agreed on goals and worked together, but Arisa never joined our meetings.

Jordan had a series of goals with which I generally agreed, beginning with getting off probation, but we differed and argued. Conduct-disordered youths can handle confrontation and disagreement with the therapist, and in fact these conflicts often engage them and strengthen the relationship. They can view the warm, sympathetic, and caring therapist as a wimp who can be easily manipulated. His grandmother and I agreed on most goals. Sometimes I sided with her and sometimes with Jordan, but mostly when they were not in agreement with each other I tried to mend the rift by highlighting their common hopes. Jordan could not agree with the therapist's and grandmother's goal of enrolling in more intensive substance abuse treatment. The strength of our relationship allowed us to continue to focus on this goal despite our differences.

Especially at the start of treatment, client goals are often a reflection of pathology. If they could have initially stated healthy goals, therapy might have been easier or not needed. As clients learn skills, abandon defenses, and develop self-esteem and trust in others, they can form healthier, more realistic goals. I tended to agree more with the parents' desires as therapy progressed. In none of these cases did therapist, parent, and youth all agree on goals, but our goals became more congruent with progress in therapy.

Peer Group Treatment Is Probably the Best Way to Teach Social Skills, When They Become Needed in Group as Problems Surface

Teresa and Arisa were "group breakers." Their controlling and mean behaviors were so toxic to the other group members that they could not be maintained in a group. At the start of treatment, Jordan lacked the anger control necessary for group involvement; only now is he ready for a group. Because they could not benefit from attending peer group, treatment of their social problems needed to be provided in individual therapy with parallel parent counseling and school consultation. Through these modalities the clients were prepared for social situations. Their unrealistic expectations, projections, and cognitive distortions were challenged by caretakers and in therapy when I had amassed enough relationship points to be heard. They were oriented to notice the consequences of their present antisocial behaviors, and prosocial behaviors were taught and reinforced. Their teachers created social opportunities that the clients processed in therapy. When the clients were ready, their parents found social experiences for them in the community and worked with the providers. Progress required a combination of interventions in several environments.

A critical component in the treatment of all the clients was the support of their caretakers and teachers. Without parents as allies, treatment of youths is difficult at best, but when parents change their parenting, dramatic changes can happen. Studies of youths discharged from residential treatment indicate that follow-up care greatly determines how long treatment gains last. Frensch and Cameron (2002) found that making gains in treatment and maintaining gains after discharge was dependent on the extent to which the family was involved in the treatment process and the availability of aftercare, including family support. Similarly, in outpatient treatment the changes can be enhanced, maintained, or eliminated by the adults in their lives. An hour of therapy a week can make a powerful impact on a person's life, but the parent's and teacher's influence can be so much greater.

There were barriers to socialization that needed to be eliminated. These clients needed to experience the parent's or therapist's caring about them before they could hope to have a healthy relationship. Teresa, Arisa, and Jordan needed to learn prosocial skills. If they tried to relate before their new skills and new expectations for others were on line, they would fail. They were experts at protecting themselves and novices at being intimate. Even if they could produce friendly behaviors and could tolerate closeness, healthier peers would flee at their neediness, control, and anger or odd behaviors when defenses were threatened. It was a catch-22 situation. They needed to be healthier to have a relationship, and they needed a relationship to be healthier. It was in the therapeutic relationship that some of their resocialization could be shaped, practiced, and then generalized to other relationships.

Therapy focused on helping Teresa, Arisa, and Jordan understand that their strategies to protect themselves from anticipated rejection caused rejection and that friendlier behaviors might lead to friendships. Their strategies had been previously somewhat successful in protecting them but became their problems. This common process exemplifies a theory of therapy that emphasizes that our past solutions become our present problems. I repeatedly explained this to them, sometimes by exploring a metaphor about knights:

> In the Middle Ages there were knights who went to battle to defend their castles. They learned that the thicker their armor, the more

successful they were in battle. Then the environment changed, because the armor-piercing crossbow was invented. In this new environment the knights with the thickest armor became the heaviest and slowest, so they were the easiest targets for a serf to run up to and shoot. What worked before became the problem when the environment changed.

This nonblaming lesson applies to most clients.

Cassi's Treatment Required One Therapist to See the Caretaker While Another Saw the Identified Patient

Cassi's grandmother received child guidance counseling, which is different from individual therapy. The purpose of the grandmother's sessions was to treat the identified patient, her granddaughter. For instance when the grandmother said that she was ashamed of Cassi's wearing spikes, rather than explore the causes of the grandmother's shame, I emphasized understanding how her feelings influenced her parenting and Cassi.

Separate therapists generate two countertransferences, which require ongoing consultation to control. Without frequent meetings, each therapist is at risk for identifying with his or her client and seeing the other family member only from his or her client's point of view. Therefore when these therapists meet, they typically say, "Your client needs to change. It's because of her that my client ..." In this case the initial meeting went something like, "Can't you get Cassi to stop being so unreasonable and accept a few simple house rules?" "Well, can't you get her grandmother to stop being so strict? She wants Cassi to come right home after school." As we discussed the situation, we both understood our client's contribution, and we could be more objective. As John Meeks (1980) wrote, the greatest obstacle to reducing an adolescent's anger at his or her parents is the therapist's countertransference. Similarly the parents might not become closer to their adolescent if the parents' therapist identifies with the apparently victimized parents and sees their parenting as an understandable reaction to the unreasonable adolescent. It is through ongoing consultation that progress can be made and disaster averted.

The Therapy for These Clients Did Not Fit the Evidenced-Based, Linear, Medical Model in Which a Treatment of Choice Is Selected for a Problem

The literature indicates that exposure is the treatment of choice for trauma resolution. However, none of these clients could have tolerated being exposed to more anxiety. Their lives were too chaotic, and they lacked the social support and ability to use relationships to handle more stress. They were not motivated to acquire the skills to manage anxiety, and they rejected anything too didactic, so information was presented slowly in the context of our relationship.

I generally tried a range of treatments for each problem, until one captured the clients' interest. I worked on the ABCs of problem behaviors: the antecedents, the behaviors, and their consequences. I focused on correcting misconceptions from the past, removing triggers and stressors in the environment, confronting nonproductive behaviors, calling attention to their negative consequences, and teaching, modeling, cajoling, and pleading to instill new behaviors and coping skills. I also tried to encourage home and school environments to teach and reward similar behaviors. When the clients would allow, I focused on problems, fostered understanding, and taught alternatives. Sometimes I ignored problems and worked on building skills and increasing self-esteem by exposing the clients to successes and approval and by fostering a relationship in which they liked me and saw that I felt the same way about them. Enjoying them and helping them accept and incorporate my positive view of them felt like a critical part of treatment and allowed the other parts to progress. I was always guided by trying to deepen the therapeutic relationship, or at least control damage to it.

These cases did not fit the linear model:

- Assessment leads to
- engagement that results in
- disclosing presenting concerns that leads to
- identifying problems to treat and
- developing a strong therapeutic alliance that supports the
- selection of interventions that compose the treatment plan that results in
- problem resolution,
- mutual appreciation, and termination.

This linear process may work best for clients who have the capacity to form trusting relationships and have or can rapidly develop a realistic understanding of their emotions, problems, and the therapy process so it does not become sabotaged by their unrealistic thinking and emotions.

Progress in therapy can be dependent on the depth of the therapeutic relationship, which is not highly valued in the medical model. The client's trust, self-disclosure, goals, ability to abandon defenses and resistances, ability to adopt new skills and expectations, depth of understanding, and frustration tolerance can all vary with the depth of the therapeutic relationship. The therapeutic relationship provides a venue in which problems can be expressed and resolved and new aspects of the client can be presented. These were clients with strong needs to protect themselves; they had been hurt by relating to others. They learned to use or avoid others; therefore, they lacked the skills and desire to form and maintain a therapeutic relationship. These clients took a long time to develop a strong enough relationship to allow the therapist some leeway in confronting or frustrating them. The relationship interacts with each step in therapy. Each step becomes a microcosm of the entire process, in the same way that each part of a hologram contains the entire picture.

The medical model is most effective with problems that are independent of each other. In my practice I rarely work with a client who presents with a single circumscribed problem that can be ameliorated with a treatment technique. Most clients present with a series of interconnected concerns. Sometimes as one problem is struggled with and the therapeutic relationship deepens, another problem is brought to light. I have worked with clients who felt comfortable sharing their deepest concerns only after a year of contact and with clients who never were able to verbalize their difficulties. Young clients may not be aware of their problems or may be vague or unable or unwilling to reveal them until well into the process. Initial presenting problems may not be the most robust or useful issues to focus on. Sometimes treatment initially focuses on problems that the client is most motivated to work on. As these cases illustrate, changes create new challenges to work on, and previously resolved problems resurface in new situations. So rather than expect the list of problems developed at the start of treatment to define the process, I anticipate working on several issues in each session, some familiar and long term, some new, some that are readily solvable, and others that will require repeated revisiting.

These Cases Give a Feeling of the Pace of Progress That I Have Come to Expect

With longer term clients, small changes in course direction, rather than U-turns, are typical. It is difficult to know specifically what led to the changes seen in these 3 months and whether the changes will be temporary or the beginnings of greater growth. For instance Teresa became less hostile to her parents and peers, perhaps because she could see herself as more loveable and therefore did not need to protect herself with anger and attacks to keep them away. She also trusted enough to risk sharing a cause of her anger at her mother and make an attempt to forgive. Arisa moved from manipulating and avoiding contact to talking about feelings, from projecting blame and responsibility and presenting herself as a victim to admitting she contributed a little to problems by controlling and manipulating others, and from being needy and demanding to accepting some limits and doing some school assignments and homework. She made a great deal of progress in a short time; however, it had been preceded by 1 year of little movement and a long hiatus from therapy during which she matured and became more used to her parents.

Treatment for Arisa and Alex exemplifies the model of therapy delivery that has become increasingly popular with the advent of managed care. It is similar to the way medical problems are treated. Clients work on specific goals and then stop treatment. If problems recur or new ones appear, the client might return for further services. These clients received services episodically over a long period with significant breaks in contact. I have been pleased with how rapidly engagement and therapeutic alliance are reestablished with returning clients and their caretakers. When continuity of care and reasonable treatment allowances are possible, this model has the potential to take advantage of the benefits of long-term therapy (trust, in-depth knowledge of the client, history of mutually shared experiences over different developmental stages and problems) as well as the goal-directness and heightened motivation generated by time-limited treatment.

Termination Is Usually Difficult for the Client and Me

I have to adjust to the pace of our progress and what we did not accomplish. Barn and Alex terminated while Cassi approached termination, and Jordan's therapy hinged on reestablishing funding and making a major change in his attitude toward residential substance abuse treatment. It is ideal for termination to occur when symptoms are ameliorated and when the client has attained a heightened capacity for happiness through improved functioning in love, work, and/or recreation. Termination for Barn and Alex was not upsetting to them, because Barn was seen only two times and did not form a relationship, and Alex attended only two peer group meetings over the summer because of a busy family schedule.

Jordan has been seen for almost a year and a half. I feel sad and powerless that he may not continue treatment. He has really used therapy well. There have been times when I felt him almost absorbing me, and in subsequent sessions I would hear my words coming back to me in the form of his thoughts about controlling anger and accepting the frustration of having to deal with another's needs in a relationship. Probably the most important goal of termination involves helping the client understand that stopping is not a rejection. I am hopeful that Jordan will be able to end knowing how much I have admired his strengths.

I get a particular satisfaction from being able to form a strong relationship with a youth who enters treatment fighting it because he or she is court ordered or made to attend by parents. These clients are often the ones who find termination the most difficult, because they can attach so strongly when they discover that I am not the authoritarian clone of the court or parents that they were expecting. In addition, they often are so alienated that they have few other relationships. Jordan lost most of his family, so I expect that termination will generate abandonment issues, unlike typical conduct disorders. I hope that he can continue; he could benefit from another year of treatment, with several months of processing his termination.

My favorite kind of termination is when the youth starts cancelling appointments because he or she is involved in relationships, school, and community activities that become more important than our meetings.

I want to know how these stories end, but I cannot have closure. The clients live on. Their stories do not end.

Notes

Chapter 1

1. Westen and Morrison (2001) found that 2 out of 3 patients could not be included in the studies they reviewed because of comorbid conditions (p. 880); and exemplifying the pre-screening of subjects, a frequently cited study on the treatment of depression, March et al. (2004), excluded 85% of potential subjects from their sample for various reasons.
2. The authors reviewed 236 peer-reviewed studies from 1962 to 2002 and reported that only 13% of studied populations were treatment seeking or referred, and 60% of the studies used "no-treatment" controls. They found that only 1% of the studies were clinically representative, "i.e., including at least some clinically referred children, some practicing clinicians and some treatment in a clinical service setting."
3. Depressed adults recovering from an initial episode of depression have a 50% chance of a second episode. When clients have a history of two or more episodes, their rate of recurrence increases to 70% to 80%.

Chapter 2

1. This product of the task force of the American Psychological Association's Division 12 Section on Clinical Child Psychology identified 25 empirically supported treatments for youths to consider for inclusion in treatment plans.
2. See http://www.aacap.org/cs/root/member_information/practice_informa tion/practice_parameters/practice_parameters.
3. Despite the evidence, President Bush declared April 10, 2008, to be National D.A.R.E. Day. On January 8, 2008, the D.A.R.E. Web site (http://www.dare. com/home/about_dare.asp) stated, "It is now being implemented in 75 percent of our nation's school districts and in more than 43 countries around the world."
4. Leading researchers polled by Boisvert and Faust also strongly agreed that therapy is helpful to the majority of clients. Most people achieve some change

relatively quickly in therapy. People change more because of "common factors" than because of "specific factors" associated with therapies. In general, therapies achieve similar outcome. The relationship between the therapist and client is the best predictor of treatment outcome. Most therapists learn more about effective therapy techniques from their experience than from the research. Placebo control groups and wait-list control groups are not as effective as psychotherapy. Therapist experience is not a strong predictor of outcome. Long-term therapy is no more effective than brief therapy for the majority of clients.

5. These researchers concluded that active treatments were just as effective as structurally equivalent controls when the controls were similar in the number and length of sessions, the modality (group or individual), and the training of the therapists and when the interventions were similar in allowing the clients to discuss topics related to their problems and treatment.

6. The number of types of patients excluded correlated highly with the improvement that the remaining subjects demonstrated on various outcome measures in studies of depression and in panic attack treatments.

7. On the basis of comparisons of active psychotherapies for adults, these researchers meta-analyzed 17 meta-analyses and found a "low and nonsignificant" difference between treatments (Cohen's $d = .20$), which was further reduced after correcting for the researcher's alliance ($d = .12$). Miller, Wampold and Varhely (2008) replicated these findings in outcome studies on youth.

8. The authors found publication rates of 94% for studies showing that antidepressants work and 8% for studies showing they do not work. Therefore, these drugs are less effective than the research reports.

9. The authors stated, "According to a report recently issued by the British House of Commons, 'Approximately 75% of clinical trials published in *The Lancet, the New England Journal of Medicine (NEJM)*, and the *Journal of the American Medical Association (JAMA)* are industry funded.'" They noted, "Most specialty medical societies and large nonprofit health advocacy organizations like the American Heart Association, the Arthritis Foundation, and the American Diabetes Association receive a large part of their funding from the drug companies. And approximately 70% of physicians' continuing medical education is now paid for by the drug and other medical industries."

10. "Fifty-eight percent had received financial support to perform research and 38% had served as employees or consultants for a pharmaceutical company. On average, CPG [clinical practice guideline] authors interacted with 10.5 different companies."

11. The authors found, "Most physicians (94%) reported some type of relationship with the pharmaceutical industry [those handsome and attractive detailers], and most of these relationships involved receiving food in the workplace (83%) or receiving drug samples (78%). More than one third of the respondents (35%) received reimbursement for costs associated with professional meetings or continuing medical education, and more than one quarter (28%) received payments for consulting, giving lectures, or enrolling patients in trials" (p. 1742).

12. They found that therapist collaboration behaviors can predict higher child and observer ratings of the therapeutic alliance when the therapist presents

treatment as a team effort with words such as *we, us,* and *let's;* encourages the youth to set goals; presents his or her work as a way to help with the child's worries and concerns; and encourages the youth's participation, involvement, and feedback. The study suggested that "finding common ground" by highlighting similarities with the child and "pushing the child to talk" beyond the point where "the child seemed interested or comfortable" were therapist behaviors that were markers that indicated that the alliance was in trouble and the child might be feeling alienated.

13. He estimated that for psychotherapy versus no treatment, the NNT is 3.

14. In the treatment of children with internalizing disorders, the more empathy, warmth, and genuineness the therapist offered, the more the clients improved.

15. These researchers reported a correlation of $r = .82$ between therapist empathy and 6-month-later drinking behavior, $r = .71$ at 1 year, and $r = .51$ 2 years posttreatment. Similarly, a confrontive approach (arguing from the facts) predicted a negative outcome in that "the more the therapist confronted the more the client drank" ($r = .65$) at 1 year (Miller, Benefield, & Tonigan, 1993). The therapeutic power of an empathetic therapist versus a confrontive therapist was also shown in family treatment, where Patterson and Forgatch (1985) found that a teaching-confronting (nonempathetic) therapist led to client resistance whereas a supporting-facilitating therapist diminished client noncompliance.

16. This review of 25 studies concluded that therapist personal characteristics of flexibility, honesty, respectfulness, trustworthiness, confidence, clarity, warmth, interest, openness, collaborativeness, involvement, hopefulness, expertise, friendliness, and protectiveness fostered the therapeutic alliance. Therapists' techniques of facilitating the expression of affect, exploration, reflection, noting past therapy successes, accurate interpretation, and attending to the patients' experience contributed to the alliance. The authors noted that the same characteristics were useful in identifying and repairing ruptures in the alliance, such as maintaining an affirming, understanding, and nurturing stance; validating the client's feelings; and admitting the therapist's contribution to the rupture. In a previous article Ackerman and Hilsenroth (2001, p. 171) reported, "Being rigid, uncertain, critical, distant, tense, distracted ... over structuring the therapy, inappropriate self-disclosure, unyielding use of transference interpretation, and inappropriate use of silence ... contribute negatively to the alliance."

17. Based on data from the Norwegian Multisite Project on Process and Outcome of Psychotherapy, the correlation between patient and therapist ratings of the strength of the therapeutic alliance was $r = .37$, indicating considerable disagreement about the health of the alliance.

18. The Session Rating Scale and the Outcome Rating Scale (2002) can be downloaded free at http://www.talkingcure.com.

19. The instrument is available at http://www.med.upenn.edu/cpr/instruments.html.

20. The instrument is available from David Burns at http://www.feelinggood.com.

21. The instrument is available free of charge at http://peabody.vanderbilt.edu/PTPB.

Chapter 3

1. *Medical necessity* is a technical term defined by governmental agencies that includes and excludes certain diagnostic groups. Meeting medical necessity indicates that the client is at risk of developing, or presently has, a significant impairment in life functioning that limits developmentally appropriate functioning in an important part of life and that the intervention provided will diminish the impairment, or prevent significant deterioration, so that the client can progress developmentally. To meet medical necessity, the client's condition must be one that will not respond to physical health-care-based treatment.
2. "USA PATRIOT Act" is an acronym for Uniting and Strengthening America by Providing Appropriate Tools Required to Intercept and Obstruct Terrorism Act of 2001.
3. Kepner provided a creative and insightful description of teaching clients the skills for grounding and pacing of experience.
4. Stress reduction CDs and tapes are available from Dr. Kabat-Zinn at POB 547, Lexington, MA 02420.
5. See http://www.guidetopsychology.com/pmr.htm. This is one of many sites that can help clients understand and use the cognitive-behavioral techniques being taught in therapy.
6. See A. Lazarus, *Brief but Comprehensive Psychotherapy: The Multimodal Way.* This cassette tape is available from David Lima Associates, (800) 810-9011.
7. Keel and Klump (2003) contended that anorexia appears to be so related to genetic factors and uniformly found across time and cultures that it probably is not a culture-bound disorder; however, bulimia can be viewed as highly related to the culture that spawns it.
8. Similar to my caseload, Hawley and Weisz (2003) found in their large sample of 7- to 17-year-old referrals to Los Angeles community mental health centers between 1991 and 1999, 23% lived with both parents, 63% lived with their mothers (of this group 35% lived with their mothers alone, 16% lived with mothers and their partners, and 11% lived with mothers and other relatives), 5% lived with fathers alone, and 9% lived in other situations (e.g., in foster care, with grandparents).

Chapter 5

1. Commenting on caseloads becoming dominated by the resistant and difficult to treat, Tom Kiresuk, the developer of Goal Attainment Scaling, jokingly suggested that for therapists to preserve their sanity, they need to move every 5 years.
2. These studies have strengths, but they also have a combination of deficits, such as having raters complete outcome measures that were designed for parents, using global outcome measures that were not related to the specific presenting complaints, supplying unknown methods and methods of unknown effectiveness, basing conclusions on a small portion of clients who complete postsession testing, not controlling for problem severity,

not distinguishing between improvement caused by the passage of time and improvement due to treatment, not using control groups, combining and not distinguishing between a wide array of treatment modalities, and searching for a dose-response relationship in cases that did not show improvement.

3. Dropouts were distinguished from completers by seven items related to the therapeutic relationship and one item related to money issues. "Dropouts had higher ratings on (a) 'the therapist didn't seem to be doing the right things,' (b) 'The therapist did not spend enough time with my child alone,' (c) 'The therapist didn't seem to be helping,' (d) 'My child's treatment was not clearly explained to me,' (e) 'One or more of the staff members did not seem competent,' (f) 'There was something about the clinic that my child or I did not like,' (g) 'I decided that going to the clinic would not help my child,' and (h) 'Services cost too much'" (Garcia & Weisz, 2002, p. 442). Therapists need to be vigilant to these issues to keep clients in treatment.

4. They found only 38% of parent–child pairs agreed on a specific problem in need of intervention. They found that parents generally described problems within the youths, whereas youths indicated problems in the parents and in family relationships.

5. They found that 23% of child–parent–therapist triads agreed on a single target problem, and only 56% agreed on a broad general category of behavior to focus on.

6. When parent, outpatient adolescent, and therapist were asked to generate three desired outcomes, only 38% of the triads could agree on one desired outcome.

Chapter 6

1. The authors concluded that impulse control, planning and decision making, the ability to change opinions, and the ability to think about consequences and their impact on others are functions of particular sites in the brain that typically develop at different times and rates during adolescence.

2. In their study of well-educated, high-functioning, long-term clients, the authors found that the most frequent termination problem was "the emotional pain for the loss of a meaningful and close relationship." Subjects also reported that not processing the termination contributed to their negative feelings about it.

3. See http://www.communitycouncil.org/level-2/children.pdf.

4. See AARP's online kinship care support group database at http://www.aarp.org/grandparents/search support/.

Chapter 7

1. See http://www.volunteermatch.org/results/. This site is a useful resource to clients who wish to volunteer.

2. They concluded that it is not how high or how low the aspirations are but whether they are realistic and accomplishable.

3. The authors found that 44 pairs of monozygotic twins that were reared apart had a with-in-pair correlation of .48 on the well-being scale of the Multidimensional Personality Questionnaire, indicating that a significant proportion of their general sense of well-being was probably inherited.
4. Dobson presents advice "inspired by the Creator Himself" (2003, p. xiv).

Chapter 8

1. For a beautiful description of the "lies we tell ourselves," see Kottler's (2003) *On Being a Therapist.*

References

Ablon, J., & Marci, C. (2004). Psychotherapy process: The missing link; Comment on Westen, Novotny, and Thompson-Brenner (2004). *Psychological Bulletin, 130*(4), 664–668. Retrieved from http://www.massgeneral.org/prp/cvs/Ablon%20%20Marci%202004.pdf

Abramson, J., & Starfield, B. (2005). The effect of conflict of interest on biomedical research and clinical practice guidelines: Can we trust the evidence in evidence-based medicine? *Journal of the American Board of Family Practice, 18,* 414–418.

Ackerman, S., Benjamin, L., Beutler, L., Gelso, C., Goldfried, M., Hill, C., et al. (2001). Empirically supported therapy relationships: Conclusions and recommendations of the Division 29 Task Force. *Psychotherapy: Theory, Research, Practice, Training, 38,* 495–497.

Ackerman, S., & Hilsenroth, M. (2001). A review of therapist characteristics and techniques negatively impacting the therapeutic alliance. *Psychotherapy: Theory, Research, Practice, Training, 38*(2), 171–185.

Ackerman, S., & Hilsenroth, M. (2003). A review of therapist characteristics and techniques positively impacting the therapeutic alliance. *Clinical Psychology Review, 23*(1), 1–33.

Adelman, H., Kaser-Boyd, N., & Taylor, L. (1984). Children's participation in consent in psychotherapy and their subsequent response to treatment. *Journal of Clinical and Child Psychology, 13*(2), 170–178.

Ahn, H., & Wampold, B. E. (2001). Where oh where are the specific ingredients? A meta-analysis of component studies in counseling and psychotherapy. *Journal of Counseling Psychology, 48*(3), 251–257.

American Academy of Pediatrics Committee on Drugs. (1996). Unapproved uses of approved drugs: The physician, the package insert, and the Food and Drug Administration. *Subject Review, 98,* 143–145.

American Psychiatric Association. (1994). *Diagnostic and statistical manual of mental disorders* (4th ed.). Washington, DC: Author.

American Psychological Association. (2002). *Ethical principles of psychologists and code of conduct.* Retrieved from http://www.apa.org/ethics/code2002.html

American Psychological Association. (2007). Record keeping guidelines. *American Psychologist, 62*(9), 993–1004.

Amrhein, P., Miller, W., Yahne, C., Palmer, M., & Fulcher, L. (2003). Client commitment language during motivational interviewing predicts drug use outcomes. *Journal of Consulting and Clinical Psychology, 71*(5), 862–878.

Anderson, C. A. (2004). An update on the effects of playing violent video games. *Journal of Adolescence, 27,* 113–122.

Andrade, A., Lambert, E., & Bickman, L. (2000). Dose effect in child psychotherapy: Outcomes associated with negligible treatment. *Journal of the American Academy of Child and Adolescent Psychiatry, 39*(2), 161–168.

Andrews, G., et al. (2002). Deconstructing co-morbidity: Data from the Australian National Survey of Mental Health and Well-being. *British Journal of Psychiatry, 181,* 306–314.

Angold, A., Costello, E., Burns, B., Erkanli, A., & Farmer, E. (2000). Effectiveness of nonresidential specialty mental health services for children and adolescents in the "real world." *Journal of the American Academy of Child and Adolescent Psychiatry, 39*(2), 154–160.

Antonuccio, D., Danton, W., & McClanahan, T. (2003). Psychology in the prescription era: Building a firewall between marketing and science. *American Psychologist, 58*(12), 1028–1043.

Arnkoff, D., Glass, C., & Shapiro, S. (2002). Expectations and preferences. In J. C. Norcross (Ed.), *Psychotherapy relationships that work: Therapist contributions and responsiveness to patients* (pp. 335–356). New York: Oxford University Press.

Attride-Stirling, J., Davis, H., Farrell, L., Groark, C., & Day, C. (2004). Factors influencing parental engagement in a community child and adolescent mental health service: A qualitative comparison of completers and non-completers. *Clinical Child Psychology and Psychiatry, 9*(3), 347–361.

Bachelor, A. (1995). Client's perception of the therapeutic alliance: A qualitative analysis. *Journal of Counseling Psychology, 42,* 323–337.

Bachelor, A., & Horvath, A. (1999). The therapeutic relationship. In M. Hubble, B. Duncan, & S. Miller (Eds.), *The heart and soul of change: What works in therapy* (pp. 133–178). Washington, DC: American Psychological Association.

Barber, J. (2000). Alliance predicts patient's outcome beyond in-treatment change in symptoms. *Journal of Consulting and Clinical Psychology, 68,* 1027–1032.

Barkham, M., Connell, J., Stiles, W., Miles, J., Margison, F., Evans, C., & Mellor-Clark, J. (2006). Dose-effect relations and responsive regulation of treatment duration: The good enough level. *Journal of Consulting and Clinical Psychology, 74*(1), 160–167.

Baskin, T., Tierney, S., Minami, T., & Wampold, B. (2003). Establishing specificity in psychotherapy: A meta-analysis of structural equivalence of placebo controls. *Journal of Consulting and Clinical Psychology, 71*(6), 973–979.

Beck, A., Rush, A., Shaw, B., & Emery, G. (1979). *Cognitive therapy of depression.* New York: Guilford.

Bedi, R., Davis, M., & Williams, M. (2005). Critical incidents in the formation of the therapeutic alliance from the client's perspective. *Psychotherapy: Theory, Research, Practice, Training, 42*(3), 311–323.

Beitman, B., & Soth, A. (2006). Activation of self-observation: A core process among the psychotherapies. *Journal of Psychotherapy Integration, 16*(4), 383–397.

Berman, J., & Norton, N. (1985). Does professional training make a therapist more effective? *Psychological Bulletin, 98,* 401–407.

Bernier, A., & Dozier, M. (2002). The client–counselor match and the corrective emotional experience: Evidence from interpersonal and attachment research. *Psychotherapy: Theory, Research, Practice, Training, 39*(1), 32–43.

Beutler, L. E., & Clarkin, J. (1990). *Differential treatment selection: Toward targeted therapeutic interventions.* New York: Brunner/Mazel.

Beverly, J. (1989). *Treating traumatized children.* Lexington, MA: Lexington Books.

Bickman, L., Andrade, A., & Lambert, E. (2002). Dose response in child and adolescent mental health services. *Mental Health Services Research, 4*(2), 57–70.

Blatt, S., & Zuroff, D. (2005). Empirical evaluation of the assumptions in identifying evidence based treatments in mental health. *Clinical Psychology Review, 25,* 459–486.

Bloom, B. (2001). Focused single-session psychotherapy: A review of the clinical and research literature. *Brief Treatment and Crisis Intervention, 1*(1), 75–86.

Bohart, A. (2007). An alternative view of concrete operating procedures from the perspective of the client as active self-healer. *Journal of Psychotherapy Integration, 17*(1), 125–137.

Boisvert, C., & Faust, D. (2003). Leading researchers' consensus on psychotherapy research findings: Implications for the teaching and conduct of psychotherapy. *Professional Psychology: Research and Practice, 34*(5), 508–513.

Bonner, B., & Everett, F. (1986). Influence of client preparation and problem severity on attitudes and expectations in child psychotherapy. *Professional Psychology: Research and Practice, 17,* 223–229.

Boyd, C., McCabe, S., Cranford, J., & Young, A. (2006). Adolescents' motivations to abuse prescription medications. *Pediatrics, 118*(6), 2472–2480.

Bradley, R., Greene, J., Russ, E., Dutra, L., & Westen, D. (2005). A multidimensional meta-analysis of psychotherapy for PTSD. *American Journal of Psychiatry, 162,* 214–227.

Braswell, L., Kendall, P., Braith, J., Carey, M., & Vye, C. (1985). "Involvement" in cognitive-behavioral therapy with children: Process and its relationship to outcome. *Cognitive Therapy and Research, 9,* 611–630.

Bratton, S., Ray, D., Rhine, T., & Jones, L. (2005). The efficacy of play therapy with children: A meta-analytic review of treatment outcomes. *Professional Psychology: Research and Practice, 36*(4), 376–390.

Braun, B. (1988). The BASK model of dissociation. *Dissociation, 1*(1), 4–10.

Breen, R., & Thornhill, J. (1998). Noncompliance with medication for psychiatric disorders: Reasons and remedies. *CNS Drugs, 9*(6), 457–471.

Brent, D., et al. (1998). Predictors of treatment efficacy in a clinical trial of three psychosocial treatments for adolescent depression. *Journal of the American Academy of Child and Adolescent Psychiatry, 37*(9), 906–914.

Breslau, N., et al. (1998). Trauma and posttraumatic stress disorder in the community: The 1996 Detroit area survey of trauma. *Archives of General Psychiatry, 55,* 626–632.

Brickman, P., Coates, D., & Janoff-Bulman, R. (1978). Lottery winners and accident victims: Is happiness relative? *Journal of Personality and Social Psychology, 36*(8), 917–927.

Briere, J. (1996). *Therapy for adults molested as children* (2nd ed., exp. and rev.). New York: Springer.

Burke, B., Arkowitz, H., & Menchola, M. (2003). The efficacy of motivational interviewing: A meta-analysis of controlled clinical trials. *Journal of Consulting and Clinical Psychology, 71*(5), 843–861.

Campbell, E. G., et al. (2007). A national survey of physician–industry relationships. *New England Journal of Medicine, 356,* 1742–1750.

Carr, L., Iacoboni, M., Dubeau, M., Mazziotta, J., & Lenzi, G. (2003). Neural mechanisms of empathy in humans: A relay from neural systems for imitation to limbic areas. *Proceedings of the National Academy of Sciences, USA, 100,* 5497–5502.

Casey, R., & Berman, J. (1985). The outcome of psychotherapy with children. *Psychological Bulletin, 98,* 388–400.

Castonguay, L., Goldfried, M., Wiser, S., Raue, P., & Hayes, A. (1996). Predicting the effect of cognitive therapy for depression: A study of unique and common factors. *Journal of Consulting and Clinical Psychology, 64,* 497–504.

Chaffin, M., et al. (2006). Report of the APSAC task force on attachment therapy, reactive attachment disorder, and attachment problems. *Child Maltreatment, 11*(1), 76–89.

Chambless, D. (2002). Beware the dodo bird: The dangers of overgeneralization. *Clinical Psychology: Science and Practice, 9*(1), 13–16.

Choudhry, N., Stelfox, H., & Detsky, A. (2002). Relationships between authors of clinical practice guidelines and the pharmaceutical industry. *Journal of the American Medical Association, 287,* 612–617.

Chu, B., & Kendall, P. (2004). Positive association of child involvement and treatment outcome within a manual-based cognitive-behavioral treatment for children with anxiety. *Journal of Consulting and Clinical Psychology, 72*(5), 821–829.

Church, E. (1994). The role of autonomy in adolescent psychotherapy. *Psychotherapy, 31,* 101–108.

Compton, S., Burns, B., Egger, H., & Robertson, E. (2002). Review of the evidence base for treatment of childhood psychotherapy internalizing disorders. *Journal of Consulting and Clinical Psychology, 70*(6), 1240–1266.

Consensus Development Panel. (1985). NIMH/NIH Consensus Development Conference statement: Mood disorders; Pharmacologic prevention of recurrence. *American Journal of Psychiatry, 142,* 469–476.

Constantino, M., Arnow, B., Blasey, C., & Argras, W. (2005). The association between patient characteristics and the therapeutic alliance in cognitive-behavioral and interpersonal therapy for bulimia nervosa. *Journal of Consulting and Clinical Psychology, 73*(2), 203–211.

Costantino, G., Malgady, R., & Rogler, L. (1986). A culturally sensitive modality for Puerto Rican children. *Journal of Consulting and Clinical Psychology, 54,* 639–645.

Creed, T., & Kendall, P. (2005). Therapist alliance-building behavior within a cognitive-behavioral treatment for anxiety in youth. *Journal of Consulting and Clinical Psychology, 73*(3), 498–505.

Crits-Christoph, P., & Mintz, J. (1991). Implications of therapist effects for the design and analysis of comparative studies of psychotherapies. *Journal of Consulting and Clinical Psychology, 59,* 20–26.

Csikszentmihalyi, M. (1990). *Flow: The psychology of optimal experience.* New York: HarperPerennial.

Csikszentmihalyi, M., & Csikszentmihalyi, I. (1988). *Optimal experience: Psychological studies of flow in consciousness.* New York: Cambridge University Press.

Davidson, J., Martinez, K., & Thomas, C. (2006). *Validation of a new measure of functioning and satisfaction for use in outpatient clinical practice.* Chicago: Association for Behavioral and Cognitive Therapies.

DeAngelis, C. D., Fontanarosa, P. B., & Flanagin, A. (2001). Reporting financial conflicts of interest and relationships between investigators and research sponsors. *Journal of the American Medical Association, 286,* 89–91.

DelBello, M., Schwiers, M., Rosenberg, H., & Strakowski, S. (2002). A double-blind, randomized, placebo-controlled study of Quetiapine as adjunctive treatment for adolescent mania. *Journal of the American Academy of Child and Adolescent Psychiatry, 41*(10), 1216–1223.

Diamond, G., Liddle, H., Hogue, A., & Dakof, G. (1999). Alliance-building interventions with adolescents in family therapy: A process study. *Psychotherapy, 36*(4), 355–368.

DiClemente, C., Schlundt, D., & Gemmell, L. (2004). Readiness and stages of change in addiction treatment. *American Journal on Addictions, 13*(2), 103–119.

Diener, E., & Fujita, F. (1995). Resources, personal strivings, and subjective well-being: A nomothetic and idiographic approach. *Journal of Personality and Social Psychology, 68,* 926–935.

Diener, E., Suh, E., Lucas, R., & Smith, H. (1999). Subjective well-being: Three decades of progress. *Psychological Bulletin, 125*(2), 276–302.

DiGiuseppe, R., Linscott, J., & Jilton, R. (1996). Developing the therapeutic alliance in child and adolescent psychotherapy. *Applied and Preventive Psychology, 5*(2), 85–100.

Dishion, T., McCord, J., & Poulin, F. (1999). When interventions harm: Peer groups and problem behavior. *American Psychologist, 54,* 755–765.

Dobson, J. (2003). *Parent's answer book.* Carol Stream, IL: Tyndale House.

Downing, J. (2004). Psychotherapy practice in a pluralistic world: Philosophical and moral dilemmas. *Journal of Psychotherapy Integration, 14*(2), 123–148.

Drew, S., & Bickman, L. (2005). Client expectancies about therapy. *Mental Health Services Research, 7*(1), 21–33.

Duncan, B., Hubble, M., & Miller, S. (1997). Stepping off the throne. *Family Therapy Networker, 21*(4), 22-33. Available at http://www.talkingcure.com

Duncan, B., Miller, S., & Sparks, J. (2004). *The heroic client: A revolutionary way to improve effectiveness through client-directed, outcome-informed therapy* (Rev. ed.). San Francisco: Jossey-Bass.

Dunkle, J., & Friedlander, M. (1996). Contribution of therapist experience and personal characteristics to the working alliance. *Journal of Counseling Psychology, 43,* 456–460.

Durlack, J.A., Fuhrman, T., & Lampman, C. (1991). Effectiveness of cognitive-behavioral therapy for maladapting children: A meta-analysis. *Psychological Bulletin, 110*, 204–217.

Eells, T. (1997). Psychotherapy case formulation: History and current status. In T. D. Eells (Ed.), *Handbook of psychotherapy case formulation* (pp. 1–25). New York: Guilford.

Elkin, I., et al. (1989). National Institute of Mental Health treatment of depression collaborative research program—General effectiveness of treatments. *Archives of General Psychiatry, 46*, 971–982.

Elkin, I., Yamaguchi, J., Arnkoff, D., Glass, C., Sotsky, S., & Kruprick, J. (1999). "Patient-treatment fit" and early engagement in therapy. *Psychotherapy Research, 9*, 437–451.

Ellis, A. (1984). Expanding the ABCs of RET. *Journal of Rational-Emotive and Cognitive-Behavior Therapy, 2*(2), 20–24.

Emmons, R. (1986). Personal strivings: An approach to personality and subjective well-being. *Journal of Personality and Social Psychology, 51*, 1058–1068.

Emmons, R., & McCullough, M. (2003). Counting blessings versus burdens: An experimental investigation of gratitude and subjective well-being in daily life. *Journal of Personality and Social Psychology, 84*(2), 377–389.

Eron, J., & Lund, T. (1996). *Narrative solutions in brief therapy.* New York: Guilford.

Fernandez, A., Begley, E., & Marlatt, G. (2006). Family and peer interventions for adults: Past approaches and future directions. *Psychology of Addictive Behaviors, 20*(2), 207–213.

Finkelhor, D. (Ed.). (1986). *A sourcebook on child sexual abuse.* Beverly Hills, CA: Sage.

Frank, J. (1971). Therapeutic factors in psychotherapy. *American Journal of Psychotherapy, 25*(3), 350–361.

Frayn, D. H. (1992). Assessment factors associated with premature psychotherapy termination. *American Journal of Psychotherapy, 46*, 250–260.

Frensch, K. M., & Cameron, G. (2002). Treatment of choice or last resort? A review of residential mental health placements for children and youth. *Child and Youth Case Forum, 31*, 307–339.

Freud, S. (1912). *Recommendations for physicians on the psychoanalytic method of treatment* (Standard ed., Vol. 12). London: Hogarth.

Garcia, J. A., & Weisz, J. R. (2002). When youth mental health care stops: Therapeutic relationship and other reasons for ending youth outpatient treatment. *Journal of Consulting and Clinical Psychology, 70*, 439–443.

Gardner, R. (1971). The mutual story telling technique. *American Journal of Psychiatry, 24*(3), 419–439.

Garfield, S. (1994). Research on client variables in psychotherapy. In A. E. Bergin & S. L. Garfield (Eds.), *Handbook of psychotherapy and behavior change* (4th ed., pp. 190–228). New York: Wiley.

Garland, A., Lewczyk-Boxmeyer, M., Gabayan, B., & Hawley, K. (2004). Multiple stakeholder agreement in desired outcomes for adolescents' mental health services. *Psychiatric Services, 55*, 671–676.

Gingerich, W., & Eisengart, S. (2000). Solution-focused brief therapy: A review of the outcome research. *Family Process, 39*(4), 477–498.

Ginsburg, G. (2006). Evidence-based treatments for children and adolescents. *Journal of Clinical Child and Adolescent Psychology, 35*(3), 480–486.

Glazener, C., Evans, J., & Peto, R. (2005). Alarm interventions for nocturnal enuresis in children. *Cochrane Database of Systematic Reviews,* No. 2. (Art. No.: CD002911. DOI: 10.1002/14651858.CD002911.pub2)

Gold, S. (2004). The relevance of trauma to general clinical practice. *Psychotherapy: Theory, Research, Practice, Training, 41*(4), 363–373.

Goldfried, M. (2004). Integrating integratively oriented brief psychotherapy. *Journal of Psychotherapy Integration, 14*(1), 93–105.

Goldfried, M., & Wolf, B. (1996). Psychotherapy practice and research: Repairing a strained alliance. *American Psychologist, 51*(10), 1007–1016.

Goldstein, E. (1994). Self-disclosure in treatment: What therapists do and don't talk about. *Clinical Social Work Journal, 22*(4), 417–433.

Goldstein, J. (1971). Investigation of doubling as a technique for involving severely withdrawn patients in group psychotherapy. *Journal of Consulting and Clinical Psychology, 37*(1), 155–162.

Gordon, T. (2000). *Parent effectiveness training.* New York: Three Rivers Press.

Gossop, M., Stewart, D., & Marsden, J. (2007). Readiness for change and drug use outcomes after treatment. *Addiction, 102*(2), 301–308.

Griffen, M. (2007). Special education and related services in California schools: Basic information for therapists. *The Therapist, 19*(6), 46–49.

Grove, W., Zald, D., Lebow, B., Snitz, B., & Nelson, C. (2000). Clinical versus mechanical prediction: A meta-analysis. *Psychological Assessment, 12*(1), 19–30.

Haley, J. (1973). *Uncommon therapy: The psychiatric techniques of Milton H. Erickson.* New York: Norton.

Hallfors, D., Cho, H., Sanchez, V., Khalapoush, S., Kim, H., & Bauer, D. (2006). Efficacy versus effectiveness trial results of an indicated "model" substance abuse program: Implications for public health. *American Journal of Public Health, 96*(8), 2254–2259.

Hamilton, B., et al. (2005). *Preliminary births for 2004.* Center for Disease Control, Division of Vital Statistics. Retrieved from http://origin.cdc.gov/nchs/products/pubs/pubd/hestats/prelim_births/prelim_births04.htm

Hampton-Robb, S. (2003). Predicting first-session attendance: The influence of referral source and client income. *Psychotherapy Research, 13*(2), 223–233.

Hansen, N., Lambert, M., & Forman, E. (2002). The psychotherapy dose-response effect and its implications for treatment delivery services. *Clinical Psychology: Science and Practice, 9*(3), 329–343.

Harris, G., Carey, B., & Roberts, J. (2007, May 10). Psychiatrists, children and drug industry's role. *New York Times.* Available online at http://www.nytimes.com/2007/05/10/health/10psyche.html

Hartmann, T. (1997). *Attention deficit disorder: A different perception* (2nd ed.). Grass Valley, CA: Underwood Books.

Harwood, M., & Eyberg, S. (2004). Therapist verbal behavior early in treatment: Relation to successful completion of parent–child interaction therapy. *Journal of Clinical Child and Adolescent Psychology, 33*(3), 601–612.

Hawkins, E., Lambert, M., Vermeersch, D., Slade, K., & Tuttle, K. (2004). The therapeutic effects of providing patient progress information to therapists and patients. *Psychotherapy Research, 14*(3), 308–327.

Hawley, K. M., & Weisz, J. R. (2003). Child, parent, and therapist (dis)agreement on target problems in outpatient therapy: The therapist's dilemma and its implications. *Journal of Consulting and Clinical Psychology, 71*(1), 62–70.

Hawley, K. M., & Weisz, J. R. (2005). Youth versus parent working alliance in usual clinical care: Distinctive associations with retention, satisfaction, and treatment outcome. *Journal of Clinical Child and Adolescent Psychology, 34*(1), 117–128.

Hellerstein, D., Rosenthal, R., Pinsker, H., Samstag, L., Muran, J., & Winston, A. (1998). A randomized prospective study comparing supportive and dynamic therapies: Outcome and alliance. *Journal of Psychotherapy Practice and Research, 7*, 261–271.

Henry, D., & Metropolitan Area Child Study Research Group. (2006). Associations between peer nominations, teacher ratings, self-reports and observations of malicious and disruptive behavior. *Assessment, 13*(3), 253–265.

Henry, W., & Strupp, H. (1994). The therapeutic alliance as interpersonal process. In A. O. Horvath & L. Greenberg (Eds.), *The working alliance: Theory, research and practice* (pp. 51–84). New York: Wiley.

Hensley S. "As Drug Bill Soars, Some Doctors Get an 'Unsales' Pitch." *The Wall Street Journal.* March 13, 2006; A1.

Heres, S., et al. (2006). Why Olanzapine beats Risperidone, Risperidone beats Quetiapine, and Quetiapine beats Olanzapine: An exploratory analysis of head-to-head comparison studies of second-generation antipsychotics. *American Journal of Psychiatry, 163*(2), 185–194.

Herman, J. (1992). *Trauma and recovery.* New York: Basic Books.

Hersoug, A., Hoglend, P., Monsen, J., & Havik, O. (2001). Quality of working alliance in psychotherapy: Therapist variables and patient/therapist similarity as predictors. *Journal of Psychotherapy Practice Research, 10*(4), 205–216.

Hettema, J., Steele, J., & Miller, W. (2005). Motivational interviewing. *Annual Review of Clinical Psychology, 1*, 91–111.

Hill, C., Nutt-Williams, E., Heaton, K., Thompson, B., & Rhodes, R. (1996). Therapist retrospective recall of impasses in long-term psychotherapy: A qualitative analysis. *Journal of Counseling Psychology, 43*(2), 207–217.

Hilliard, R., Henry, W., & Strupp, H. (2000). An interpersonal model of psychotherapy: Linking patient and therapist developmental histories, therapeutic process and types of outcome. *Journal of Consulting and Clinical Psychology, 68*(1), 125–133.

Hoagwood, K., Burns, B., Kiser, L., Ringeisen, H., & Schoenwald, S. (2001). Evidence-based practice in child and adolescent mental health services. *Psychiatric Services, 52*(9), 1179–1189.

Horvath, A. (2001). The alliance. *Psychotherapy: Theory, Research, Practice, Training, 38*(4), 365–372.

Horvath, A., & Symonds, B. (1991). Relation between working alliance and outcome in psychotherapy: A meta-analysis. *Journal of Counseling Psychology, 38*, 139–149.

Howard, K., Kopta, S., Krause, M., & Orlinsky, D. (1986). The dose-effect relationship in psychotherapy. *American Psychologist, 41*(2), 159–164.

Hoyt, M., & Talmon, M. (1990). Single-session therapy in action: A case example. In M. Talmon, *Single-session therapy* (pp. 78–96). San Francisco: Jossey-Bass.

Hubble, M., Duncan, B., & Miller, S. (Eds.). (1999). *The heart and soul of change: What works in therapy.* Washington, DC: American Psychological Association.

Hutchings, P., & Dutton, M. (1993). Sexual assault history in a community mental health center clinical population. *Community Mental Health Journal, 29*(1), 59–63.

Iacoviello, B., McCarthy, K., Barrett, M., Rynn, M., Gallop, R., & Barber, J. (2007). Treatment preferences affect the therapeutic alliance: Implications for randomized controlled trials. *Journal of Consulting and Clinical Psychology, 75*(1), 194–198.

Irving, L., et al. (2004). The relationships between hope and outcomes at the pretreatment, beginning, and phases of psychotherapy. *Journal of Psychotherapy Integration, 14*(4), 419–443.

Issakidis, C., & Andrews, G. (2004). Pretreatment attrition and dropout in an outpatient clinic for anxiety disorders. *Acta Psychiatrica Scandenavica, 109*, 426–433.

Jameson, F. (1991). *Postmodernism, or the culture logic of late capitalism*. London: Verso.

Jensen, D. (2005). Unlawful and/or unethical dual relationships: A word to the wise. *The Therapist, 17*(5), 25–29.

Joyce, A., Ogrodniczuk, J., Piper, W., & McCallum, M. (2003). The alliance as mediator of expectancy effects in short-term individual therapy. *Journal of Consulting and Clinical Psychology, 71*(4), 672–679.

Kabat-Zinn, J. (1990). *Full catastrophe living: Using the wisdom of your body and mind to face stress, pain and illness*. New York: Dell Publishing.

Karver, M., Handelsman, J., Fields, S., & Bickman, L. (2006). Meta-analysis of therapeutic relationship variables in youth and family therapy: The evidence for different relationship variables in the child and adolescent treatment outcome literature. *Clinical Psychology Review, 26*(1), 50–65.

Kazantzis, N., & Ronan, R. (2006). Can between-session (homework) activities be considered a common factor in psychotherapy? *Journal of Psychotherapy Integration, 16*(2), 115–127.

Kazdin, A. (2008). Evidence-based treatment and practice: New opportunities to bridge clinical research and practice, enhance the knowledge base, and improve patient care. *American Psychologist, 63*(3), 146–159.

Kazdin, A., & Wassell, G. (1998). Treatment completion and therapeutic change among children referred for outpatient therapy. *Professional Psychology: Research and Practice, 29*, 332–340.

Kazdin, A., & Whitley, M. (2006). Pretreatment social relations, therapeutic alliance and improvements in parenting practices in parent management training. *Journal of Consulting and Clinical Psychology, 74*(2), 346–355.

Keel, P., & Klump, K. (2003). Are eating disorders culture-bound syndromes? Implications for conceptualizing their etiology. *Psychological Bulletin, 129*(5), 747–769.

Keijsers, G., Schaap, C., & Hoogduin, C. (2000). The impact of interpersonal patient and therapist behavior on outcome in cognitive behavior: A review of empirical studies. *Behavior Modification, 24*(2), 264–297.

Keller, M., Lavori, P., Lewis, C., & Klerman, G. (1983). Predictors of relapse in major depressive disorder. *Journal of the American Medical Association, 250*, 3299–3304.

Kelly, T. A. (1990). The role of values in psychotherapy: Review and methodological critique. *Clinical Psychology Review, 10*, 171–186.

Kelly, T., & Strupp, H. (1992). Patient and therapist values in psychotherapy: Perceived changes, assimilation, similarity, and outcome. *Journal of Consulting and Clinical Psychology, 60*(1), 34–40.

Kendall, P., Kipnis, D., & Otto-Salaj, L. (1992). When clients don't progress: Influences on and explanations for lack of therapeutic progress. *Cognitive Therapy and Research, 16,* 269–281.

Kendjelic, E., & Eells, T. (2007). Generic psychotherapy case formulation training improves formulation quality. *Psychotherapy: Theory, Research, Practice, Training, 44*(1), 66–77.

Kepner, J. (1995). *Healing tasks: Psychotherapy with adult survivors of childhood abuse.* San Francisco: Jossey-Bass.

Kerkorian, D., McKay, M., & Bannon, W. (2006). Seeking help a second time: Parents'/caregivers' characterizations of previous experiences with mental health services for their children and perceptions of barriers to future use. *American Journal of Orthopsychiatry, 76*(2), 161–166.

Kilmann, P., & Auerbach, R. (1979). Treatments of premature ejaculation and psychogenic impotence: A critical review of the literature. *Archives of Sexual Behavior, 8,* 81–100.

Kim, D., Wampold, B., & Bolt, D. (2006). Therapist effects in psychotherapy: A random effects modeling of the NIMH TDCRP data. *Psychotherapy Research, 16,* 161–172.

Kipper, D., & Ritchie, T. (2003). The effectiveness of psychodramatic techniques: A meta-analysis. *Group Dynamics: Theory, Research and Practice, 7*(1), 13–25.

Kirsch, I., Moore, T. J., Scoboria, A., & Nicholls, S. S. (2002). The emperor's new drugs: An analysis of antidepressant medication data submitted to the U.S. Food and Drug Administration. *Prevention and Treatment, 5,* Article 23. Retrieved from http://www.journals.apa.org/prevention/volume5/pre0050023a.html

Klein, D., Schwartz, J., Santiago, N., Vivian, D., & Vocisano, C. (2003). Therapeutic alliance in depression treatment: Controlling for prior change and patient characteristics. *Journal of Consulting and Clinical Psychology, 71*(6), 997–1006.

Knox, S., Goldberg, J., Woodhouse, S., & Hill, C. (1999). Client's internal representations of their therapists. *Journal of Counseling Psychology, 46*(2), 244–256.

Knox, S., Hess, S., Nutt-Williams, E., & Hill, C. (2003). "Here's a little something for you": How therapists respond to client gifts. *Journal of Counseling Psychology, 50*(2), 199–210.

Knox, S., & Hill, C. E. (2003). Therapist self-disclosure: Research-based suggestions for practitioners. *Journal of Clinical Psychology/In Session, 59*(5), 529–539.

Kopta, S. (2003). The dose-effect relationship in psychotherapy: A defining achievement for Dr. Kenneth Howard. *Journal of Clinical Psychology, 59,* 727–733.

Kopta, S., Howard, K., Lowry, J., & Beutler, L. (1994). Patterns of symptomatic recovery in psychotherapy. *Journal of Consulting and Clinical Psychology, 62*(5), 1009–1016.

Korotitsch, W., & Nelson-Gray, R. (1999). An overview of self-monitoring research in assessment and treatment. *Psychological Assessment, 11*(4), 415–425.

Kottler, J. (2003). *On being a therapist.* San Francisco: Jossey-Bass.

Kourany, R., Garber, J., & Tornusciolo, G. (1990). Improving first appointment attendance rates in child psychiatry outpatient clinics. *Journal of the American Academy of Child and Adolescent Psychiatry, 29,* 657–660.

Kozart, M. (2002). Understanding efficacy in psychotherapy: An ethnomethodological perspective on the therapeutic alliance. *American Journal of Orthopsychiatry, 72*(2), 217–231.

Kraemer, H., & Kupfer, D. (2006). Size of treatment effects and their importance to clinical research and practice. *Biological Psychiatry, 59,* 990–996.

Kramer, S. (1986). The termination process in open-ended psychotherapy: Guidelines for clinical practice. *Psychotherapy, 23*(4), 526–531.

Kuhl, J., Jarkon-Horlick, L., & Morrissey, R. (1997). Measuring barriers to help-seeking behavior in adolescents. *Journal of Youth and Adolescence, 26,* 637–650.

Ladany, N., Hill, C., Thompson, B., & O'Brien, K. (2004). Therapist perspectives on using silence in therapy: A qualitative study. *Counseling and Psychotherapy Research, 4*(1), 80–89.

Lambert, M. (1992). Psychotherapy outcome research: Implications for integrative and eclectical therapists. In J. Norcross & M. Goldfried (Eds.), *Handbook of psychotherapy integration* (pp. 94–129). New York: Basic Books.

Lambert, M. J., & Barley, D. E. (2001). Research summary on the therapeutic relationship and psychotherapy outcome. *Psychotherapy: Theory/Research/Practice/Training, 38,* 357–361.

Lambert, M., & Bergin, A. (1992). Achievements and limitations of psychotherapy research. In D. K. Freedheim (Ed.), *History of psychotherapy: A century of change* (pp. 360–390). Washington, DC: American Psychological Association.

Lambert, M., Whipple, J., Hawkins, E., Vermeersch, D., Nielsen, S., & Smart, D. (2003). Is it time for clinicians to routinely track patient outcome? A meta-analysis. *Clinical Psychology: Science and Practice, 19*(3), 288–301.

Lampropoulos, G., & Dixon, D. (2007). Psychotherapy integration in internships and counseling psychology doctoral programs. *Journal of Psychotherapy Integration, 17*(2), 185–208.

Lane, R. (2000). *The loss of happiness in market democracies.* New Haven, CT: Yale University Press.

Latner, J., & Wilson, G. (2002). Self-monitoring and the assessment of binge eating. *Behavior Therapy, 33*(3), 465–477.

Lazarus, A. (1989). *The practice of multimodal therapy: Systematic, comprehensive, and effective psychotherapy.* Baltimore: Johns Hopkins University Press.

Lazear, K., Worthington, J., & Detres, M. (2004). *Family experience of the mental health system—Findings compendium: Issue brief 3; Decisions and responsibilities of care* (FMHI Series Publication No. 224–3). Tampa: University of South Florida. Retrieved from http://pubs.fmhi.usf.edu

Leitner, L. (2007). Theory, technique, and person: Technical integration in experiential constructivist psychotherapy. *Journal of Psychotherapy Integration, 17*(1), 33–49.

Lewis, J. (2000). Repairing the bond in important relationships: A dynamic for personality maturation. *American Journal of Psychiatry, 157*(9), 1375–1378. Retrieved from http://ajp.psychiatryonline.org/cgi/content/full/157/9/1375

Lexchin, J., Bero, L., Djulbegovic, B., & Clark, O. (2003). Pharmaceutical industry sponsorship and research outcome and quality: Systematic review. *British Medical Journal, 326,* 1167–1170.

Lieberman, J., et al. (2005). Effectiveness of antipsychotic drugs in patients with chronic schizophrenia. *New England Journal of Medicine, 353*(12), 1209–1223.

Lilienfeld, S. (2005). Scientifically unsupported and supported interventions for childhood psychopathology: A summary. *Pediatrics, 115*(3), 761–764.

Lilienfeld, S. (2007). Psychological treatments that cause harm. *Perspectives on Psychological Science, 2*(1), 53–70.

Link, B. G., & Phelan, J. C. (2001). Conceptualizing stigma. *Annual Review of Sociology, 27,* 363–385.

Littrell, J., & Girvin, H. (2002). Stages of change: A critique. *Behavior Modification, 26,* 223–273.

Long, R. (1968). The observing ego and adolescent development. *Rev. Inst. Nac. Neurol.* (Mexico), *2,* 8–21.

Lonigan, C., Elbert, J., & Bennett-Johnson, S. (1998). Empirically supported psychosocial interventions for children: An overview. *Journal of Clinical Child Psychology, 27,* 138–145.

Luborsky, L. (1976). Helping alliances in psychotherapy. In J. Claghorn (Ed.), *Successful psychotherapy* (pp. 92–111). New York: Brunner/Mazel.

Luborsky, L., Barber, J., Siqueland, L., Johnson, S., Najavits, L., Franks, A., et al. (1996). The revised helping alliance questionnaire (HAq-ll). *Journal of Psychotherapy Practice and Research, 5,* 260–271.

Luborsky, L., & Crits-Cristoph, P. (Eds.). (1990). *Understanding transference: The CCRT method.* New York: Basic Books.

Luborsky, L., McLellan, A., Diguer, L., Woody, G., & Seligman, D. (1997). The psychotherapist matters: Comparison of outcomes across twenty-two therapists and seven patient samples. *Clinical Psychology: Science and Practice, 4*(1), 53–65.

Luborsky, L., et al. (1999). The researchers own therapy allegiances: A "wild card" in comparisons of treatment efficacy. *Clinical Psychology: Science and Practice, 6,* 95–106.

Luborsky, L., et al. (2002). The dodo bird verdict is alive and well—mostly. *Clinical Psychology: Science and Practice, 9*(1), 2–12.

Lucas, R., Clark, A., Georgellis, Y., & Diener, E. (2003). Reexamining adaption and the set point model of happiness: Reactions to change in marital status. *Journal of Personality and Social Psychology, 84*(3), 527–539.

Lueck, W. (2004). *Differential treatment response as a function of diagnostic classification.* Unpublished doctoral dissertation, Brigham Young University, Provo, Utah.

Lutz, W., Leon, S., Martinovich, Z., Lyons, J., & Stiles, W. (2007). Therapist effects in outpatient psychotherapy: A three-level growth curve approach. *Journal of Counseling Psychology, 54*(1), 32–39.

Lutz, W., Martinovich, Z., & Howard, K. (1999). Patient profiling: An application of random coefficient regression models to depicting the response of a patient to outpatient psychotherapy. *Journal of Consulting and Clinical Psychology, 67*(4), 571–577.

Lykken, D., & Tellegen, A. (1996). Happiness is a stochastic phenomenon. *Psychological Science, 7,* 186–189.

Lyubomirsky, S. (2008). *The how of happiness: A scientific approach to getting the life you want.* New York: Penguin Press.

Lyubomirsky, S., & Ross, L. (1997). Hedonic consequences of social comparison: A contrast of happy and unhappy people. *Journal of Personality and Social Psychology, 73,* 1141–1157.

Lyubomirsky, S., Sheldon, K., & Schkade, D. (2005). Pursuing happiness: The architecture of sustainable change. *Review of General Psychology, 9*(2), 111–131.

MacKenzie, D., Wilson, D., & Kider, S. (2001). Effects of correctional boot camps on offending. *Annals of the American Academy of Political and Social Science, 578,* 126–143.

Mallinckrodt, B. (1996). Change in working alliance, social support and psychological symptoms in brief therapy. *Journal of Counseling Psychology, 43*(4), 448–455.

Mallinckrodt, B., Porter, M., & Kivlighan, D. (2005). Client attachment to therapist, depth of in-session exploration, and object relations in brief psychotherapy. *Psychotherapy: Research, Practice, Training, 42*(1), 85–100.

Manjoo, F. (2008). *True enough: Learning to live in a post-fact society.* Hoboken, New Jersey: Wiley & Sons Inc.

March, J. S., et al. (2004). Fluoxetine, cognitive-behavioral therapy, and their combination for adolescents with depression study (TADS) randomized controlled trial. *Journal of the American Medical Association, 292,* 807–820.

Marci, C., Ham, J., Moran, E., & Orr, S. (2007). Physiological correlates of perceived therapist empathy and social-emotional process during psychotherapy. *Journal of Nervous and Mental Disease, 195*(2), 103–111.

Marlatt, G. (Ed.). (1998). *Harm reduction: Pragmatic strategies for managing high-risk behaviors.* New York: Guilford.

Martin, D. J., Graske, J., & Davis, M. (2000). Relation of the therapeutic alliance with outcome and other variables: A meta-analytic review. *Journal of Consulting and Clinical Psychology, 68,* 438–450.

Mayle, P. (1973). *Where did I come from?* Secaucus, NJ: Lyle Stuart.

Mayle, P. (1975). *What's happening to me?* Secaucus, NJ: Lyle Stuart.

McCann, D., et al. (2007). Food additives and hyperactive behaviour in 3-year-old and 8/9-year-old children in the community: A randomized, double-blinded, placebo-controlled trial. *The Lancet, 370*(9598), 1560–1567.

Meehl, P. (1954). *Clinical vs. statistical prediction: A theoretical analysis and a review of the evidence.* Minneapolis: University of Minnesota Press.

Meehl, P. (1959). Some technical and axiological problems in the therapeutic handling of religious and valuation material. *Journal of Counseling Psychology, 6,* 255–259.

Meeks, J. (1980). *The fragile alliance.* Malibar, FL: Krieger.

Melander, H., et al. (2003). Evidence b(i)ased medicine—Selective reporting from studies sponsored by pharmaceutical industry: Review of studies in new drug applications. *British Medical Journal, 326,* 1171–1173.

Menchola, M., Arkowitz, H., & Burke, B. (2007). Efficacy of self-administered treatments for depression and anxiety. *Professional Psychology: Research and Practice, 38*(4), 421–429.

Mental health: Does therapy help? (1995, November). *Consumer Reports,* 734–739.

Mesibov, G., & Shea, V. (2006). *Evidence-based practices, autism and the TEACCH program.* Unpublished manuscript.

Messer, S. B., & Wampold, B. E. (2002). Let's face facts: Common factors are more potent than specific therapy ingredients. *Clinical Psychology: Science and Practice, 9*(1), 18–22.

Meyer, B., Pilkonis, P., Krupnick, J., Egan, M., Simmens, S., & Sotsky, S. (2002). Treatment expectancies, patient alliance, and outcome: Further analyses from the National Institute of Mental Health treatment of depression collaborative research program. *Journal of Consulting and Clinical Psychology, 70*(4), 1051–1055.

Michael, K., & Crowley, S. (2002). How effective are treatments for child and adolescent depression? A meta-analytic review. *Clinical Psychology Review, 22,* 247–269.

Miller, M. (2007). Drug diversion by adolescents. *Harvard Mental Health Letter, 24*(1), 8.

Miller, S., Duncan, B., & Hubble, M. (1997). *Escape from Babel: Toward a unifying language for psychotherapy.* New York: Norton.

Miller, S., Duncan, B., & Hubble, M. (2004). Beyond integration: The triumph of outcome over process in clinical practice. *Psychotherapy in Australia, 10*(2), 2–19.

Miller, S., Hubble, M., & Duncan, B. (2007). Supershrinks: Who are they? What can we learn from them? *Psychotherapy Networker, 31*(6), 26–35; 56–57. Retrieved from egory=magazine&sub_cat=articles&page=1&type=article&id=Supershrinks

Miller, S., Wampold, B., & Varhely, K. (2008). Direct comparisons of treatment modalities for youth disorders: A meta-analysis. *Psychotherapy Research, 18*(1), 5–14.

Miller, W., & Baca, L. (1983). Two-year follow-up of bibliotherapy and therapist-directed controlled drinking training for problem drinkers. *Behavior Therapy, 14,* 441–448.

Miller, W., Benefield, R., & Tonigan, J. (1993). Enhancing motivation for change in problem drinking: A controlled comparison of two therapist styles. *Journal of Consulting and Clinical Psychology, 61*(3), 455–461.

Mohr, D. (1995). Negative outcome in psychotherapy: A critical review. *Clinical Psychology: Science and Practice, 2,* 1–27.

Mohr, J., & Woodhouse, S. (2001). Looking inside the therapeutic alliance: Assessing client's visions of helpful and harmful psychotherapy. *Psychotherapy Bulletin, 36,* 15–16.

Moncrieff, J., Wessely, S., & Hardy, R. (2004). Active placebos versus antidepressants for depression. *Cochrane Database of Systematic Reviews,* No. 1. (Art. No.: CD003012. DOI: 10.1002/14651858.CD003012.pub2)

Montalvo, B., & Haley, J. (1973). In defense of child therapy. *Family Process, 12*(3), 227–244.

Morrissey-Kane, E., & Prinz, R. (1999). Engagement in child and adolescent treatment: The role of parental cognitions and attributions. *Clinical Child and Family Psychology Review, 2*(3), 183–198.

Mussell, M., Mitchell, J., Crosby, R., Fulkerson, J., Hoberman, H., & Romano, J. (2000). Commitment to treatment goals in prediction of group cognitive-behavioral therapy treatment outcome for women with bulimia nervosa. *Journal of Consulting and Clinical Psychology, 68,* 432–437.

National Institute on Drug Abuse. (2007). *Monitoring the future survey, Overview of findings.* Retrieved from http://www.drugabuse.gov/newsroom/07/MTF07Overview.html

Nock, M., & Kazdin, A. (2005). Randomized controlled trials of a brief intervention for increasing participation in parent management training. *Journal of Consulting and Clinical Psychology, 73*(5), 872–879.

Norcross, J. (1997). Emerging breakthroughs in psychotherapy integration: Three predictions and one fantasy. *Psychotherapy, 34,* 86–90.

Norcross, J. (Ed.). (2002a). *Psychotherapy relationships that work: Therapist contributions and responsiveness to patient needs.* New York: Oxford University Press.

Norcross, J. C. (2002b). Empirically supported (therapy) relationships. *The Milton H. Erickson Foundation Newsletter, 22*(3), 6. Available at: http://www.erickson-foundation.org/newsletterpdfs/Vol%2022%20No%203.pdf

Norcross, J. (2006). Integrating self-help into psychotherapy: 16 practical suggestions. *Professional Psychology: Research and Practice, 37*(6), 683–693.

Norcross, J., & Goldfried, M. (2005). The future of psychotherapy integration: A roundtable. *Journal of Psychotherapy Integration, 15*(4), 392–471.

Norcross, J., Hedges, M., & Prochaska, J. (2002). The face of 2010: A Delphi poll on the future of psychotherapy. *Professional Psychology: Research and Practice, 33*(3), 316–322.

Norcross, J., Koocher, G., & Garofalo, A. (2006). Discredited psychological treatments and tests: A Delphi poll. *Professional Psychology: Research and Practice, 37*(5), 515–522.

Oetzel, K., & Scherer, D. (2003). Therapeutic engagement with adolescents in psychotherapy. *Psychotherapy: Theory, Research, Practice, Training, 40*(3), 215–225.

Okiishi, J., Lambert, M., Eggett, D., Nielsen, L., Dayton, D., & Vermeersch, D. (2006). An analysis of therapist treatment effects: Toward providing feedback to individual therapists on their client's psychotherapy outcome. *Journal of Clinical Psychology, 62*(9), 1157–1172.

Okiishi, J., Lambert, M., Nielsen, S., & Ogles, B. (2003). Waiting for supershrink: An empirical analysis of therapist effects. *Clinical Psychology and Psychotherapy, 10,* 361–373. Retrieved from http://www.interscience.wiley.com

Olfson, M., Marcus, S., Druss, B., & Pincus, H. (2002). National trends in the use of outpatient psychotherapy. *American Journal of Psychiatry, 159,* 1914–1920.

Orlinsky, D., Grawe, K., & Parks, B. (1994). Process and outcome in psychotherapy. In S. L. Garfield (Ed.), *Handbook of psychotherapy and behavior change* (4th ed., pp. 270–378). New York: Wiley.

O'Sullivan, M. J., Peterson, P., Cox, G., & Kirkeby, J. (1989). Ethnic populations: Community mental health services ten years later. *American Journal of Community Psychology, 17,* 17–30.

Oyserman, D., Bybee, D., & Terry, K. (2006). Possible selves and academic outcomes: How and why possible selves impel action. *Journal of Personality and Social Psychology, 9*(1), 188–204.

Patterson, G., & Forgatch, M. (1985). Therapist behavior as a determinant for client non-compliance: A paradox for the behavior modifier. *Journal of Consulting and Clinical Psychology, 53,* 846–851.

Paul, G. (1967). Strategy in outcome research in psychotherapy. *Journal of Consulting Psychology, 31,* 109–118.

Pavuluri, M., Luk, S., & McGee, R. (1996). Help-seeking for behavior problems by parents of preschool children: A community study. *Journal of American Academy of Child and Adolescent Psychiatry, 35,* 215–222.

Persons, J. (2007, August 16). Lecture. Director of the San Francisco Bay Area Center for Cognitive Therapy.

Peterson, C., & Seligman, M. (2004). *Character strengths and virtues: A handbook and classification.* New York: Oxford University Press.

Petrosino, A., Turpin-Petrosino, C., & Buehler, J. (2002). "Scared Straight" and other juvenile awareness programs for preventing juvenile delinquency. *Cochrane Database of Systematic Reviews,* No. 4. Retrieved from http://www.campbellcollaboration.org/doc-pdf/ssa.pdf

Phillips, E. L. (1988). Length of psychotherapy and outcome: Observations stimulated by Howard, Kopta, Krause, and Orlinsky. *American Psychologist, 43*(8), 669–670.

Piper, W., Azim, H., Joyce, A., McCallum, M., Nixon, G., & Segal, P. (1991). Quality of object relations versus interpersonal functioning as predictors of alliance and outcome. *Journal of Nervous and Mental Disease, 179,* 432–438.

Piper, W., Joyce, A., McCallum, M., & Azim, H. (1998). Interpretive and supportive forms of psychotherapy and patient personality variables. *Journal of Consulting and Clinical Psychology, 66*(3), 558–567.

Piper, W., Ogrodniczuk, J., Joyce, A., McCallum, M., Rosie, J., O'Kelly, J., & Steinberg, P. (1999). Prediction of dropping out in time-limited interpretive individual psychotherapy. *Psychotherapy, 36,* 114–122.

Pliszka, S., Matthews, T., Braslow, K., & Watson, M. (2006). Comparative effects of methylphenidate and mixed salts amphetamine on height and weight in children with attention-deficit/hyperactivity disorder. *Journal of the American Academy of Child and Adolescent Psychiatry, 45*(5), 520–526.

Popenoe, D., & Whitehead, B. (2003). *The National Marriage Project.* Rutgers. Retrieved from http://www.marriage.rutgers.edu

Prochaska, J. O., & DiClemente, C. C. (1992). The transtheoretical approach. In J. C. Norcross & M. R. Goldfried (Eds.), *Handbook of psychotherapy integration* (pp. 300–334). New York: Basic Books.

Reitzel, L., et al. (2006). Does time between application and case assignment predict therapy attendance or premature termination in outpatients? *Psychological Services, 3*(1), 51–60.

Rhule, D. (2005). Take care to do no harm: Harmful interventions for youth problem behavior. *Professional Psychology: Research and Practice, 36*(6), 618–625.

Richert, A. (2007). Concepts, processes and procedures: An introduction to the special issue on integration of concrete operating procedures. *Journal of Psychotherapy Integration, 17*(1), 1–9.

Roe, D., Dekel, R., Harel, G., Fenning, S., & Fenning, S. (2006). Clients' feelings during termination of psychodynamically oriented psychotherapy. *Bulletin of the Menninger Clinic, 70*(1), 68–81.

Rogers, C. (1957). The necessary and sufficient conditions of therapeutic personality change. *Journal of Consulting Psychology, 21,* 95–103.

Rosenfeld, G. (1976). *The effect on self-esteem of induced selective attention to successes and failures.* Unpublished doctoral dissertation, University of Minnesota.

Rosenzweig, S. (1936). Some implicit common factors in diverse methods in psychotherapy. *American Journal of Orthopsychiatry, 6,* 412–415.

Roth, A., & Fonagy, P. (2006). *A critical review of psychotherapy research: What works for whom?* (2nd ed.). New York: Guilford.

Roth, G., Assor, A., Niemiec, C., Ryan, R., & Deci, E. (2007). *The negative emotional and academic consequences of parental conditional regard: Comparing positive conditional regard, negative conditional regard and autonomy support as parenting practices.* Unpublished manuscript. Available from assor@bgu.ac.il

Ryan, R., & Deci, E. (2001). On happiness and human potentials: A review of research on hedonic and eudaimonic well-being. *Annual Review of Psychology, 52,* 141–166.

Safran, J., & Muran, J. (1996). The resolution of ruptures in the therapeutic alliance. *Journal of Consulting and Clinical Psychology, 64*(3), 447–458.

Safran, J., Muran, J., Samstag, L., & Stevens, C. (2002). Repairing alliance ruptures. In J. C. Norcross (Ed.), *Psychotherapy relationships that work.* New York: Oxford University Press.

Salzer, M., Bickman, L., & Lambert, E. (1999). Dose-effect relationship in children's psychotherapy services. *Journal of Consulting and Clinical Psychology, 67*(2), 228–238.

Samstag, L., Batchelder, S., Muran, C., Safran, J., & Winston, A. (1998). Early identification of treatment failures in short-term psychotherapy: An assessment of therapeutic alliance and interpersonal behavior. *Journal of Psychotherapy Practice and Research, 7,* 126–143.

Saul, R. (1999). *The Gutmacher report on public policy, 2*(3). Retrieved from http://www.guttmacher.org/pubs/tgr/02/3/gr020306.html

Scamardo, M., Bobele, M., & Biever, J. (2004). A new perspective on client dropouts. *Journal of Systemic Therapies, 23*(2), 27–38.

Schore, A. (1996). The experience-dependent maturation of a regulatory system in the orbital prefrontal cortex and the origin of developmental psychopathology. *Developmental Psychopathology, 8,* 59–87.

Schore, A. (1997). Early organization of the nonlinear right brain and development of a predisposition to psychiatric disorders. *Developmental Psychopathology, 9,* 595–631.

Schore, A. (2003). *Affect regulation and the repair of the self.* New York: Norton.

Schwartz, J. (1996). *Brain lock: Free yourself from obsessive-compulsive behavior.* New York: HarperCollins.

Scogin, F. R. (2003). Introduction: The status of self-help administered treatments. *Journal of Clinical Psychology, 59*(3), 247–249.

Seligman, M. (1995). The effectiveness of psychotherapy: The "Consumer Reports" study. *American Psychologist, 50*(12), 965–974.

Seligman, M. (1996). Science as an ally of practice. *American Psychologist, 51*(10), 1072–1079.

Seligman, M. (2002a). *Authentic happiness.* New York: Free Press.

Seligman, M. (2002b). Positive psychology, positive prevention, and positive therapy. In C. R. Snyder & J. L. Shane (Eds.), *Handbook of positive psychology.* New York: Oxford Press.

Seligman, M., Rashid, T., & Parks, A. (2006). Positive psychotherapy. *American Psychologist, 61*(8), 774–788.

Seligman, M., Steen, T., Park, N., & Peterson, C. (2005). Positive psychology progress: Empirical validation of interventions. *American Psychologist, 60*(5), 410–421.

Shadish, W., et al. (1997). Evidence that psychotherapy works in clinically representative conditions. *Journal of Consulting and Clinical Psychology, 65,* 355–365.

Shahar, G., Blatt, S., Zuroff, D., & Pilkonis, P. (2003). Role of perfectionism and personality disorder features in response to brief treatment for depression. *Journal of Consulting and Clinical Psychology, 71*(3), 629–633.

Shirk, S., & Karver, M. (2003). Prediction of treatment outcome from relationship variables in child and adolescent therapy: A meta-analytic review. *Journal of Consulting and Clinical Psychology, 71*(3), 452–464.

Siegel, D. (2001). Toward an interpersonal neurobiology of the developing mind: Attachment relationships, mindsight and neural integration. *Infant Mental Health Journal, 22,* 67–94.

Simmons, M., Shalwitz, J., Pollock, S., & Young, A. (2003). *Understanding confidentiality and minor consent in California: An adolescent provider toolkit* (1st rev. ed.). San Francisco: Adolescent Health Working Group, San Francisco Health Plan.

Siev, J., & Chambless, D. (2007). Specificity of treatment effects: Cognitive therapy and relaxation for generalized anxiety and panic disorders. *Journal of Consulting and Clinical Psychology, 75*(4), 513–522.

Smith, M., & Glass, G. (1977). Meta-analysis of psychotherapy outcome studies. *American Psychologist, 32,* 752–760.

Smith, M., Glass, G., & Miller, T. (1980). *The benefits of psychotherapy.* Baltimore: Johns Hopkins University Press.

Snyder, C., Ilardi, S., Michael, S., & Cheavens, J. (2000). Hope theory: Updating a common process for psychological change. In C. R. Snyder & R. E. Ingram (Eds.), *Handbook of psychological change: Psychotherapy processes and practices for the 21st century* (pp. 128–153). New York: Wiley.

Spector, J., & Read, J. (1999). The current status of eye movement desensitization and reprocessing. *Clinical Psychology and Psychotherapy, 6*(3), 165–174.

Spenser, T., Faraone, S., Biederman, J., Lerner, M., et al. (2006). Does prolonged therapy with a long-acting stimulant suppress growth in children with ADHD? *Journal of the American Academy of Child and Adolescent Psychiatry, 45*(5), 527–537.

Spielmans, G. I., Pasek, L. F., & McFall, J. P. (2007). What are the active ingredients in cognitive and behavioral psychotherapy for anxious and depressed children? A meta-analytic review. *Clinical Psychology Review, 27*(5), 642–654.

Steinbrook, R. (2008). Financial support of continuing medical education. *Journal of the American Medical Association, 299*(9), 1060–1062.

Stern, D. N., et al. (1998). Non-interpretive mechanisms in psychoanalytic therapy: The "something more" than interpretation. *International Journal of Psycho-Analysis, 79,* 903–921.

Stern, S. (1993). Managed care, brief therapy, and therapeutic integrity. *Psychotherapy: Theory, Research, Practice, Training, 30*(1), 162–175.

Steyer, J. (2002). *The other parent.* New York: Atria.

Stiles, W. B., et al. (2004). Patterns of alliance development and the rupture-repair hypothesis. Are productive relationships U-shaped or V-shaped? *Journal of Counseling Psychology, 51*(1), 81–92.

Stiles, W. B., Leach, C., Barkham, M., Lucock, M., Iveson, S., Shapiro, D., Iveson, M., & Gillian, H. (2003). Early sudden gains in psychotherapy under routine clinic conditions: Practice-based evidence. *Journal of Consulting and Clinical Psychology, 71*(1), 14–21.

Strong, S. (1968). Counseling: An interpersonal influence process. *Journal of Counseling Psychology, 15*(3), 215–224.

Strupp, H., & Hadley, S. (1979). Specific versus nonspecific factors in psychotherapy: A controlled study of outcome. *Archives of General Psychiatry, 36,* 1125–1136.

Sukhodolsky, D., Kassinove, H., & Gorman, B. (2004). Cognitive-behavioral therapy for anger in children and adolescents: A meta-analysis. *Aggression and Violent Behavior, 9*(3), 247–269.

Switzer, G., Dew, M., Thompson, K., Goycoolea, J., Derricott, T., & Mullins, S. (1999). Posttraumatic stress disorder and service utilization among urban mental health center clients. *Journal of Traumatic Stress, 12*(1), 25–39.

Tam, K., & Healy, J. (2007). The Ohio Mental Health Consumer Outcomes System, Report Number 16. *Benchmarks for reliable change and clinical significance in the Ohio Scales for Youth-Problem Severity and Functioning Scales.* Retrieved from http://www.mh.state.oh.us/oper/outcomes/reports/rpt.quarterly.16.pdf

Tang, T., & DeRubeis, R. (1999). Sudden gains and critical sessions in cognitive-behavioral therapy for depression. *Journal of Consulting and Clinical Psychology, 67,* 894–904.

Tarico, V., Low, B., Trupin, E., & Forsyth-Stephens, A. (1989). Children's mental health services: A parent perspective. *Community Mental Health Journal, 25,* 313–326.

Tatarsky, A. (2003). Harm reduction psychotherapy: Extending the reach of traditional substance use treatment. *Journal of Substance Abuse Treatment, 25,* 249–256.

Tellegen, A., Lykken, D., Bouchard, T., Wilcox, K., Segal, N., & Rich, S. (1988). Personality similarity in twins reared apart and together. *Journal of Personality and Social Psychology, 54,* 1031–1039.

Terr, L. (1983). Chowchilla revisited: The effects of psychic trauma four years after a school-bus kidnapping. *American Journal of Psychiatry, 140,* 1543–1550.

Truax, C., Altmarm, H., Wright, L., & Mitchell, K. (1973). Effects of the therapeutic conditions in child therapy. *Journal of Community Psychology, 1,* 313–318.

Turner, E., Matthews, A., Linardatos, E., Tell, R., & Rosenthal, R. (2008). Selective publication of antidepressant trials and its influence on apparent efficacy. *New England Journal of Medicine, 358*(3), 252–260.

Tyron, G., & Winograd, G. (2002). Goal consensus and collaboration. In J. Norcross (Ed.), *Psychotherapy relationships that work: Therapist contributions and responsiveness of patients* (pp. 106–122). New York: Oxford University Press.

U.S. Bureau of the Census. (2002). *Census 2000 Summary File 3 (SF 3)—Sample data*. Retrieved from http://factfinder.census.gov/home/en/datanotes/expsf3.htm

Vedantam, S. (2006a). Comparison of schizophrenia drugs often favors firm funding study. *Washington Post*. Retrieved from http://www.washingtonpost.com

Vedantam, S. (2006b). Psychiatric guide has drug firm ties. *Sacramento Bee*, p. A10.

Vervaeke, G., Vertommen, H., & Storms, G. (1997). Client and therapist values in relation to dropout. *Clinical Psychology and Psychotherapy, 4*(1), 1–6.

Vocisano, C., et al. (2004). Therapist variables that predict symptom change in psychotherapy with chronically depressed outpatients. *Psychotherapy: Theory, Research, Practice, Training, 41*(3), 355–365.

Wade, N. (1996). The spin doctors. *Illinois Medicine*, 8(5). Cited in Kasdan, M., et al. (1999). The nocebo effect: Do no harm. *Journal of the Southern Orthopaedic Association*, 8(2), p.109.

Wampold, B. E. (2001). *The great psychotherapy debate: Models, methods and findings*. Mahwah, NJ: Lawrence Erlbaum.

Wampold, B. E. (2007). Psychotherapy: The humanistic (and effective) treatment. *American Psychologist, 62*(8), 857–873.

Wampold, B. E., & Brown, G. (2005). Estimating variability in outcomes attributable to therapists: A naturalistic study of outcomes in managed care. *Journal of Consulting and Clinical Psychology, 73*(5), 914–923.

Wampold, B. E., Minami, T., Baskin, T. W., & Tierney, S. C. (2002). A meta-(re)analysis of the effects of cognitive therapy versus "other therapies" for depression. *Journal of Affective Disorders, 68*, 159–165.

Wampold, B., Minami, T., Tierney, S., Baskin, T., & Bhati, K. (2005). The placebo is powerful: Estimating placebo effects in medicine and psychotherapy from randomized clinical trials. *Journal of Clinical Psychology, 61*(7), 835–854.

Weddington, W., & Cavenar, J. (1979). Termination initiated by the therapist: A counter transference storm. *American Journal of Psychiatry, 136*, 1302–1305.

Weinberger, D., Elvegag, B., & Giedd, J. (2005). *The adolescent brain: A work in progress*. National Campaign to Prevent Teen Pregnancy. Retrieved from http://www.teenpregnancy.org/resources/reading/pdf/BRAIN.pdf

Weiss, B., Caron, A., Ball, S., Tapp, J., Johnson, M., & Weisz, J. (2005). Iatrogenic effects of group treatment for antisocial youth. *Journal of Consulting and Clinical Psychology, 73*(6), 1036–1044.

Weiss, J. (1993). *How therapy works*. New York: Guilford.

Weisz, J. R., Doss, A., & Hawley, K. (2005). Youth psychotherapy outcome research: A review and critique of the evidence base. *Annual Review of Psychology, 56*, 337–363.

Weisz, J. R., & Hawley, K. (2002). Developmental factors in the treatment of adolescents. *Journal of Consulting and Clinical Psychology, 70*(1), 21–43.

Weisz, J. R., & Jensen, P. (1999). Efficacy and effectiveness of child and adolescent psychotherapy and pharmacotherapy. *Mental Health Services Research, 1*, 125–157.

Weisz, J. R., Jensen-Doss, A., & Hawley, K. (2006). Evidence-based youth psychotherapies versus usual clinical care. *American Psychologist, 61*(7), 671–689.

Weisz, J. R., McCarty, C. A., & Valeri, S. M. (2006). Effects of psychotherapy for depression in children and adolescents: A meta-analysis. *Psychological Bulletin, 132*(1), 132–149.

Weisz, J. R., Weiss, B., Alicke, M., & Klotz, M. (1987). Effectiveness of psychotherapy with children and adolescents: A meta-analysis for clinicians. *Journal of Consulting and Clinical Psychology, 55*(4), 542–549.

Weisz, J. R., Weiss, B., Han, S., Granger, D., & Morton, T. (1995). Effects of psychotherapy with children and adolescents revisited: A meta-analysis of treatment outcome studies. *Psychological Bulletin, 117,* 450–468.

Westen, D., & Morrison, K. (2001). A multidimensional meta-analysis of treatments for depression, panic, and generalized anxiety disorder: An empirical examination of the status of empirically supported therapies. *Journal of Consulting and Clinical Psychology, 69*(6), 875–899.

Wexler, D. B. (1991). *The adolescent self: Strategies for self-management, self-soothing and self-esteem in adolescents.* New York: Norton.

Whipple, J., Lambert, M., Vermeersch, D., Smart, S., Neilsen, S., & Hawkins, E. (2003). Improving the effects of psychotherapy: The use of early identification of treatment failure and problem-solving strategies in routine practice. *Journal of Counseling Psychology, 50*(1), 59–68.

White, M. (1988–1989). The externalizing of the problem and the re-authoring of lives and relationships. *Dulwich Centre Newsletter.*

Whitlock, J., Powers, J., & Eckenrode, J. (2006). The virtual cutting edge: The Internet and adolescent self-injury. *Developmental Psychology, 42*(3), 407–417.

Whittaker, J., & Garbarino, J. (1983). *Social support networks: Informal helping in the human services.* New York: Aldine.

Williams, D., & Levitt, H. (2007). A qualitative investigation of eminent therapists' values within psychotherapy: Developing integrative principles for moment-to-moment psychotherapy practice. *Journal of Psychotherapy Integration, 17*(2), 159–184.

Williams, E., Polster, D., Grizzard, B., Rockenbaugh, J., & Judge, A. (2003). What happens when therapists feel bored or anxious: A qualitative study of distracting self-awareness and therapists' management strategies. *Journal of Contemporary Psychotherapy, 33*(1), 5–18.

Wilson, D., MacKenzie, D., & Mitchell, F. (2005). *Effects of correctional boot camps on offending.* A Campbell collaboration systematic review. Retrieved from http://www.campbellcollaboration.org/doc-pdf/wilson_bootcamps_rev.pdf

Wittchen, H., et al. (1998). Prevalence of mental disorders and psychological impairments in adolescents and young adults. *Psychological Medicine, 28,* 109–126.

Wolak, J., Mitchell, K., & Finkelhor, D. (2007). Unwanted and wanted exposure to pornography in a national sample of youth Internet users. *Pediatrics, 119*(2), 247–257.

Wong, Y. (2006). Strength-centered therapy: A social constructivist, virtues-based psychotherapy. *Psychotherapy, Theory, Research, Practice, Training, 43*(2), 133–146.

Yeh, M., & Weisz, J. R. (2001). Why are we here at the clinic? Parent–child (dis)agreement on referral problems. *Journal of Consulting and Clinical Psychology, 69,* 1018–1025.

Zhang, S. (1999). *An evaluation of the Los Angeles County Drug Treatment Boot Camp* (Final report, NCJ 189787). San Marco: California State University, and the U.S. Department of Justice, National Institute of Justice.

Zuroff, D., & Blatt, S. (2006). The therapeutic relationship in brief treatment of depression: Contributions to clinical improvement and enhanced adaptive capacities. *Journal of Consulting and Clinical Psychology, 74*(1), 130–140.

Zuvekas, S., Vitiello, B., & Norquist, G. (2006). Recent trends in stimulant medication use among U.S. children. *American Journal of Psychiatry, 163*(4), 579–585.

Index

A

AA (Alcoholics Anonymous), 55, 63, 75, 199, 221
ABCs (antecedents, behaviors, and consequences), 69, 70, 234
abstinence-based programs (AA and NA), 221
abuse, 137, 231. *See also* domestic violence
  reporting of suspected, 55
  sibling, 180
  treatment for, 136
abuse, sexual, 156, 180. *See also* molestation
  parents and,
    157
academic failure, 221
academic placement, 164
active listening, 127, 151
addiction, 230. *See also* substance abuse
adjustment disorder, 43
Adolescent Health Working Group, 139
adolescents, 157. *See also* clients, adolescent; youth
  anxiety and, 128

autonomy-seeking, 151
emancipating, 151, 214
embarrassment and, 128
empowering, 152
highly sexualized girls, 102
hostility and, 151
molested, 102
oppositional, 151
parents and, 138
sensitivity to criticism, 152
sexually active, 102
stigma and, 128
subversion of treatment and, 128
treatment for, 24
adults. *see* clients, adult
advice, giving, 92
affect regulation, faulty, 27
African American, 199
Alateen, 202
alcohol, 62
Alex (case study), 229, 230, 237
  medication and, 230
  three-month follow-up, 216
  typical day of therapy, 192–194
Alice in Wonderland, 20
all-or-none reasoning, 88
American Academy of Pediatrics Committee on Drugs, 22